Really Reading
Gertrude Stein

Really Reading Gertrude Stein

A Selected Anthology With Essays by Judy Grahn

The Crossing Press
Freedom, California 95019

Cover design by Betsy Bayley
Cover photograph of Gertrude Stein from the Sophia Smith Collection,
Smith College
Cover photograph of Judy Grahn © 1984 by Chris Felver
Typesetting by Wordwise
Printed in the United States of America

Library of Congress Cataloging-in-Publicatin Data

Grahn, Judy, 1940-
    Really reading Gertrude Stein : a selected anthology with
essays by Judy Grahn.
            p.   cm.
    Bibliography: p.
    ISBN 0-89594-381-6 (cloth)   ISBN 0-89594-380-8 (pbk.)
    1. Stein, Gertrude, 1874-1946—Criticism and nterpretation.
I. Stein, Gertrude, 1874-1946. II. Title.
PS3537.T323Z618   1989
818'.5209—dc20   89-17478
                                               CIP

Acknowledgments

It is rare, I think, that a writer has a chance to thank her own mentor in words, as these essays are an expression of my great love for Gertrude Stein. I feel honored and as always, awed by the contribution of Stein to world thought.

I wish to thank those who have written about her ideas, and kept her work available in its great variety, Carl Van Vechten, Thornton Wilder, Donald Sutherland, Patricia Meyerowitz, Robert Bartlett Haas, John Malcolm Brinnin, Sam Steward, Ron Silliman, Jane Rule, Catharine Stimpson, and many others.

I want to express thanks also for stimulating and helpful converstations about her with Wendy Cadden, Kris Brandenburger (who helped also with editing), the late Robert Duncan, Joe Barry, Sam Steward, Maria Jutasi Coleman, and Barbara Hoke. Thanks also to Fran Winant for early illumination of the Lesbian content in "Lifting Belly," in her own writings. And here's a toast to the spirit of my beloved Papa for quoting me Stein phrases in my childhood.

Special thanks to New College Poetics Department for sponsoring my three lectures, especially Robert Duncan, Diane Di Prima, David Meltzer, Duncan Mc Noughton, Louis Patler, and Michael Palmer. Thanks to the English Department and John J. Winkler of the Classics Department at Stanford University for sponsoring my Stein class. Thanks to helpful librarians at the Collection of American Literature, the Beinecke Rare Book and Manuscript Library, Yale University, and to my publishers Elaine Goldman Gill and John Gill.

Contents

Section III

Section One

By Judy Grahn

The There That Was And Was Not There

Essence, Value, Commonality and Play

Whenever a person, and especially a woman, calls herself great, or the greatest, of writers, that is of idea-formers, this is a signal to pay her some attention since either she is lying or she is telling the truth. And if she is lying we shall know it soon, as her work quickly fades and her effect never materializes. But if she is telling the truth her work will gradually expand its influence and power within our culture, and what on earth could be more exciting than to have a woman's philosophical work expand its influence and power within our culture after so many centuries of profound silence.

Gertrude Stein said that she was great, at least the writer of our century, and others have said that she is comparable to, say, Spinoza, and still others have belittled her and trivialized her work, and many people have heard of her and want to read her.

Yet she remains difficult to understand; some people try and soon give up. I have considered her my mentor for more than thirty years and I still can not always read an entire book at a time. Every single person I know finds her difficult. At the same time I have gotten so much from her, more than from anyone, and I believe we need her philosophy more than ever.

Let's suppose you've heard so much of her, you think you ought to take her on, or perhaps you have tried in the past and now again you plow right into something long and tasty looking, something that looks like a regular novel, such as *The Making of Americans*, trying to read it in a dutiful, forthright, sincere manner.

At first, while you are perhaps puzzled at the odd frames of reference, the elliptical sentences that swirl back upon themselves, you are also delighted with the psychological insights. Then gradually the interest wanes as you feel annoyance with the enveloping loops of repetition, your readings become tedious, then you admit to a burrowing rage at the lack of resolution, the refusal of the stories to have orgasmic conclusion, the endless tickling of the brain's senses with no fusion of progression. Perhaps (as I have done a few times) you slam the book down resentfully, feeling exhausted and stupid, betrayed again by this intriguing-looking woman with the erratic though persistent reputation for greatness.

You are, I think, reacting typically to Gertrude Stein, and not differently than many a scholar and wise person. Is she merely making fun of us, as some people have believed? I don't think this, of course, but I butted my head against her work for years, and it was because my expectations were so different from her fulfillment.

Poet, novelist, playwright, essayist, philosopher and in her own definition of artists-as-modern-versions-of-saints— saint. By this she did not mean that artists are religious or belong in a Christian context. She meant that artists bear the same focus of leadership and shamanic interpretation of the cosmos to human perceptions, in our age, as saints did for their societies in the Middle Ages.

Completely self-centered in her work, she had the apparent audacity to define herself as the one great writer/thinker of our time. She placed herself well above the men she most

immediately influenced during her lifetime: Ernest Hemingway, Thornton Wilder, Richard Wright, for instance. She
placed herself, as a literary figure, in the company of the men
who have most influenced Western literature, Marcel Proust,
William Shakespeare, Walt Whitman; and finally she placed
herself alone.

And there she sits as we approach her, finding again as
always, no one to compare her to, no one to help us
understand her in terms of....anyone else's mind. She is not
"like" anyone, her writing is unique. We are left with her
words, and ourselves, alone.

Since Gertrude Stein's death in 1946 increasing numbers of her books have been put into print, her plays are
performed, her ideas are explored more seriously than during her lifetime, when her style was as often mocked as it was
emulated and absorbed into the common language.

Suppose she was telling the truth when she said that she
is the most important writer of our time, then the adage about
Muhammed going to the mountain applies here. In going to
her mountain, the mountain of work that she left us, we find
that she is with some justification considered obscure for
much of her work seems indirect, and its meaning veiled, and
this even though her vocabulary is scrupulously "accessible."

For years I thought: "She is difficult," until one day it
occurred to me to say it the other way: "She is easy. I am
difficult."

Suppose it is not that she is veiled and obscure but that
we, her readers, are. We are veiled by our judgments. We
come to writing prepared to compare it to other writing we
have known. Since there is no one to compare her with, this
method doesn't work for Gertrude Stein.

We have been taught by most of our writers to expect
certain functions of writing: that it model emotion for us, as
blues singing also does, allowing us to explore feeling; that it

provide tension-relief in the form of solved mysteries, cliff-hanging adventures and will-she-won't-she romances; that it recreate foreign and exotic places, and fantasy landscapes; that we be reflected back to ourselves in sociological form or slice-of-life photographs. Stein's work does not perform any of these social functions nor did she ever intend that it would.

Stein spent much effort distinguishing for herself the difference between identity and essence. "Am I I because my little dog knows me?" she asked.

Or stated this way: Can I enter her or anyone's writing only if I already recognize myself and my own past experiences in it? Can I experience the writing as current event rather than reflection?

By suspending judgment about how a story, poem or play "should go" and by agreeing with myself to keep reading even when I can't find a way to recognize myself, I have begun to muddle into the landscape of her mind.

No other writer I know, while using a totally simple and accessible vocabulary, has coordinated so many of the terms of the writing to her own unique sensibilities. She is completely willful in this regard, requiring at times complete surrender, not of the reader's will, but of her/his identity and preconceptions, and not only of how a piece of literature goes, but even that it needs to go anywhere at all.

We are veiled from her whenever we have perceptions of philosophy as dense, of great writers as condescending, biting, derisive; consequently we also believe ourselves too "dense" to understand philosophy, and hence inferior to "greatness." Stein, however, operated from the premise of our intelligence and our worth. We often cannot believe the open-heartedness that is in her writing.

Because we are veiled we misinterpret. Large numbers of the reading public know that Stein said, "a rose is a rose is a rose is a rose," and believe she meant that roses are tedious, tiresomely all alike, when she meant the opposite, that every time you see a rose it is a different experience because it is located at a different place in the "sentence" of your life; and moreover that a rose "is," has existence beyond our cliches about it.

Many people in Oakland, California and the heavily populated surrounding area know that she said of Oakland, where she grew up, that "there is no there there," and believe she meant that Oakland is dull and shabby, lacking in culture. They believe this because San Francisco, across the Bay from Oakland, is considered classy and artful by contrast to the industrialized, heavily working class Oakland. A San Francisco joke is that Oakland exists because "they had to put the other end of the Bay Bridge down somewhere."

But Stein's comment was made after she returned home from her long self-exile in France, looking for the house that she grew up in, and finding it torn down, and the ten acres of fruit trees turned into avenues: "there is no there there," meaning she went looking for the old home and couldn't find it—a pensive and even sad statement, not a class judgement of Oakland.

Stein is a writer in ideas, not judgments; and she writes in ideas, they are thread and fabric of her works. To help us unveil ourselves to her, let me unravel my way into the fabric of her unique mind by introducing some terms for her ideas: equality, commonality, essence, value, continual present, play, and transformation.

Equality, or Commonality

Although her name is associated with French, especially cubist painters and other modern painters because she, and more especially her brothers Leo and Michael collected paintings, the painter who actually influenced her own work was Cezanne. Of an older generation and already becoming established when she became enthralled with his particular vision, this painter broke with nineteenth century classicism to produce paintings in which every square inch of picture mattered as much as any other. The whole field of the canvas is important, rather than the older vision in which central characters dominate, with a sky above and ground below.

Stein in her work with words used the entire text as a field in which every element mattered as much as any other, every part of speech, every word and, good poet that she was, every space and punctuation mark.

Equality is the term she used for this, though I prefer to suggest another, commonality, an idea I have been developing since the act of writing the Common Woman Poems in 1969. Using the idea of commonality means standing exactly where you and/or your group (of whatever current definition) are, and noticing what part of you overlaps with others who are standing exactly where they are.

Commonality differs from "universality" by having infinite numbers of changeable centers, where "universal" by definition and by usage, has only one—"uni," one. When universality is the principle, we search in another's work for that portion we can identify with—and dismiss the remainder as not relevant (because not "ours"). When commonality is the principle, we search for what overlaps with ourselves, then learn what we can from the remainder and leave it alone with respect as a whole that belongs to, that is, is centered in, someone else, not "us."

Commonality is more complex than equality because it has a subjective and a collective meaning in addition to the leveling action of equality. Equality of the whole field says that each element equally matters and is centered in itself. Commonality says that each element in the field equally matters and is centered in itself and in addition is in continual overlapping relation to every other element.

"What do we have in common" means how are we related subjectively and objectively, whereas "how are we equal" means how are we seen as similar by outside eyes. In Stein, shortly the outside eye of observation begins dancing in relation to an inside eye centering within the elements of the sentences.

Stein said of herself that she was not an efficient person but that she was good-humored and that she was democratic. "If you are like that anybody will do anything for you. The important thing is that you must have deep down as the deepest thing in you a sense of equality." Having a deep down sense of equality, she liked to talk to all kinds of people, she learned some things about her art from watching animals, and she believed children should have the right to vote.

She began developing her literary ideas of equality in her first novel, Q.E.D., with three female characters, using a perspective she called "fairness" to describe an intense love triangle that included herself as one character. Soon after in *Three Lives* she extended equality of perspective to include the class and age of the characters, two of them being portraits of servants, one an old woman; while in the third and best known, Melanctha, she extended somewhat shakily across the great chasm in American life—race—by centering in the life of a working class "Negro" woman of Baltimore, Md.

Equality in writing characters in a whole field means being able to locate a centrality of worth in another person outside the sociological categories of religion, race and class, of women and men, of people and dogs, of dogs and trees, of stones and chairs and even or especially of paragraph and word, and word and letter.

In college Stein's most influential teacher, William James, had said that the moment one excludes anything from consciousness is the moment when one begins to cease being an intellectual. Stein expanded her sense of inclusiveness, and her fascination with "everyone" by including characters and subjects situated in daily life, the most mundane and ordinary everyday events becoming for her the stuff of philosophy and meaningful being:

A Box

A large box is handily made of what is necessary to replace any substance. Suppose an example is necessary, the plainer it is made the more reason there is for some outward recognition that there is a result. (*Tender Buttons*)

She included the participation of the reader as part of "the whole field." She wanted us to work our minds, so much so that she discarded use of the comma in much of her work because, she said, a comma is like a servant, always holding your coat and opening the door for you. She thought this was condescending to and undermining of the independence of mind of the reader.

As she worked out her ideas of equality, she applied them to the nature of writing and thinking, and increasingly explored grammatical structures, allowing parts of speech usually relegated to "inferior" or dependent status to have equality in sentences, and to speak from their own centers in sentences based entirely in them and their relationships to other words.

The usually overlooked articles, for instance: "When is and thank and is and and and is when is when is and when thank when is and when and thank." ("Patriarchal Poetry")

And the usually overlooked prepositions: "Put it with it with it and it and it in it in it add it add it at it at it with it with it put it put it to this to understand." ("Patriarchal Poetry")

And the usually overlooked adverbs: "Able able nearly

nearly nearly nearly able able finally nearly able nearly not now finally finally nearly able." ("Patriarchal Poetry")

It is no wonder we are taking our time understanding her, given that she is challenging our very basic patterns of relationship, at the level of linguistic relationship, for how we speak is how we think, and how we think is how we are.

In Stein's work the linear plot inherent in English language sentences falls away. The noun is no longer the all-important main character surrounded by subservient modifiers and dependent articles and clauses, the verb is no longer a mounted hero riding into the sentence doing all the action, while the happy or tragic ending of objective clause waits in the wings with appropriate punctuation to lead us through the well-known plot to the inevitable end period.

She let the characters (which in some of her writing are parts of speech or numbers, not people or other creatures) spin out from their own internal natures as she let them happen from within themselves rather than placing them in an externally directed context. She discovered them as she uncovered them layer by layer through the rhythms of their speech or parts of speech, and the patterns of their daily lives, she listened to them as her eyes listened to Cezanne's intensity of color, carrying this idea of equality further to when everything in a given field is seen as equally vital, life is perceived as a dance in which every element contributes to every other. In a painting of a woman sitting by a bush in a chair the sky is alive the bush is alive the woman is alive the tips of her hair are alive the dress is alive the shoe is alive the ground is alive the chair is alive, and when this is done in a paragraph rather than a painting the word chair is alive the word the is alive the word is is alive and the word alive is alive and they are all dancing with each other in common. They are not telling a story that we already know or can already know and certainly not in a progressive linear manner.

Essence

In addition to equality Stein used what she called essence. Searching for the "bottom nature" or essence of a character, and then later of an object or archetype, or part of speech, she found the repeated themes of characters being revealed in repeated ordinary phrases they use in speaking, and in the themes of their behavior and apparent inner motivation. After much close listening, Stein selected these repetitions as the essential rhythms of meaning that underlie all life/thought forms.

I once lived with a parakeet who "named" humans using a similar method as Gertrude Stein. At the time I lived not only with the appealing parakeet but also with a woman whose constant smoking had given her a severe chronic cough, while my nose ran continually as I was allergic to her smoke.

The parakeet was very responsive to and imitative of our language, entertaining us often with lengthy mumbled versions of human speech. He also identified us with special noises. Every time the parakeet saw the smoking woman he made this noise: cough-cough, cough-cough. Whenever he saw me he made this noise: sniff-sniff, sniff-sniff. He used these sounds to greet us in his bright-eyed and friendly fashion, exactly as we greeted him with his name, Gloriana.

I was only amused and a little embarrassed by this until I listened carefully and realized that cough-cough and sniff-sniff were in fact the sounds we made most often. He had called us by the noises we made the most consistently and repetitively in our everyday lives, revealing in both of us, very tellingly, our essence during that period of time.

Stein, believing that everything has its own "bottom nature," set out to write the biographical history of her family and all their neighbors by revealing the essences of all the characters, an effort that turned into *The Making of Americans*:

"As I was saying mostly all children have in them loving repeating being as important in them to them and to every one around them. Mostly growing young men and growing young women have to themselves very little loving repeating being, they do not have it to each other then most of them, they have it to older ones then as older ones have it to them loving repeating being, not loving repeating being but repeating as the way of being in them, repeating of the whole of them as coming every minute from them." *(The Making of Americans)*

Though the lengthy book has many psychological insights, her explorations of essence in *The Making of Americans* led her to much generalized and almost sociological cataloguing of kinds of people: "Independent dependent men and women have attacking as a natural way of fighting in them." She included the narrator in the whole field by repeating clauses characteristic of the role of storyteller: "As I was saying," and "There will be now a history of her."

Using the idea of everything belonging to a whole field and mattering equally, as well as each being having an essence of its own, she inevitably wrote patterns rather than linear sequences. This centers her squarely in a "feminine," that is to say, not in a traditional patriarchal construction, for she is a cosmic quiltmaker of essential relationships rather than a chronicler of linear heroic adventures.

Value

Plot and imagery are the elements that very often give a piece of writing cohesion, enabling the individual sentences to hold together and to hold our interest. In the absence of both plot and comparative imagery, what gives the work integrity within itself?

Stein answered this question for herself by borrowing a technique from painters known as value. The intensity of color after it is applied to a canvas is called tone; and there is great variety in the tone of pigments as they are made of such diverse substances in nature as metals and plants and petroleums. To coordinate this wild variety painters add a single color to each of the others, an undertone they all have in common, just as jellies all have added sugar in common. This added color is usually zinc white; painters use a scale known as a grey scale to decide how much white to add to each color on their palette, in order for all the colors to have value, or harmony with each other, once they are applied to the canvas.

Words get their "color intensity" by the emotion and circumstance of their social usage. Stein worked out her idea of value as she wrote Tender Buttons in a series of still life portraits based in everyday life with titles such as "Roast Beef" and "Milk":

A Method of a Cloak

A single climb to a line, a straight exchange to a cane, a desperate adventure and courage and a clock, all this which is a system, which has feeling, which has resignation and success, all makes an attractive black silver. (*Tender Buttons*)

To acquire *value*, Stein carefully chose a particularly physical vocabulary, not in the sense of gross physical imagery (blood dripping guts), but in the sense of not so many Latin-based words, and many more Anglo-Saxon. Because Latin is no longer a living language we memorize its syllables without knowledge of their original physical basis, and thus Latin based words have little physical associative *value*. So: "sanguine" is the Latin for "blood"; blood is the more physically immediate Anglo-Saxon. The use of more immediately experienced (in the synaptic connections of the brain) Anglo-Saxon words gives her work a physical basis that lives in the vocabulary itself, and is not dependent on dramatic body imagery for its physical grounding.

On the other hand she decided that words with "too much association" did not work to establish the overall *value* she was after, either. Socially prohibited or violently loaded words such as "stench" and "nigger," and pathological physical images such as "yellow pus," she decided no longer to use—they did not harmonize with her overall intent.

One consequence of developing *value* and *essence* as the basis of her work, rather than social themes, dramatic imagery or linear plots, is that she developed a remarkable objective voice. To an uncanny degree at times, social judgment is absent in her author's voice, as the reader is left the power to decide how to think and feel about the writing.

Her paragraphs appeal to an esthetic of the mind that is harmonic, almost pastoral, and deeply meditative. Anxiety, fear and anger are not played upon, and this alone sets her apart from most modern authors. Her work is harmonic and integrative, not alienated; at the same time it is grounded and useful, not wistful or fantastic.

Grounding and the Continuous Present

Her use of time in grammatical structures that center in "ing" words, participles of current happening rather than past or future verbal constructs, results in what she called the use of the *continuous present*. This spinning of time within the text itself and on a word by word basis grew very naturally out of her understanding of her other principles: that everything matters equally, that everything has an essential nature; the establishment of a harmonic coordination of vocabulary, and the decision not to pursue linear plot. She used these tools plus current observation to ground her work in the physical present.

Concentration on such matters automatically places us in the present and grounds us directly wherever we are.

When someone is distracted from his immediate environment it is because he has something "more important" on his mind, some other story going on in his head that is not connected to where he is. Stein did not have any "more important story" going on; she centered her writing on everything that was happening within it at the time, so the words are in the time appropriate to their current relationship to each other, rather than being pushed around in accordance to a previously known "story."

To the extent that we do not feel familiarity in being so immediately grounded in any writing we get impatient in reading her because the details and the essences do not seem "as important" as some other idea of story, or fantasy that we have in our minds to take us away from our current state. And to the extent that we don't recognize her patterns, we try to stay connected to the "content" of information, to some objective state, and wander off from her subjectivity and patterned connectedness to find a "more important story."

Stein was not "experimental" in her work, she was very deliberate and had a solidly scientific methodology of observation and theory each time over the years as she developed new aspects of her art. She set out in college in a science field, medicine, and when she gave that up for writing she retained her scientific methods and her interest in subjects such as the human mind, geography, being, time, and the nature of language.

She criticized her younger self once when she said of a few of the still-life verbal portraits written in 1912-1914 and collected as *Tender Buttons* that they are "too much fantasy," they were not successful to her intent. She succeeded in her own view when she was grounded with an objective eye, looking at real beings in real life, as the basis for her portraits, however far-reaching the effects of her verbal patterning.

To create portraits of words based in observed reality, she and her lifelong companion, Alice B. Toklas, drove a cow around a field so she could observe it and construct a verbal portrait. Accounts vary as to which of the pair actually drove the cow.

Because she was rooted thoroughly in a scientific method of observing and listening, everyone who attempts to imitate her style sounds thin and artificial; they are fantasizing, making up what she was doing. She wasn't "making up" anything; she was using theories and observations of real life and real relationships in grammatical structures.

Stein's friend Pablo Picasso said that the artist is never experimental, experimentation is for those who don't know what they are doing. Gertrude Stein always knew what she was doing as can be seen from her essays and lectures which so precisely describe her theories and intentions.

Stein grew continuously and exponentially in her artistic life along the dimensions she laid down early on. The plots of stories, she believed, had already been told by the literature of the last century so why tell them again? Having rejected the Western literary plot mechanisms of conflict and resolution, hero-victim-rescue, and linear cause and effect progressions, she exchanged plot in the sense of linear progression of events for a more intriguing and difficult sense of it as place, context, field, entirety. Everything that is present in this place, matters. Without a linear plot, past and future merge and time spins in an endless present. What happens is happening at the time of the reading, the *continuous present*, the only time that exists in Stein's writing. As you read it is when it is happening, it is happening in its entirety, and it is happening right here at this moment inside you.

Play

A primary characteristic of Stein's work is that she does not emotionally manipulate. We are as readers very dependent on emotional manipulation giving us the clues to appropriate inner response, laid down by most authors, especially those least influenced by Stein.

Stein does not instruct how to feel about her subjects, often we cannot tell if "tragedy" or "comedy" is the appropriate emotional mask for us to wear while reading. As no guiding plot directs us through familiar action so we can feel joy when the hero succeeds and despair when he fails, no judging or tension-dripping dramatic voice of value shines through the vocabulary to tell us what the social, moral and emotional implications are.

What I have noticed in doing oral presentations of Stein's work is the individuality of audience response to her. Some people will look baffled, some serious, some whimsical and some will be in hysterics with laughter during the exact same passage; two minutes later, similar responses but not from the same people. Everyone is responding to her from inside the self, rather than the entire group laughing and saddening at points of narrative so predictable actors and speakers can mark them as places to go slow so as to allow for the response.

Rather than the emotional manipulation that is a characteristic of linear writing, Stein uses *play*.

This use of *play* operates with spontaneity and openness, and in addition with much space for movement. There is such leeway of interpretation in her work, such layering of relationship, such room to feel a variety of feelings and incongruities, to have insights and bursts of expression that seem to be a release as though energy collects, spirals and then spurts out in fresh insight or a catching of oneself in an old absurd thought. These outbursts are responses to what could be called doorway humor, that is, the humor spins on incongruities and contradictions of thought that accumulate in her repeating, finally acting to open a doorway in the mind through which a new idea can bubble or an old idea exit in a wheeze of delight. Just as the cervix also opens, on its own time schedule, for the releasing of a new thought (a baby), or the release, in bubbles and dribbles, of old thoughts in the built-up lining of the uterus.

Of the very particularly Steinian humor, "It isn't wit," Alice said, "the English have wit." Stein humor is not used to dissect, mellow, or disarm a situation. Rather it is used to further the described situation, and reveal the multiplicity of its nature.

Her humor is that of the essential geni, the "idiot" or king's fool who sees the emperor naked and finds this nakedness wonderfully interesting, or who finds something else entirely about the situation wonderfully interesting. Honesty, being the ability to admit—to let in some intelligence—honesty and humor are related. Being open to information means not placing moral straitjackets on it or processing it. Taking in new information completely honestly means believing it *and* not believing it at the same time, taking it for accurate and not accurate at the same time. Information being something new, the gathering of intelligence is related to humor. It is a state of being "in formation," in the act of being, of admitting. This is a transformational state, a state of possibly changing one's mind.

The continual play of Stein's language shakes our everyday belief that reality is hard-edged and fixed, and at the same time so fragile that we feel our version of reality must be taken seriously lest it crumble and our relationship to it and to our own personalities also crumble into madness. Allowing new dimensions of thought through, however, does not result in madness, but in an endless spiral of creative, motion-filled worlds—worlds of overlapping events.

Reality in Stein's work is never fixed, it is by definition and usage always in motion, taking its meanings from evershifting relationships which the humor aids by sparking our courage—through the shifts of ever moving text.

Transformation

I realize that one reason I have taken so many years to read her work, besides the sheer volume of it, is also the intensity of its effect on me. As a writer, I am sensitive to my own originality and embarrassed if I think I am imitating others. Especially when I was younger, in my twenties and thirties, I could not go near Stein without turning into her. Although I went to her as a starting point for two major projects, *She Who* and *Mundane's World*, I entered her work and then quickly pulled away as soon as I was able to make use of her forms and theories, lest my own work sound hopelessly imitative of her powerful style.

The time is long past for trying to consider her "experimental" or out at some fringe of literature. *Three Lives*, her first published work, was written in 1903, her last work was written in 1946, at the end of her life. Now as I write late in the century she helped form, she is central not only to American literature, but she continues deeply to influence American thought, and to further the development, begun by Walt Whitman, of a unique American literary language. And as a woman-centered language philosopher, she gives us the foundation of a new theosophy. Decade by decade her readership deepens and comprehends her more fully, as though we change along a continuum of her own thought.

She is not marginal, not experimental, not randomly selective, not just letting her mind wander, not nonsensical and not making fun of us. Most importantly she is not alienated. She is integrative and by being centrally located rather than linear her work is central to itself and to its own principles; it is referential to itself and to the ideas that she used to form it; as such it is philosophical, and it is what it is.

Her use of commonality leads to each element being seen from its own perspective. Meanings are drawn from the interaction of overlapping commonalities, and the refractive humor. Her use of essence coordinates with scientific ideas of energy, of waves. And her use of value leads to harmony and integration.

The question of how to "understand" her now clarifies itself, as the wrong question. To *under*stand, to get to the basis, the root or hidden meaning, is the wrong tool to bring to Stein as she so rarely uses symbolic imagery that has meaning beyond what happens between reader and the immediate language on the page. Perhaps *inter*stand is what we do, to engage with the work, to mix with it in an active engagement, rather than "figuring it out." Figure it in.

Now perhaps we have some answers to the puzzle of our difficulty in reading such intense simplicity. She is transformational—extremely so, entering as she does so freely the brain of language at the level of the synaptic connections establishing syntax, and hence, the essential meanings we each interpret as "my life." Stein is subversive at this level, given the extreme linearity of the plots of our society, so subversive that too much absorption of her thought-forms would render the reader dysfunctional, especially if we try instantly to implement them. Our own safety mechanisms cut us off from her before this happens, with the defense, "boredom, confusion."

Secondly, the work is subversive at the level of fundamental social relationships, postulating a field in which everything is equal. While this field description is as perfectly true a description as any other, it also flies in the face of every functional social moment we experience outside the experience of reading Stein. The moment we put "Patriarchal Poetry" or "Advertisements" down the cup does not equal the wall which does not equal the human sitting on the couch which does not equal the one shuffling down the street which does not equal the which or the not or the does or the sitting or the the or the or.

Not yet, anyhow.

Essential Clues for Really Reading Her:

1. Play with her.

Let her happen in you. One of the best approaches to Gertrude Stein is to play with her, and to allow her to play inside your mind without trying to guide her into any preconceived notion of sense. I think it is when she is approached with too much seriousness of intent, that her seriousness most eludes. When you get tired of playing, stop.

2. When she gets tedious, skip around.

Get over the embarrassment of not being able to read her easily, if, as it is with me, this is true. One reason for her tediousness is that she did not edit herself for length, and we often read as if we don't know when to stop until we feel we have eaten some candy. As philosophers often do, she left her work intact for the most part, in the bright little notebooks she used, thus leaving us with her complete, unaltered writing mind. Just as it is up to us to feel our own feelings as we read her, so we must also take some responsibility for editing her, reading what connects at the moment and leaving the rest for later, and without feeling either stupid in ourselves or resentful of the fact that she thought of every word she wrote as a gift of equal merit.

3. Read aloud with a friend or two.

I have found that reading her aloud deepens my interaction with the words, allows me to keep a watchful eye floating on top of her words while the rest of me waits to see what happens inside myself. And it is wonderful to see how someone else reacts differently, surfaces with an entirely different set of impressions and insights.

4. Pick a sentence as a mantra or daily meditation.

"How easily we ask for what we are going to have." This is a pleasing and provocative sentence to me, one of zillions of hers, and zillions are overwhelming. By concentrating for days on just one, I can make a practical use of her.

5. Sing the lines.

Reading with a group of friends increases enjoyment, but singing her lines is the most enjoyment of all, requiring as it does complete entry into her sense of expressive play and delight in life. You do not need melodic sense to do this, chanting and rhythmic howling of the words do just as well.

By Gertrude Stein

If You Had Three Husbands

1915

If you had three husbands.

If you had three husbands.

If you had three husbands, well not exactly that.

If you had three husbands would you be willing to take everything and be satisfied to live in Belmont in a large house with a view and plenty of flowers and neighbors, neighbors who were cousins and some friends who did not say anything.

This is what happened.

She expressed everything.

She is worthy of signing a will.

And mentioning what she wished.

She was brought up by her mother. She had meaning and she was careful in reading. She read marvelously. She was pleased. She was aged thirty-nine. She was flavored by reason of much memory and recollection.

This is everything.

Foreword.

I cannot believe it.

I cannot realize it.

I cannot see it.

It is what happened.

First there was a wonder.

Really wonder.

Wonder by means of what.

Wonder by means of measures.

Measuring what.

Heights.

How high.

A little.

This was not all.

There were well if you like there were wonderful spots such as were seen by a queen. This came to be a system. Really it was just by a treasure. What was a treasure. Apart from that.

Surely.

Rather.

In their beginning what was a delight. Not signing papers or anything or indeed in having a mother and two sisters. Not nearly enough were mentioned by telegraphing. It was a choice.

I ramble when I mention it.

Did she leave me any money.

I remember something.

I am not clear about what it was.

When did I settle that.

I settled it yesterday.

Early Life

They were not miserably young they were older than another. She was gliding. It is by nearly weekly leaning that it comes to be exact. It never was in dispute.

They were gayly not gaily gorgeous. They were not gorgeous at all. They were obliging. If you think so. If you think so glow. If you believe in light boys. They were never another.

It came to be seen that any beam of three rooms was not showy. They were proud to sit at mother. Slowly walking makes walking quicker. They have toys and not that in deceiving. They do not deceive them. No one is willing. No one could be cool and mother and divided and necessary and climatical and of origin and beneath that mean and be a sun. It was strange in her cheek. Not strange to them or that.

A young one.

Not by mountains.

Not by oysters.

Not by hearing.

Not by round ways.

Not by circumference again.

Not by leaving luncheon.

Not by birth.

It doesn't make any difference when ten are born. Ten is never a number. Neither is six. Neither is four.

I will not mention it again.

Early days of shading.

Make a mouse in green.

Make a single piece of sun and make a violet bloom. Early piece of swimming makes a sun on time and makes it shine and warm today and sun and sun and not to stay and not to stay or away. Not to stay satin. Out from the whole wide world he chose her. Out from the whole wide world and that is what is said.

Family.

What is famine. It is plenty of another. What is famine. It is eating. What is famine. It is carving. Why is carving a wonderful thing. Because supper is over. This can happen again. Sums are seen.

Please be polite for mother. Lives of them. Call it shall it clothe it. Boil it. Why not color it black and never red or green. This is stubborn. I don't say so.

No opposition.

If you had a little likeness and hoped for more terror. If you had a refusal and were slender. If you had cuff-buttons and jackets and really astonishing kinds of fever would you stop talking. Would you not consider it necessary to talk over affairs.

It was a chance that made them never miss tea. They did not miss it because it was there. They did not mean to be particular. They invited their friends. They were not aching. It was noiseless and beside that they were clever. Who was clever. The way they had of seeing mother.

Mother was prepared.

They were caressing.

They had sound sense.

They were questioned.

They had likeness. Likeness to what. Likeness to loving. Who had likeness to loving. They had likeness to loving. Why did they have a likeness to loving. They had a likeness to loving because it was easily seen that they were immeasurable.

They were fixed by that, they were fixed, not licensed, they were seen, not treasured, they were announced, not restless, they were reasoning, not progressing. I do not wish to imply that there is any remedy for any defect.

I cannot state that anyone was disappointed. I cannot state that any one was ever disappointed by willingly heaping much confusion in particular places. No confusion is reasonable. Anybody can be nervous.

They were nervous again.

This is wishing.

Why is wishing related to a ridiculous pretence of changing opposition to analysis. The answer to this is that nearly any one can faint. I don't mean to say that they don't like tennis.

Please be capable of sounds and shoulders. Please be capable of careful words. Please be capable of meaning to measure further.

They measured there.

They were heroes.

Nobody believed papers.

Everybody believed colors.

I cannot exercise obligation.

I cannot believe cheating.

I cannot sober mother.

I cannot shut my heart.

1 cannot cherish vice.

I cannot deceive all.

I cannot be odious.

I cannot see between.

Between what and most.

I cannot answer either.

Do be left over suddenly.

This is not advice.

No one knows so well what widening means. It means that yards are yards and so many of them are perfect. By that I mean I know. This is not so.

I am not telling the story I am repeating what I have been reading.

What effects tenderness.

Not to remember the name.

Say it.

The time comes when it is natural to realize that solid advantages connect themselves with pages of extreme expression. This is never nervously pale. It is finely and authentically swollen by the time there is any rapid shouting.

I do not like the word shouting. I do not mean that it gives me any pleasure. On the contrary I see that individual annoyances are increased by it but nevertheless I am earnestly persuasive concerning it. Why soothe why soothe each other.

This is not at all what is being said.

It happened very simply that they were married. They were naturally married and really the place to see it was in the reflection every one had of not frightening not the least bit frightening enthusiasm. They were so exact and by nearly every one it was encouraged soothed and lamented. I do not say that they were interested.

Any years are early years and all years are occasions for recalling that she promised me something.

This is the way to write an address.

When they were engaged she said we are happy. When they were married she said we are happy. They talked about everything they talked about individual feeling. This is not what was said. They did not talk about disinterested obligation. They did not talk about pleasantness and circumstances. I do not mean to say that there was conversation. I do not organize a revision. I declare that there was no need of criticism. That there was no criticism. That there was breathing. By that I mean that lights have lanterns and are not huddled together when there is a low ceiling. By that I mean that it was separate. The ceiling was separated from the floor. Everywhere.

I could say that devotion was more merited than walking together. What do you mean. I mean that we all saw it.

When not by a beginning is there meadows and music, you can't call it that exactly, when not by a beginning, there is no beginning, I used to say there was a beginning, there is no beginning, when there is no beginning in a volume and there are parts, who can think.

This pencil was bought in Austria.

Length of time or times.

He agreed. He said I would have known by this time. I don't like to think about it. It would have led to so much. Not that I am disappointed I cannot be disappointed when I have so much to make me happy. I know all that I am to happiness, it is to be happy and I am happy. I am so completely happy that I mention it.

In writing now I find it more of a strain because now I write by sentences. I don't mean that I feel it above, I feel it here and by this time I mention it too. I do not feel the significance of this list.

Can you read a book.

By the time artificial flowers were made out of feathers no pride was left. Any one is proud if the name of their house is the name of a city.

I remember very well the time I was asked to come up and I said I did not want to. I said I did not want to but I was willing not quite to understand why after all there need be poison. Do not say more than a word.

No this is wrong.

Cousins and cousins, height is a brother. Are they careful to stay.

If you had three husbands I don't mean that it is a guess or a wish. I believe finally in what I saw in what I see. I believe finally in what I see, in where I satisfy my extreme shadow.

Believing in an extreme dream. This is so that she told her mother. I do not believe it can be mentioned. I do not believe it can be mentioned.

Astonishing leaves are found in their dread in their dread of that color. Astonishing leaves can be found in their dread not in their dread of that color. Astonishing leaves can be found in their dread in their dread of that color.

When it came to say I mean a whole day nobody meant a whole day. When it came not to say a whole day nobody meant a whole day. There never was a single day or a single murmur or a single word or a single circumstance or sweating. What is sweating. Not distilling. Distilling necessitates knowing. Knowing necessitates reasons and reasons do not necessitate flowers. States are flowers.

Brother to birthdays.

Twenty four days.

Not a beginning.

By politeness. It is not really polite to be unworthy. Unworthy of what unworthy of the house and of the property adjoining.

Let me describe the red room. A red room isn't cold or warm. A red room is not meant to be icy. A red room is worthy of articles.

He pleased she pleased everybody. He pleased her.

He pleased her to go. She was attracted by the time. I do not remember that there were any clocks.

I don't wish to begin counting.

All this was after it was necessary for us to be there all the time. Who were we. We were often enlivening. By way of what. By way of steps or the door. By way of steps. By way of steps or the door.

I remember very well the day he asked me if I were patient. Of course I was or of course I was patient enough, of course I was patient enough.

When it was easy to matter we were all frames not golden or printed, just finely or formerly flattered. It was so easy easy to be bell. Belle was her name. Belle or Bella. I don't mean relations or overwhelming. I don't even mean that we were fond of healthy trees. Trees aren't healthy by yesterday or by roots or by swelling. Trees are a sign of pleasure. It means that there is a country. A country give to me sweet land of liberty.

One can easily get tired of rolls and rows. Rows have one seat. Rolls are polite. In a way there is no difference between them. Rolls and rows have finished purses. Rows and rolls have finished purses.

It isn't easy to be restless.

If sitting is not developed.

If standing is not open.

If active action is represented by lying and if piles of tears are beside more delight, it is a rope.

By that we swim.
Capture sealing wax not in or color.
Ceilings.
I like that dwelling.
All the same sound or bore.
Do it.
Try that.
Try.
Why.
Widen.
Public speaking is sinister if cousins are brothers. We were a little pile.
Buy that.
There is no such sense.

Pleasant days.

So to speak.
Sand today.
Sunday.
Sight in there.
Saturday.
Pray.
What forsooth.
Do be quiet.
Laugh.
I know it.
Shall we.
Let us go ten.
One must be willing.
If one loves one another by that means they do not perish. They frequent the same day and nearly that it was six months apart.
Three and three make two.
Two twenty.
I was not disappointed.

Do as you please, write the name, change it, declare that you are strong, be annoyed. All this is not foolish.

She was doubtless not old.

Pleasant days brother. I don't mean this thing. I don't mean calling aloud, I never did so, I was not plaintive. I was not even reached by coughing. I was splendid and sorrowful. I could catch my breath.

I don't feel that necessity.

They came home.

Why did they come home.

They come home beside.

All of it was strange, their daughter was strange, their excitement was strange and painfully sheltered. Quiet leaning is so puzzling. Certainly glasses makes cats a nuisance. We really have endured too much. Everybody says the same thing.

I do not see much nesessity for believing that it would have occurred as it did occur if sun and September and the hope had not been mentioned. It was all foolish. Why not be determined. Why not oppose. Why not settle flowers. Settle on flowers, speak cryingly and be loath to detain her. I don't see how any one can speak.

I am not satisfied.

Present Homes.

There then.

Present ten.

Mother and sister apples, no not apples, they can't be apples, everything can't be apples, sounds can't be apples. Do be quiet and refrain from acceptances.

It was a great disappointment to me.

I can see that there is a balcony. There never was a sea or land, there never was a harbor or a snow storm, there never was excitement. Some said she couldn't love. I don't believe anybody said that. We were all present. We could be devoted. It does make a different thing. And hair, hair should not be deceiving. Cause tears. Why tears, why not abscesses.

I will never mention an ugly skirt.

It pleased me to say that I was pretty.

Oh we are so pleased.

I don't say this at all.

Consequences are not frightful.

Pleasure in a home.

After lunch, why after lunch, no birds are eaten. Of course carving is special.

I don't say that for candor.

Please be prepared to stay.

I don't care for wishes.

This is not a success.

By this stream.

Streaming out.

I am relieved from draught. This is not the way to spell water.

I cannot believe in much.

I have courage.

Endurance.

And restraint.

After that.

For that end.

This is the title of a conclusion which was not anticipated.

When I was last there I smiled behind the car. What car showed it.

By that time.

Believe her out.

Out where.

By that.

Buy that.

She pleased me for. Eye saw.

Do it.

For that over that.
We passed away. By that time servants were memorable.
They came to praise.
Please do not.
A blemish.
They have spans.
I cannot consider that the right word.
By the time we are selfish, by that time we are selfish.
By that time we are selfish.
It is a wonderful sight,
It is a wonderful sight to see.
Days.
What are days.
They have hams.
Delicate.
Delicate hams.
Pounds.
Pounds where.
Pounds of.
Where.
Not butter dogs.
I establish souls.
Any spelling will do.
Beside that.
Any spelling will do beside that.
If you look at it.
That way.
I am going on.
In again.
I am going on again in in then.
What I feel.
What I do feel.
They said mirrors.
Undoubtedly they have that phrase.
I can see a hat.

I remember very well knowing largely.

Any shade, by that I do mean iron glass. Iron glass is so torn. By what. By the glare. Be that beside. Size shall be sensible. That size shall be sensible.

Fixing.

Fixing enough
Fixing up.
By fixing down, that is softness, by fixing down there.

Their end.

Politeness.

Not by linen.

I don't wish to be recalled.

One, day, I do not wish to use the word, one day they asked to buy that.

I don't mean anything by threads. It was wholly unnecessary to do so. It was done and then a gun. By that stand. Wishes.

I do not see what I have to do with that.

Any one can help weeping.

By wise.

I am so indifferent.

Not a bite.

Call me handsome.

It was a nice fate.

Any one could see.

Any one could see.

Any one could see.

Buy that etching.

Do be black.

I do not mean to say etching. Why should I be very sensitive. Why should I matter. Why need I be seen. Why not have politeness.

Why not have politeness.

In my hair.

I don't think it sounds at all like that.

Their end.

To end.

To be for that end.

To be that end.

I don't see what difference it makes

It does matter.

Why have they pots.

Ornaments.

And china.

It isn't at all.

I have made every mistake.

Powder it.

Not put into boxes.

Not put into boxes.

Powder it.

I know that well.

She mentioned it as she was sleeping.

She liked bought cake best. No she didn't for that purpose.

I have utter confusion.

No two can be alike.

They are and they are not stubborn.

Please me.

I was mistaken.

Any way.

By that.

Do not refuse to be wild.

Do not refuse to be all.

We have decided not to withstand it.

We would not rather have the home.

This is to teach lessons of exchange endurance and resemblance and by that time it was turned.

Shout.

By.

Out.

I am going to continue humming.

This does not mean express wishes.

I am not so fanciful. I am beside that calculated to believe in whole pages. Oh do not annoy me.

Days.

I don't like to be fitted. She didn't say that. If it hadn't been as natural as all the rest you would have been as silly as all the rest.

It's not at all when it is right.

I wish for a cake.

She said she did.

She said she didn't.

Gloom.

There was no gloom.

Every room.

There was no room.

There was no room.

Buy that chance.

She didn't leave me any money.

Head.

Ahead.

I don't want to be visible or invisible.

I don't want a dog named Dick.

It has nothing to do with it.

I am obliged to end.

Intend.

My uncle will.

By Gertrude Stein

Rooms

from Tender Buttons

Act so that there is no use in a centre. A wide action is not a width. A preparation is given to the ones preparing. They do not eat who mention silver and sweet. There was an occupation.

A whole centre and a border make hanging a way of dressing. This which is not why there is a voice is the remains of an offering. There was no rental.

So the tune which is there has a little piece to play, and the exercise is all there is of a fast. Then tender and true that makes no width to hew is the time that there is question to adopt.

To begin the placing there is no wagon. There is no change lighter. It was done. And then the spreading, that was not accomplishing that needed standing and yet the time was not so difficult as they were not all in place. They had no change. They were not respected. They were that, they did it so much in the matter and this showed that that settlement was not condensed. It was spread there. Any change was in the ends of the centre. A heap was heavy. There was no change.

Burnt and behind and lifting a temporary stone and lifting more than a drawer.

The instance of there being more is an instance of more. The shadow is not shining in the way there is a black line. The truth has come. There is a disturbance. Trusting to a baker's boy meant that there would be very much exchanging and anyway what is the use of a covering to a door. There is a use, they are double.

If the centre has the place then there is distribution. That is natural. There is a contradiction and naturally returning there comes to be both sides and the centre. That can be seen from the description.

The author of all that is in there behind the door and that is entering in the morning. Explaining darkening and expecting relating is all of a piece. The stove is bigger. It was of a shape that made no audience bigger if the opening is assumed why should there not be kneeling. Any force which is bestowed on a floor shows rubbing. This is so nice and sweet and yet there comes the change, there comes the time to press more air. This does not mean the same as disappearance.

A little lingering lion and a Chinese chair, all the handsome cheese which is stone, all of it and a choice, a choice of a blotter. If it is difficult to do it one way there is no place of similar trouble. None. The whole arrangement is established. The end of which is that there is a suggestion, a suggestion that there can be a different whiteness to a wall. This was thought.

A page to a corner means that the shame is no greater when the table is longer. A glass is of any height, it is higher, it is simpler and if it were placed there would not be any doubt.

Something that is an erection is that which stands and feeds and silences a tin which is swelling. This makes no diversion that is to say what can please exaltation, that which is cooking.

A shine is that which when covered changes permission. An enclosure blends with the same that is to say there is blending. A blend is that which holds no mice and this is not because of a floor it is because of nothing, it is not in a vision.

A fact is that when the place was replaced all was left that was stored and all was retained that would not satisfy more than another. The question is this, is it possible to suggest more to replace that thing. This question and this perfect denial does make the time change all the time.

The sister was not a mister. Was this a surprise. It was. The conclusion came when there was no arrangement. All the time that there was a question there was a decision. Replacing a casual acquaintance with an ordinary daughter does not make a son.

It happened in a way that the time was perfect and there was a growth of a whole dividing time so that where formerly there was no mistake there was no mistake now. For instance before when there was a separation there was waiting, now when there is separation there is the division between intending and departing. This made no more mixture than there would be if there had been no change.

A little sign of an entrance is the one that made it alike. If it were smaller it was not alike and it was so much smaller that a table was bigger. A table was much bigger, very much bigger. Changing that made nothing bigger, it did not make anything bigger littler, it did not hinder wood from not being used as leather. And this was so charming. Harmony is so essential. Is there pleasure when there is a passage, there is when every room is open. Every room is open when there are not four, there were there and surely there were four, there were two together. There is no resemblance.

A single speed, the reception of table linen, all the wonder of six little spoons, there is no exercise.

The time came when there was a birthday. Every day was no excitement and a birthday was added, it was added on Monday, this made the memory clear, this which was a speech showed the chair in the middle where there was copper.

Alike and a snail, this means Chinamen, it does there is no doubt that to be right is more than perfect there is no doubt and glass is confusing it confuses the substance which was of a color. Then came the time for discrimination, it came then and it was never mentioned it was so triumphant, it showed the whole head that had a hole and should have a hole it showed the resemblance between silver.

Startling a starving husband is not disagreeable. The reason that nothing is hidden is that there is no suggestion of silence. No song is sad. A lesson is of consequence.

Blind and weak and organised and worried and betrothed and resumed and also asked to a fast and always asked to consider and never startled and not at all bloated, this which is no rarer than frequently is not so astonishing when hair brushing is added. There is quiet, there certainly is.

No eye-glasses are rotten, no window is useless and yet if air will not come in there is a speech ready, there always is and there is no dimness, not a bit of it.

All along the tendency to deplore the absence of more has not been authorised. It comes to mean that with burning there is that pleasant state of stupefication. Then there is a way of earning a living. Who is a man.

A silence is not indicated by any motion, less is indicated by a motion, more is not indicated it is enthralled. So sullen and so low, so much resignation, so much refusal and so much place for a lower and an upper, so much and yet more silence, why is not sleeping a feat why is it not and when is there some discharge when. There never is.

If comparing a piece that is a size that is recognised as not a size but a piece, comparing a piece with what is not recognised but what is used as it is held by holding, comparing these two comes to be repeated. Suppose they are put together, suppose that there is an interruption, supposing that beginning again they are not changed as to position, suppose all this and suppose that any five two of whom are not separating suppose that the five are not consumed. Is there an exchange, is there a resemblance to the sky which is admitted to be there and the stars which can be seen. Is there. That was a question. There was no certainty. Fitting a failing meant that any two were indifferent and yet they were all connecting that, they were all connecting that consideration. This did not determine rejoining a letter. This did not make letters smaller. It did.

The stamp that is not only torn but also fitting is not any symbol. It suggests nothing. A sack that has no opening suggests more and the loss is not commensurate. The season gliding and the torn hangings receiving mending all this shows an example, it shows the force of sacrifice and likeness and disaster and a reason.

The time when there is not the question is only seen when there is a shower. Any little thing is water.

There was a whole collection made. A damp cloth, an oyster, a single mirror, a mannikin, a student, a silent star, a single spark, a little movement and the bed is made. This shows the disorder, it does, it shows more likeness than anything else, it shows the single mind that directs an apple. All the coats have a different shape, that does not mean that they differ in color, it means a union between use and exercise and a horse.

A plain hill, one is not that which is not white and red and green, a plain hill makes no sunshine, it shows that without a disturber. So the shape is there and the color and the outline and the miserable centre, it is not very likely that there is a centre, a hill is a hill and no hill is contained in a pink tender descender.

A can containing a curtain is a solid sentimental usage. The trouble in both eyes does not come from the same symmetrical carpet, it comes from there being no more disturbance than in little paper. This does show the teeth, it shows color.

A measure is that which put up so that it shows the length has a steel construction. Tidiness is not delicacy, it does not destroy the whole piece, certainly not it has been measured and nothing has been cut off and even if that has been lost there is a name, no name is signed and left over, not any space is fitted so that moving about is plentiful. Why is there so much resignation in a package, why is there rain, all the same the chance has come, there is no bell to ring.

A package and a filter and even a funnel, all this together makes a scene and supposing the question arises is hair curly, is it dark and dusty, supposing that question arises, is brushing necessary, is it, the whole special suddenness commences then, there is no delusion.

A cape is a cover, a cape is not a cover in summer, a cape is a cover and the regulation is that there is no such weather. A cape is not always a cover, a cape is not a cover when there is another, there is always something in that thing in establishing a disposition to put wetting where it will not do more harm. There is always that disposition and in a way there is some use in not mentioning changing and in establishing the temperature, there is some use in it as establishing all that lives dimmer freer and there is no dinner in the middle of anything. There is no such thing.

Why is a pale white not paler than blue, why is a connection made by a stove, why is the example which is mentioned not shown to be the same, why is there no adjustment between the place and the separate attention. Why is there a choice in gamboling. Why is there no necessary dull stable, why is there a single piece of any color, why is there that sensible silence. Why is there the resistance in a mixture, why is there no poster, why is there that in the window, why is there no suggester, why is there no window, why is there no oyster closer. Why is there a circular diminisher, why is there a bather, why is there no scraper, why is there a dinner, why is there a bell ringer, why is there a duster, why is there a section of a similar resemblance, why is there that scissor.

South, south which is a wind is not rain, does silence

choke speech or does it not.

Lying in a conundrum, lying so makes the springs restless, lying so is a reduction, not lying so is arrangeable.

Releasing the oldest auction that is the pleasing some still renewing.

Giving it away, not giving it away, is there any difference. Giving it away. Not giving it away.

Almost very likely there is no seduction, almost very likely there is no stream, certainly very likely the height is penetrated, certainly certainly the target is cleaned. Come to sit, come to refuse, come to surround, come slowly and age is not lessening. The time which showed that was when there was no eclipse. All the time that resenting was removal all that time there was breadth. No breath is shadowed, no breath is painstaking and yet certainly what could be the use of paper, paper shows no disorder, it shows no desertion.

Why is there a difference between one window and another, why is there a difference, because the curtain is shorter. There is no distaste in beefsteak or in plums or in gallons of milk water, there is no defiance in original piling up over a roof, there is no daylight in the evening, there is none there empty.

A tribune, a tribune does not mean paper, it means nothing more than cake, it means more sugar, it shows the state of lengthening any nose. The last spice is that which shows the whole evening spent in that sleep, it shows so that walking is an alleviation, and yet this astonishes everybody the distance is so sprightly. In all the time there are three days, those are not passed uselessly. Any little thing is a change that is if nothing is wasted in that cellar. All the rest of the chairs are established.

A success, a success is alright when there are there rooms and no vacancies, a success is alright when there is a package, success is alright anyway and any curtain is wholesale. A curtain diminishes and an ample space shows varnish.

One taste one tack, one taste one bottle, one taste one fish, one taste one barometer. This shows no distinguishing sign when there is a store.

Any smile is stern and any coat is a sample. Is there any use in changing more doors than there are committees. This question is so often asked that squares show that they are blotters. It is so very agreeable to hear a voice and to see all the signs of that expression.

Cadences, real cadences, real cadences and a quiet color. Careful and curved, cake and sober, all accounts and mixture, a guess at anything is righteous, should there be a call there would be a voice.

A line in life, a single line and a stairway, a rigid cook, no cook and no equator, all the same there is higher than that another evasion. Did that mean shame, it meant memory. Looking into a place that was hanging and was visible looking into this place and seeing a chair did that mean relief, it did, it certainly did not cause constipation and yet there is a melody that has white for a tune when there is straw color. This shows no face.

Star-light, what is star-light, star-light is a little light that is not always mentioned with the sun, it is mentioned with the moon and the sun, it is mixed up with the rest of the time.

Why is the name changed. The name is changed because in the little space there is a tree, in some space there are no trees, in every space there is a hint of more, all this causes the decision.

Why is there education, there is education because the two tables which are folding are not tied together with a ribbon, string is used and string being used there is a necessity for another one and another one not being used to hearing shows no ordinary use of any evening and yet there is no disgrace in looking, none at all. This came to separate when there was simple selection of an entire pre-occupation.

A curtain, a curtain which is fastened discloses mourning, this does not mean sparrows or elocution or even a whole preparation, it means that there are ears and very often much more altogether.

Climate, climate is not southern, a little glass, a bright winter, a strange supper an elastic tumbler, all this shows that the back is furnished and red which is red is a dark color. An example of this is fifteen years and a separation of regret.

China is not down when there are plates, lights are not ponderous and incalculable.

Currents, currents are not in the air and on the floor and in the door and behind it first. Currents do not show it plainer. This which is mastered has so thin a space to build it all that there is plenty of room and yet is it quarreling, it is not and the insistance is marked. A change is in a current and there is no habitable exercise.

A religion, almost a religion, any religion, a quintal in religion, a relying and a surface and a service in indecision and a creature and a question and a syllable in answer and more counting and no quarrel and a single scientific statement and no darkness and no question and an earned administration and a single set of sisters and an outline and no blisters and the section seeing yellow and the centre having spelling and no solitude and no quaintness and yet solid quite so solid and the single surface centred and the question in the placard and the singularity, is there a singularity, and the singularity, why is there a question and the singularity why is the surface outrageous, why is it beautiful why is it not when there is no doubt, why is anything vacant, why is not disturbing a centre no virtue, why is it when it is and why is it when it is and there is no doubt, there is no doubt that the singularity shows.

A climate, a single climate, all the time there is a single climate, any time there is a doubt, any time there is music that is to question more and more and there is no politeness, there is hardly any ordeal and certainly there is no tablecloth. This is a sound and obligingness more obligingness leads to a harmony in hesitation.

A lake a single lake which is a pond and a little water any water which is an ant and no burning, not any burning, all this is sudden.

A canister that is the remains of furniture and a looking-glass and a bed-room and a larger size, all the stand is shouted and what is ancient is practical. Should the resemblance be so that any little cover is copied, should it be so that yards are measured, should it be so and there be a sin, should it be so then certainly a room is big enough when it is so empty and the corners are gathered together.

The change is mercenary that settles whitening the coloring and serving dishes where there is metal and making yellow any yellow every color in a shade which is expressed in a tray. This is a monster and awkward quite awkward and the little design which is flowered which is not strange and yet has visible writing, this is not shown all the time but at once, after that it rests where it is and where it is in place. No change is not needed. That does show design.

Excellent, more excellence is borrowing and slanting very slanting is light and secret and a recitation and emigration. Certainly shoals are shallow and nonsense more nonsense is sullen. Very little cake is water, very little cake has that escape.

Sugar any sugar, anger every anger, lover sermon lover, centre no distractor, all order is in a measure.

Left over to be a lamp light, left over in victory, left over in saving, all this and negligence and bent wood and more even much more is not so exact as a pen and a turtle and even, certainly, and even a piece of the same experience as more.

To consider a lecture, to consider it well is so anxious and so much a charity and really supposing there is grain and if a stubble every stubble is urgent, will there not be a chance of legality. The sound is sickened and the price is purchased and golden wheat is golden, a clergyman, a single tax, a currency and an inner chamber.

Checking an emigration, checking it by smiling and certainly by the same satisfactory stretch of hands that have more use for it than nothing, and mildly not mildly a correction, not mildly even a circumstance and a sweetness and a serenity. Powder, that has no color, if it did have would it be white.

A whole soldier any whole soldier has no more detail than any case of measles.

A bridge a very small bridge in a location and thunder, any thunder, this is the capture of reversible sizing and more indeed more can be cautious. This which makes monotony careless makes it likely that there is an exchange in principle and more than that, change in organization.

This cloud does change with the movements of the moon and the narrow the quite narrow suggestion of the building. It does and then when it is settled and no sounds differ then comes the moment when cheerfulness is so assured that there is an occasion.

A plain lap, any plain lap shows that sign, it shows that there is not so much extension as there would be if there were more choice in everything. And why complain of more, why complain of very much more. Why complain at all when it is all arranged that as there is no more opportunity and no more appeal and not even any more clinching that certainly now some time has come.

A window has another spelling, it has "f" all together, it lacks no more then and this is rain, this may even be something else, at any rate there is no dedication in splendor. There is a turn of the stranger.

Catholic to be turned is to venture on youth and a section of debate, it even means that no class where each one over fifty is regular is so stationary that there are invitations.

A curving example makes righteous finger-nails. This is the only object in secretion and speech.

To being the same four are no more than were taller. The rest had a big chair and surveyance a cold accumulation of nausea, and even more than that, they had a disappointment.

Nothing aiming is a flower, if flowers are abundant then they are lilac, if they are not they are white in the centre.

Dance a clean dream and an extravagant turn up, secure the steady rights and translate more than translate the authority, show the choice and make no more mistakes than yesterday.

This means clearness it means a regular notion of exercise, it means more than that, it means liking counting, it means more than that, it does not mean exchanging a line.

Why is there more craving than there is in a mountain. This does not seem strange to one, it does not seem strange to an echo and more surely is in there not being a habit. Why is there so much useless suffering. Why is there.

Any wet weather means an open window, what is attaching eating, anything that is violent and cooking and shows weather is the same in the end and why is there more use in something than in all that.

The cases are made and books, back books are used to secure tears and church. They are even used to exchange black slippers. They can not be mended with wax. They show no need of any such occasion.

A willow and no window, a wide place stranger, a wideness makes an active center.

The sight of no pussy cat is so different that a tobacco zone is white and cream.

A lilac, all a lilac and no mention of butter, not even bread and butter, no butter and no occasion, not even a silent resemblance, not more care than just enough haughty.

A safe weight is that which when it pleases is hanging. A

safer weight is one more naughty in a spectacle. The best game is that which is shiny and scratching. Please a pease and a cracker and a wretched use of summer.

Surprise, the only surprise has no occasion. It is an ingredient and the section the whole section is one season.

A pecking which is petting and no worse than in the same morning is not the only way to be continuous often.

A light in the moon the only light is on Sunday. What was the sensible decision. The sensible decision was that notwithstanding many declarations and more music, not even notwithstanding the choice and a torch and a collection, notwithstanding the celebrating hat and a vacation and even more noise than cutting, notwithstanding Europe and Asia and being overbearing, not even notwithstanding an elephant and a strict occasion, not even withstanding more cultivation and some seasoning, not even with drowning and with the ocean being encircling, not even with more likeness and any cloud, not even with terrific sacrifice of pedestrianism and a special resolution, not even more likely to be pleasing. The care with which the rain is wrong and the green is wrong and the white is wrong, the care with which there is a chair and plenty of breathing. The care with which there is incredible justice and likeness, all this makes a magnificent asparagus, and also a fountain.

By Gertrude Stein

from The Making of Americans

(excerpt)

To begin again then with some description of the meaning of loving repeating being when it is strongly in a man or in a woman, when it is in them their way of understanding everything in living and there are very many always living of such being. This is now again a beginning of a little description of it in one.

The kinds and ways of repeating, of attacking and resisting in different kinds of men and women, the practical, the emotional, the sensitive, the every kind of being in every one who ever was or is or will be living, I know so much about all of them, many of them are very clear in kinds of men and women, in individual men and women, I know them so well inside them, repeating in them has so much meaning to knowing, more and more I know all there is of all being, more and more I know it in all the ways it is in them and comes out of them, sometime there will be a history of every one, sometime all history of all men and women will be inside some one.

Now there will be a little description of the coming to be history of all men and women, in some one. This is then to be a little history of such a one. This is then now to be a little description of loving repeating being in one.

This is then a beginning of the way of knowing everything in every one, of knowing the complete history of each one who ever is or was or will be living. This is then a little description of the winning of so much wisdom.

Many have loving repeating being in them, many never come to know it of them, many never have it as a conscious feeling, many have in it a restful satisfaction. Some have in it always more and more understanding, many have in it very little enlarging understanding. There is every kind of way of having loving repeating being as a bottom. It is very clear to me and to my feeling, it is very slow in developing, it is very important to make it clear now in writing, it must be done now with a slow description. To begin again then with it in my feeling, to begin again then to tell of the meaning to me in all repeating, of the loving there is in me for repeating.

There are many that I know and always more and more I know it. They are all of them repeating and I hear it. They are all of them living and I know it. More and more I understand it, always more and more it has completed history in it.

Every one has their own being in them. Every one is of a kind of men and women. Always more and more I know the whole history of each one. This is now a little a description of such knowing in me. This is now a little a description of beginning of hearing repeating all around me.

As I was saying learning, thinking, living in the beginning of being men and women often has in it very little of real being. Real being, the bottom nature, often does not then in the beginning do very loud repeating. Learning, thinking, talking, living, often then is not of the real bottom being. Some are this way all their living. Some slowly come to be repeating louder and more clearly the bottom being that makes them. Listening to repeating, knowing being in every one who ever was or is or will be living slowly came to be in me a louder and louder pounding. Now I have it to my feeling to feel all living, to be always listening to the slightest changing, to have each one come to be a whole one to me from the repeating in each one that sometime I come to be understanding. Listening to repeating is often irritating, listening to repeating can be dulling, always repeating is all of living, everything in a being is always repeating, always more and more listening to repeating gives to me completed understanding. Each one slowly comes to be a whole one to me. Each one slowly comes to be a whole one in me.

Now this is the way I hear repeating. This is the way slowly some men and some women, each one, comes to be a whole one to me.

There are many that I know and always more and more I know it. They are always all of them always repeating themselves and I hear it. Always I stop myself from being too quickly sure that I have heard all of it. Always I begin again to listen to it. Always I remember all the times I thought I had heard all of it all the repeating in some one and then there was much more to it. Always I remember every way one can hear only a part of it, the repeating that is the whole history of any one and so always I begin again as if I had never heard it.

Always I love it, sometimes I get a little tired of it, mostly I am always ready to do it, always I love it. Listening up to completed understanding of the repeating that sometime is a completed history of each one is all my life and always I live it. I love it and I live it. Sometimes I am tired in it, mostly I am always ready for it.

Everybody is a real one to me, everybody is like some one else too to me. Every one always is repeating the whole of them. Each one slowly comes to be a whole one to me. Each one slowly comes to be a whole one in me.

This is now a description of learning to listen to all repeating that every one always is making of the whole of them. This is now some description of learning to hear, see and feel all repeating that each one always is making of the whole of them. Each one as I was saying sometimes comes to be a whole one in me, each one sometime comes to be a complete being to me. Sometimes after they are this to me I keep on knowing it inside me, sometimes I lose it, sometimes I doubt it, it is too clear or too vague or too confused inside me. Sometime then I have it all to do again. Always I keep on hearing, feeling, seeing all repeating in each one for always it has more and more being to my feeling.

This is now then some description of my learning. Then there will be a beginning again of Martha Hersland and her being and her living. This is now then first a little studying and then later Martha Hersland will begin living. Now then to do this little studying.

There is a certain feeling one has in one when some one is not a whole one to one even though one seems to know all the nature of that one. Such a one then is very puzzling and when sometimes such a one is a whole one to one all the repeating coming out of them has meaning as part of a whole one. When some one is not a clear one to one, repeating coming out of them has not this clear relation. Then such a one is puzzling until they come to be a whole one. Then repeating coming out of them has clear meaning.

Always then I am hearing, feeling, seeing the repeating always coming out of every one. Loving repeating being is in me always every moment in my living. Sometimes as I was saying hearing repeating is very irritating. Always sometime it comes to be to me a completed history of each one I am ever knowing.

Sometimes I know and hear and feel and see all the repeating in some one, all the repeating that is the whole of some one but it always comes as pieces to me, it is never there to make a whole one to me. Some people have it in them to be in pieces in repeating the whole of them, such of them almost come never to be a whole one to me, some come almost all their living in repeating to be succession not a whole one inside me. Sometimes sometime such a one has a way of loving which makes a whole one of such a one long enough to hear the whole repeating in such a one as a complete one by some one. Such a one comes then sometime to be a whole one and then one loses the whole one repeating of them and they are pieces then of repeating and always it is changing back to pieces of repeating from the little time of loving that a little time makes of them a whole one. There are very many of them and this is now a little a description of the nature in this kind of them, this is now a little a description of learning to know them to make of them a complete one.

There are then a kind of them, a kind of men and women, there are very many of them always living who have it in them to be inside them to be mostly to every one, to be always to mostly every one pieces coming out of them, pieces that never make of them a whole one, not because of complication in them, not because of difficulty of envisaging them but because really such of them are in pieces inside them, always in their living. This kind then of men and women have it to have it to be true of them that nothing in them dominates them, not mind, nor bottom nature in them, nor other nature or natures in them, nor emotion, nor sensitiveness, nor suggestibility, nor practicalness, nor weakness, nor selfishness, nor nervousness, nor egotism, nor desire, nor whimsicalness, nor cleverness, nor ideals, nor stimulation, nor vices, nor indifference, nor beauty, nor eating, nor drinking, nor laziness, nor energy, nor emulation, nor envy, nor malice, nor pleasure, nor skepticism. It is not as it is in some that there is contradictory being in them, there is not in such of these of them domination of anything in them to make contradiction, to make changing of one thing to another in them. Always they are in pieces then but pieces are not disconcerting to them or any one, hardly not puzzling. Some of such of them sometimes then make melodrama of themselves to themselves to hold themselves together to them. Some of such of them make of themselves to themselves and sometimes to other ones that know them a melodrama of themselves to make to themselves each one of themselves a

whole one to themselves and sometimes to make of themselves a whole one to others around them. This is a very
interesting thing, this is sometimes the explanation of melodrama in some one.

Some then some men and some women are not whole
ones inside me for long times together. Sometime one of such
a one was a whole one in me and then it was clear to me why
such a kind of one was not for long times continually a whole
one in me.

This is now then a little a description of my telling of it.
As I was saying mostly always when some one is entirely and
completely a whole one to me, I know it and I tell it, sometimes
I tell it to that one that is then entirely and completely a whole
one inside to me, sometimes I tell it to any one who will listen
to it.

As I was saying each one is sometimes a whole one to me,
is a whole one inside me, each one then sometimes gives to
me a sense of being filled up inside me with that one, then a
whole one inside me. Each one then is sometime a whole one
in me, I know it and I tell it, I am filled up then with that whole
one inside me and I tell it and then it settles down inside me
to always hearing it repeating in such a one, filling in and
changing and being a completer and completer history of that
one and always then it is quietly there in me and I like it.
Sometimes it is disturbed in me and again completely fills me
and then again it settles down in me. Then again it is quietly
there in me and I always like it. Always I am then learning
more and more the history of that one, always more and more
there is then meaning in all the repeating coming out of that
one but there is then not so much need in me to tell it, it is
then steady pleasant, sometimes exciting, learning in me and
always I enjoy it but then it is quieter inside me and I am then
not all filled up with it and so then though always often I tell
it, all of it, pieces of it to any one who will listen to it, I am not
then all filled up with it and I can then really be without really

needing to tell it, I can then get along without really then ever telling it.

As I was saying each one sometime is a whole one to me. As I was saying mostly when it is complete to me and I first really know it, really and completely and filled up with it then I tell it. Mostly then I have to tell it. Mostly then I am filled up with it and it comes out of me then as telling it, sometimes to the one that is then a whole one to me, sometimes then to any one who will then listen to me.

As I was saying I know many women and many men. I know many of them as babies, as children as growing men and growing women as grown men and grown women as growing old men and growing old women, as grown old men and grown old women, and every kind of being they ever have in them. I know many then of them very many of them and sometime each one is a whole one to me, each one is a whole one inside me, each one then has real meaning for me. Sometime then each one is a whole one to me, sometime then each one of them has a whole history of each one for me. Everything then they do in living is clear then to me, their living, loving, eating, pleasing, smoking, scolding, drinking, dancing, thinking, working, walking, talking, laughing, sleeping, suffering, joking, everything in them. There are whole beings then, they are themselves inside them to me. They are then, each one, a whole one inside me. Repeating of the whole of them always coming out of each one of them makes a history always of each one of them always to me.

By Gertrude Stein

Marguerite
Or A Simple Novel Of High Life

In northern countries a child is often adopted. When it is. There is often something else that happens and either the child is not well or very well and something else happens. It is very likely that it is a girl.

Should it be about what they care.

Once once or twice in the northern countries they adopted a girl. She had a happy childhood and nothing else matters. A childhood is not happy if nothing else matters. It is just what they like.

In northern countries if they adopt a child they will be satisfied to be unhappy. If nothing else matters.

In a southern country if a child is well a father is nervous that is if it is well born as it is well. And they will be seriously well. Just as it does. It will if it does. It can take any amount of care.

If she could remember that she was adopted would it be more than any other pleasure or sadness. She was never distressed.

One at a time they being the only one left and so a home is formally what they do often feel to be very well but not established.

It has often happened that they have been adopted. One may say it is better to be brought up by one parent than to be adopted. One may say and no one does say or refuses to be thought to be welcomed by any such thing.

In the northern countries they often adopt a child particularly when a couple have been childless.

It was their habit to be childless and so they adopted had adopted one. She was raised as their daughter although in a way it was the one who had adopted her as their legal daughter who was with it as one.

It is her name which is of importance. Sometimes they are legally adopted and in any case they are known by the name. And in this case it was so.

After a little while it ended not disagreeable which made it not a matter of indifference:

She was not appointed nor was she chosen to leave home.

Should she be chosen in adoption not any one is chosen. They adopt one this is often happening in a northern country where it is not very cold and no one is ever frozen. They often adopt a child and they think nothing of having never been accustomed not to have had a child without adoption. And so much for that.

After the adoption the child is with them and there is no difficulty about any one leaving them when either one or the other need not have been left without either one or some other one and without explaining and so they are necessarily bad and they have been very good. It is a satisfaction to come from a small country which is not a big country and which is never really frozen nor is it the country where they will have never been cold in the summer nor hot in the winter the winter is not only cold but the summer which is after the winter is hot and everybody is not certain that it is possible to have a cold winter colder and a warm summer hotter and so they are equal to anything.

It is the custom to adopt a child in a northern country if the couple have not either of them wanted a child and they have not have one earlier and then when it is later they have adopted one. This is not an advantage but it is happy without there being any more than one without any objection and the other not wanting it either.

She was used to callousness, she could be tenderly mused she could accustom and in they are always made comfortable in a different letter.

After adopting they are very kind to the child they have adopted. They do not mean anything or if they are fortunate fortunate and fortunately is a good reason.

From the beginning she and they were likely or just as likely to be adopting.

The way they were happy was this. They were colder and warmer and they were always ready to go in and come out as often and this is altogether. Once in a while they were not more than always careful but this made no difference to Marguerite. No one could adopt oftener. They adopted once. As it happens they adopted she was adopted. This makes her.

It is my might.

One.

Marguerite was chosen and once when she was younger she was not so promising.

Now to like her.

She could be happy in not hurrying.

Or could she be happy in not hurrying.

After she left her adopted father and her adopted mother she had not left them. They would never know anything about anything and she would not care nor were they there nor nearly anything. This is natural when it has happened and is happening that she is sad but not worrying. How many can inherit money when some have some and really no one knows anything. And this is not a grievance in believing. She was very happy. Any one is sad. And any one is no one worrying. I like to look at cushions.

See one.

It is a sea where they are near a lake and she said they swam there from their nightgown. Or all. They swam there. Not on the sea they were not on the sea. A land that is not on the sea is all that is so nearly that in living she was not threatening but really saying a river to be sad is nearer. And so this was not late in life. But even later.

It is very pretty to have straight hair made curly.

The thing that happened was that she had a habit. Not of being adopted or adopting but really truly would she like it now was not it dreadful that any one could often only not be sent away. And stay.

The real story of a northern winter is and a northern summer and which they might in vanish. She could always be called for.

In the northern countries adoption is not everything because they are not ever careless. She was adopted when she was quite a little thing. This does not matter. Who always does not matter. Alike does not matter. Who has been never been careless. All about does not matter.

She was adopted and it does not matter. She is now known as never having been careless which they may declare should she be here.

Oh why can they be cared for.

A change of scene and she comes to England.

Why is England not a northern country. It is not a northern country.

She will call either selfish if they come either as selfish.

After or a little other after she is adopted she likes to change about. What does she change about. Nothing at all. She stays as she is.

Once in a while if she likes it not only not better but always as often not better she feels that it is not even a wish. And so she calls money often money. Which made get leave strangeness to be selfish and their on their account their wish. After she had been adopted it might be that she was born always there as not so easily can any one remember anything or not after a while.

It is always their meaning which is a difference between often and open.

In the Northern countries they adopt children and children have them to ask everything in the way and at the time and when they have or have been as a morning. And in this way easily of course and in consequence and it was most of the time. She could not remember any trouble.

After she was adopted she lived there. It could not know. They could not change by chance. Any one could get to be twenty-one. Almost more.

After a while any one knew that no one not on account of come again. It is very true that an adopted one is never glad to see her mother because she has not got one. They need never regret everything. She will not be cautious to close.

After she had been adopted they will be thought to swim and sing. They will be light in summer and dark in winter. They will be all alike in respect to everything just as they choose. It is why they had one then. There is plenty of favoritism in singing and swimming but she remembered them both.

Once once or twice the mother.

Or very happy with a girl.

She could in one year every time it would they would be that they had a girl.

Three a girl they adopted a girl. In a northern country.

In a southern country a girl. It made the parents sad. That they had that she had a girl. She was not their parents.

To go back now to the one who was an adopted one going to England. It is very likely that in going to England she went from them. They were not there to be ready. And she left. She did not. Not leave them. They were inquiring. Not if she was leaving. No one could enquire. If she were leaving. Because she had not. Left then. To leave them.

The thing she did was to go to England. And there the struggle for life was not severe.

Just who has been whose.

Marguerite there could expect care. She could be very much better everywhere. Everywhere and there.

After Margurite had been adopted nobody spoke.

Consider how agreeable adoption is also consider how many hours from England also to please to never to be able to achieve the ambition of really going where they desired it if not any longer they could have been hoped to have her come. After adoption going is going. As much can be said of coming. She was an adopted one. She felt finely.

After every little while she saw why it was not once in a while. He changed while they changed. She was left alone. England was not as far and she could go. This was after she was left that is to say adopted means having been adopting. There is no reason why they should stop choosing. Who could she called one and one.

It is easy to feel better.

Marguerite did not feel better. She had been adopted and then later she went to England and there she remained until she left England.

After she returned from England she knew who hesitated.

She was often told that they were wretched. And she made their wishes their wishes. Can any one leave Finland. She did and came to England. After that they will be acquainted.

As I was saying she had been adopted as is the habit in Northern countries and after every little while they will beware of their English. They have it very well taught. They will go. They will not decide about everything. It is always thought well that she should go away which she did and stay away which she does. She will be happy if she can say I mean.

And they will respect having been in England. And now she is not far away.

She will resume her voyages. She will leave England for France.

And having left England for France she has come to France and having come to France she will long to have been in England as is natural to her station. She will be unique in asking and receiving and not being only but also desired. And so they may go. She has been in England and from England she has come to France and having come to France she will be in a state of enlightenment and no one need because it is prettily desirable and very successful to mention swans and sparrows. Sparrows are not younger than swans.

And so here we are in France and so they say there are more pleasures than rather very often they are separately undertaken to be anxious.

In this way one may unite before and after and because of their betterment.

The melody of which they like they must be always used to be welcome. And love to rush and pleasantly come back. Or they will. This may be better than their chance of leaving it very well fastened as in a plan.

She may be thought to be thoughtful but she was adopted as is the custom in northern countries.

Be very carefully acquainted with anxiety.

Or do not expose yourself to this as a wish.

Can you see how readily not to agree not to say not to manage to say not to bewilder not to favor or not to gently mind which piously makes theirs be sewn. All of which they will all go to arrange it so.

The three countries in which they have been acquainted but she has not been acquainted with them is or are England Finland and France and Finland comes first.

Every little while they know her better.

It was not only known but it was told. That she knew. That

in northern countries they did adopt and were adopted very young or anything. And they plainly made it as difference to have no one like it which is why they were willing to be feeling. It is not strange to be feeling. They will answer and answer anything that is no one who can would ask and answer a question or not at all which is just as returned as vehement they will kindly cry. Or known as announcement. Or complying with custom. The custom. In a northern country is something. Not entirely nothing. Not either just as well. Not with. Or without. Or with them. They will please do.

After she had been adopted she was plainly not wishing but very little in it as it is to do very likely. She could be just as well. And so much a reason for a treasure. They may use treasure and pleasure alike. It is in their way not selfish or grasping.

She may be after a while there.

Remember in Finland Finland is a country, England is a country that is a country which is a comfort and they say they may not only have been but who can say where. England is there. She came to France to stay. And she did.

No one reasons for her reflect what reasons are. Or just did. She make it be. As well as in they say.

And so we begin.

She will change hands because. They will welcome her. And she will be very capable.

They will make theirs be often. That she is not responsible for being left. And going after all to have them ask what might they do if she had been disappointed. All of which it is in a way inevitable and how dreadful.

Could she be adopted by a country without hope. In a country where they feel that going away is welcome. Does she feel that they will ask. Oh yes and no.

Does all who have been met in vain come with for recuperation.

All made by their meaning. All made without with and

also by nor for just as with their meaning. In how to place.

Say why she will welcome surely and be as welcome. A survival of their interesting and after all the north can be called less as very farewell.

She was adopted as if with and by for her father and her mother which she had.

I do borrow and borrows her so and so.

Let us remember that she learned finnish as she was born there of a finnish father and a finnish mother or rather. After the adoption.

Now she went away. Older. After that please mind the cross. And be always with and might have missed her mother. Might not. She had no father. She had no mother.

In England she did not like weddings either. She felt very well.

So may she ask why any one had a blessing all which all of which may be true.

Why will England be happy there. Or might they be there. For in which it is neat or not obliged. It is a cloud that they will exactly furnish meat for butter. And never question why they make messages older. It is not because of their willingness believing rested not as well all of which are allowed. It is by their own way. Own may and is. Being taking. Shall refreshment have with them a time. All this makes adoption forgotten.

Gradually they will lie.

Marguerite prefers to be annoyed to be impatient. She prefers to be disturbed to be here. And here means there. But which she can call. Every little while they are out of it. And she can be remembered and so she is by this never wakened. Any little gift is lighter than at first. And so Marguerite has been in finland in England and in France. Or be polite.

Can nobody know.

Of why do they. Be always there. For which. They will plan. More of it.

Often not only was she not adopted but not at all. Oh or not at all. They were so indifferent. By that time it was not alone that they were careless. Should he mean to be. It was just that. And just as likely.

She could not betray or doubt. Nor could they betray or doubt.

Like that.

It was not often why they went away.

For this for them for which for what they do.

Or just to mention it.

It does not make.

They like it though.

That it could not make not any at all. A difference.

Could having not gone away leave it to them. Or could it. Just as well as they choose. By which I mean. Have I it do at all or very likely. It is by all this that they ought. Which is very well as neglected.

It does not make any difference by what they mean. They like to say hammer.

All of which they could be not out loud. Or very well careful.

Marguerite has no friends. She is not very tall. She will have a sight of there being there. Or not at all.

She is never anxious. To be quite. Persuaded. Or may be. Would they like it if. It was not all of it more than just as much better. It is very quiet when they like.

All this is Marguerite.

And now what does she say.

Marguerite is capable of being born and adopted and leaving just as you like. Or might it be what they will as occasion. Or will they be willing to go. Or might. She be not only without mention. Not of this. Nor only anything. And so they like. What is it that makes everything useful. These are all the day. And this is what she can say. Marguerite can say. That they may. Be alike.

What should Marguerite mean by missing.

All of it by the time they do.

Marguerite was left she does not know by whom. Nor does she know that she was an orphan. She was adopted as is the custom of Northern countries very often. She was adopted at once and lived there with and without care. Not that it made any difference. Or was just alike. She had many gifts and was very often. With them. As they like. Neither do they mean that. Which is why they are not careless or very often thinking. That it should be all as well. And so Marguerite was not mistaken nor could be more an object of their seeing. Which could it do. She was not only never married. But they were. Not mistaken. It is not on account. Of this. They can protect and recognise and organise this from that. Which is what is obliging. And so often. Marguerite could often mean known.

Could it be happen to be selfish. And are they comfortable in England. And do they. Ever. Dance after going to their churches where they pray. Or like it. Or how. Do they like it. By which means. They are never after. What I like. Best.

In this way Marguerite has told all she knew. And now she knew that it is in France. Not where they dance. But just as likely.

After a little while she managed to leave a parade. That is they were taught about glasses. And very well if they came back. Could Marguerite be first in her class or lonesome or anxious or pitiful or will not crying or just as much and very nearly eating. Oh thank you.

It is now known that there are hours in Sweden. Also which they like. It is now known that Finland is not a part of Sweden and England is a way. To which they please. Making it do. Like. And alike. By which it is more than forever it is well. To have it known.

By the time that they were English and not far away.

By the time that they were not English.

All of which does not recall it more French.

Or every little while.

By a more or who little while.

Marguerite was Finnish she admired everything English she was able not to like the French and in a little while she was here. And had come to stay.

This was not what Marguerite had to say.

Marguerite had been adopted whether she was little or very little and she had been to say so or better. It is not only better not only not to have not to say so. Oh no. She was adopted and was there when she had not been there. There.

In the northern countries and Finland is northern adopting is not often everything. Might they say anything if they might. Please do.

Marguerite was painted pale not while light not white. It is not her wish. She has no wish. She is leaving adopted.

And they like it very well. And they might have it to do. And they will not have it declared. And they will. Once in when there is time. In which. It is so much. As much. Of interest.

When she came.

Marguerite who has or had adopted Marguerite.

Do be or do.

She had an adventure. She came nervously. Or left by that. Where they went in. Or to please.

Every one was patient.

One can.

One cannot lose ones Marguerite.

And she was prayed there. She likes what they can. And do. Go.

Or not.

What can Marguerite do better.

She had done better.

She to find no effort on Saturday to be too much either in England in Finland nor in France. And should be very tired.

Not here nor very well there. But mainly with which they will well and never as well though they admire this. She does not know what ten years are.

And so they do not neglect to arrange not a pattern but dishes not a swan but roses not a swan but carrots and nobody laughs.

Or well.

However will they leave it as a finish.

And so how many hours are ours.

Who has been heard to hurry. She will be always not or selfish. They will claim doors.

How can hours or ours be different in Finnish in English and or or in French.

How often do they burst open.

Not white or blue she could be tired on Sunday.

Marguerite was selfish she asked could it be dreadful.

Then they went where they went in.

After all who has not lost ones Marguerite. Or found the time.

Marguerite pleases better than ever. She is more homo-genious.

Could any one guess how many countries are known as present.

Three countries are known as present. In each one I have forgotten but I do not forget.

They will not eliminate industry nor practice. They have manners and places and additions. They will also come as they can.

How are they careful. They are careful not as they are told.

A conversation in English in Finnish and in French can not be held at the same time nor with indifference ever or after a time. They will be proud to be nearly or may they be ever after just like nor either just the same find and finally like it. Might it make no difference to anybody.

Could she sigh by being half of the time just there.

And so may be to doubt it.

She alone knows and there is not that difference. Before they were alike now they are not. May be they are before. Before they are not they are alike. And only often before.

She could have a chance by being just and not only there. It made no difference. It was always why. And they could worry. Just by all of it.

Finland is far away. It is easily reached. They will be there. They often cause it to come. England is not far away. Who will not be not only just as they went there. Almost all which. They are alike. It should and did they have it which made it only only is allowed. They will often always which is likely. Once in a while they will not be there. Two are to them.

This way English Finnish and French. Now can all who speak. Speak it.

Marguerite can come every day or else. By the time which they know.

Should have been tries.

That is nice. To not like what she tries.

And so the home of truth is Finland. It is also England. Is it also France.

It is very difficult to remember and forget adoption.

In northern countries who adopted whom. Or would they be refused or would they be worshipped or would they be just as dark as a dog or just as fair as a ribbon and would they like it best if it cost nothing or if it did would they not be better able to be glad if they could not kneel nor either if they did which they could like and alike is fastened. Then they may be fairly said to be often together. Not more than the mother and daughter or is it fair to leave an adopted daughter not home alone only home alone. She could not be called cried. They will be often near to when they cost not in that. No one can lose a daughter not in Finland which is one of those northern countries. Neither one of these is made why they are which is they are happy just which is whether more than they do either not even more only just alike. This is why they pay.

Come in and come to study.

Marguerite a seat.

Is it nicely to be in doubt if it is warmer within and without. Any doubt is dear. She can be hoped.

Finland is a country where purses are given to women or are given to men or are either given often as enough to children. They will play with purses.

Marguerite was adopted she was often not a mother nor indeed either. She was pure and easily frightened. She had been a little girl. Who were not old were not told nor was she told nor will. They may have been seen to know that a lake in the morning is not near a sea at night. She would so like to cross an ocean and be good humored.

She was a part of readiness. And yet she could not arrange. She was told she was brave and she looks it. For them do they dislike.

How often could no one remember.

She was endowed and not painful she made it prettily and fatigue she was meaning that they would like their taste her taste was shown. It was admired and all who were complimented were please.

Marguerite could think well of any noon. She was often called not to come but to stay awhile. And like it.

Could they be sure that by adoption any religion changes. Marguerite never asked or asks herself this. This which in a way means that as it is she could never have been to a mountain. Nor will she think that it is that that is lost. Alright who like to-morrow and with it at night. She has never been painfully timid just timid.

All who can like a house can like a house.

Marguerite will she be sweet in living or failing. Will she be sweet.

Marguerite feels nicely about adopting. She will know better not to adopt often. She will be miserable or just round.

She will be nicely spared. Or well. How is it a cunning to have fine hair. Or be just well. Or not impatient. Or easily lost. Or with them. It might make time to have them around.

Marguerite was famous. They talked about her. They said will she she has might it mean that and who has been often wanted. Could she be alike. They will not often do more than they do. All who are ours.

Marguerite was made a maid.

She exchanged and came again. She was adopted had been known in the north. They will all like her like that.

No one can ever think any minute.

Marguerite is a life what and then which adopted. A northern country. Is one. In which. They are adopting. They leave it to me.

It is easy to be hours apart. And never move.

She liked it all the time.

When she first began. To smile. It was. Not. All the while. Pretty soon she did not begin. She did not smile oftener.

After every once in a while. They made their happen to make. Have made the any arrangement. It was often just what they had. No one could be more like. It is often very convenient. All who make hour glasses. She might try.

It could not be seen that they were often selfish.

What could she did she having back. Leave all of it at once. We have known that she never left them. They were partly mine. She knew. Which she could.

It is often why they obtain.

Make I make it right with Marguerite.

Marguerite was not stolen. She could come alone.

And so they knew which ever she was having first.

It was always how they liked and often. Knowing as well as she did. Whose could she arrange for. And plead. Might they not just as often try. Just as often as not.

Marguerite was not as often fond of first.

Just why should union try. And may she be called. In

union there is strength but more break it. She has passed part of her life here.

Who knows Marguerite. When she comes.

She can forget three countries Finland England and France. Every little while is most.

Can any one forget who has been here. Why certainly in asking them the questions. How many are there who do not come with her. Or will they leave her most. She will apply. And it is their having her here. Which is for them whether. An adoption is clever. It is easy to finish. Without which.

Marguerite was early to bed but she read.

Shall it be why they thought. Does it make any difference when they eat. Will they interfere as they came. Could they come as they would. Who will hope that they do.

Marguerite would never like to mean. She would. She could be seized with displeasure. It is not only but also avoided but not by which they pause. She could. Have heard. Of another country. Which was. Not Finland. Not England. Nor France. Earlier she could. And then she could. And now she could.

All that she could. She either would. And so it pleases and well dreadful. No one should ever quote. Or have it help her.

Marguerite was adopted. So she says. And why should she say she was adopted. People in northern countries can adopt and be adopted.

After that they will leave them. Or if they have. They will leave them. I like that dog. Or they will leave them. But whichever they are. They do not like it. Or going away. Will they be strange. Will they be. Alike.

It is easy to have a difficulty in hearing when they were where. She is went to be here. She came to be here. If they came not to be where. They came to be at most where. They were. And so alike.

It is very easy to love wealth and poverty, riches and money conveniences and plenty, arrangements and anything which they are sure to have there. And they so one like it. Could she be other. Than not happy. In spite of which. She can smile. Wanly. With them. Left at last. Along. Oh why do they like. It.

This is what she had to happen.

Who could remember where she had been could she remember who had been there. Will she remember that she has not been where it is not more than she can have been with known.

Marguerite cannot ask a question.

That is the power of adoption.

So many hours so many houses so many countries so many cities. And with all of them one. Nobody knows London is in England.

She cannot be as fresh as a daisy.

Think wonderfully of there being or so dreadful with wondering of their being which they are wondering or with not only their being. The country that is well-known.

And so. Often.

Every time she says anything she smiles. Nor will she like them. What is there between with them. And we might do. Or say. For them.

And so she came to come. Marguerite is here.

Once there came in these difficult times to sit not at all because she was querulous. Not at all. She was not annoyed or a nuisance. She had a rosy life. She had been adopted and she was not indeed bothered to be devined. They will also call clad. She can be so often particular. Nor will it do that she like dolls. Anybody can hear for her. She was ready to say not younger. It is too often too made too known too well. Anybody can hear needing. Nor can they if they have enough. All these who can hear or need in to meet. Marguerite. It often makes an impression. It should be time to be often. To not to like to that.

Please have Marguerite fancy. More or this which is not

only met as known. It is their nicely live.

It is easy to forget a country and counties and to remember for them.

Marguerite has been held mainly for them. She can cook well. So she says. Does. And may be.

It is not nicely to need why they ask.

No one can or does lose their Marguerite. Here she is.

Just why Marguerite was carefully to be known as never seated. And she was not in acres. But she could. Justify please it for them.

No one could think that she would be sure to place a time with that. She was often just as willing as if she were orphan where. There were no orphans. Could she be if she were older. Just as old. She might if she were asked be more than just where. There were but had been one to declare. And now he wants his ball. She would not be interested. She would say. How dreadful. But does this express any emotion. Have adopted children that is a child of adoption have any emotion. Marguerite was never one of three.

She could help this. And like this. With them with for this. Never thank them for this and this. Remember an adoption. And she could not tell when.

She could say she never knew. To whom she could be grateful. And therefor. She was not grateful before. She was able. Not to think more. Than she had. In time. She was very selfish to be welcome.

Once in a while she could remember that her mother and her father had a mother and grandmother. But she never knew. She knew that they were not only more but moreover. She could not feel careless of repair or of despair. Nor could she love those she loved the most. Who can lie. They can easily be cheerful as they say. It is not only that she looks but that she does not look alike. Who can for it say it. Made them not fasten or favorite or aching. She liked why she ate and why she did not eat. She was often fastening and fasting.

They may be all be awkward. Or who can be kind. Should it leave it made it that it does not matter or like that.

Once in a while they think well to distinguish. Marguerite can and should be debated. She can be often or for more. And then how is or when it is or when is it or if it is. She can be often with and beside almost met. It is as happy they will find as happy or may be they will accord a crowd. It is not only theirs are silent.

Marguerite was fastened by having been a birthday. She knows the day so in that sense she was not adopted. And by it. They are leaving it in might they can be very should it be mine too. How many years can you be adopted. She never asked that yet although and though all that is well past.

Marguerite was so she said having had given what she said. She was as often a little way in each. A country is a country gone and known. And often. They will celebrate not to like and like that.

Please mind me.

Marguerite is often placed in a seat and by herself if she sits.

Gracious and to be kind.

They will abolish a stool.

And she will change a day for a chair. She might be thought for a festival. But no. Northern countries have adoptions. And with a little while. Northern countries do. They may be cold. They may be warm and sunshine. Also which is what she may as like. She can conceal her pause.

Marguerite was wishing. She was not wishing. She was not white and wishing. She was not pale nor brown and wishing. And if it is not night.

Marguerite may be taught right.

She can come away.

It is what happened by a seat. With and will it when she says did. They may do that. The same.

What can conceal a border.

Here we are well.

Anybody having no apprehension and nor intention nor in regard to right or with as by their please. She was always ready to be then to that. I like it. But hours of going aghast. It is very ease to be well with less. Less is it.

No one has the right to whistle in a court.

She could not be wrong. In the wrong.

Oh Marguerite will they be ever told just why they are not bold why they are in the fold. Why they are adopted and who they are like. Marguerite is like Amelia.

Marguerite when she is in pain is plain. When she is heard she is safe then she is blest she is best.

Marguerite is very much indeed why they. Can be best of it as a place wherein they can. It is often they who make the sound that they have not a pleasure in hearing.

Marguerite is very much what they have.

Now all who think about adopting adopt.

She may be very careful that not only all who think about adopting adopt but which they can in all of the way that they disturb.

Why will she be all English all Finnish all French why will she be all Finnish all English all French. Marguerite has the time to hear.

Oh Marguerite will you be planned. Or will you be very much a place. Or will you be a fastening. Or will you be their home.

Oh Marguerite who will have been here known for him for them. Or will it be just what they need.

Marguerite for which will they acknowledge.

All who can be just sit still together.

It happened that she had known but was discouraged.

But she was sure and then they came that is she came. To them.

Oh will they miss. It.

It is not only that they know but that she knows that she

can be a little more than extra.

Marguerite believe me. That you are sweet.

No Marguerite. Believe me that you are there.

Marguerite believe or not as you like.

Marguerite just why should all who are here open the door and declare.

I wonder at it.

Marguerite when can you connect the past with the past. The adopted past with the or a adopted past. And then they will not beside because she moves fairly surely although she may forget.

If caught and coercion are not alike.

Marguerite be careful that you have thought so.

Or Marguerite be careful that you have thought either that they did come or that they have come.

Or could they or could they smile so well.

Marguerite was often right. She said there would be more light.

Indeed she was not often colored to be night. And then she smiled as well as never more. Very often that is. As a place.

Could fifty times they think of Marguerite.

Marguerite was there or she. Was pleasant not as to hair. Not pleasant there. That is delicately fair and yet as dark as when they knew there was a park. Where they were like. A great deal of light is some resemblance.

I like it. Marguerite could be like it.

She could also like it. Although very nearly she at first.

And then arrange. Mountains are a range and also stoves and also will they be so sweet to cattle. Not if they are kept clean.

It is often thought that they will know their merriment.

Marguerite was stationed and was questioned. One thought she could be was frightened. But no. In the morning she was low. But by evening she was really earning morning noon and evening and just alike. She could be frightened of their having meant to dike and not like Finland England and France or so much.

She was often naturally historic.

Or just at a glance.

Now how is there a story without a history. Or a history.

How is there a history without a story.

Her story was that she knew history. She knew when Finland was born not only within but again. She also did know not to know England then not even France.

Afterwards she was in request.

What could more do than South. Not north. Not north or South. Which they may aim. Or commit to claim.

Marquerite never did claim. She asks for a thing in unison. She bestowed pale as their part. And they will. It is either otherwise or they may as well as will. Why they are wholesome. Or just as well apart.

Can she Marguerite be a mean. Between which is that there is a stream. Or with as well.

It is more than kind of her to be here.

Marguerite can almost dream that to be adopted is a dream of not a queen. Or just shortly. She can also prevail upon no one to come when where they will if it is either here or there. Or just alike. Why will they not mean. Come with them quickly. She has been there. Not as it were there.

It is surprising than any one like her could be what is it if they do not ask.

Or just much a chance.

Can any one think future when they will. She is not to be known as when they come either.

Does she like all who have been here. Marguerite cannot ask questions.

That is not the reason of not adopted or not in the past.

If it could that they were the children she had not almost forgotten.

It is often by that that they will include excursion. Nor will they call not coming again. Anything is ours like that. So not only with where they and do not it has been often all brought.

Marguerite was a child not younger than most. She will be tall as not tall as less than for most. She will is already shown. That they touch. Or will think it a resolve with fair and very pleased to be a principle. She could not think well of further but further than it went. Should all who come back go. Or stay.

Anyone cannot be adopted and registered. Or not polite in courteousness or just why they will better able to love to have it be. Just what it was not. Like and like for them.

Thank you in kind.

Marguerite no one knows.

It is not often ready to have part three partly. No will she just like having it with not a trouble. It is no trouble.

How do you like what they did.

By why they will be pale.

She is pale. Not as pale. Because it is not known. Why she is not. Oh love to be so.

Marguerite was slowly changing to circumstances. She might be dangerous if she changed. And do they do think so.

It is often called Marguerite to be forgotten.

Why could not Marguerite think that when she came there it would be open. Because she has had experience that when she came there it would be open. Just as get yes.

It is not why she was as she was but only longer.

Marguerite in fruition. And all of it not a distress to a pleasure.

She could be called not nor another careful nor caution. In syllables no one renounces.

Marguerite all filled with then. She has been dangerous not to danger nor to weather.

All who have been told nothing are not knowing. All of it doubtless.

Marguerite will she mean that nobody knows she has no adventures but experience. Nobody knows. She knows. She knows all made of knows or knowledge all will be known as knows. It is of no importance.

All white is not alike or paleness increasing.

Should it have shown or shone with accents brighten she could be happy if she was not better known. How is she better known. By having been in many places without their cost.

And now act as if Marguerite could converse and have things happen.

She was adopted and not starved.

She was born before she was adopted and not starved.

She was born and not starved.

She was left more than adopted and not starved and not here known.

All apples all dogs all suns and all places and all oranges and all dinners and all dears are not starved and all not adopted and all not known and all not clouded and all not taken and all not a trouble and all not liked and all not beside and all not kind. And all.

She was born and not starved adopted and not starved here and not starved there and not starved known and not starved again and not starved and only. She was not starved and so a heroine.

This is a story of Marguerite.

From head to feet.

And a love of what she asked. Was why they came.

But she might be just as well be happy.

Marguerite was mentioned as sweet.

But not as sweet Marguerite because just for this. Or with just for this.

All out to be inclined to be praised for. What she does. Or not.

Marguerite then had this happen.

Just why they like what they say.

Marguerite was always there in not a disappointment. If they went away to stay or to go. Could she go. When they went away to stay. This would happen not to go. It would happen that she was not only not to go but not to stay. This is how Marguerite could find out.

How could she like what she did.

Marguerite when she was sure could learn Finnish that is to say she was Finnish and could learn English if she did learn English she could learn french. And as much.

All who are around are reasonable.

And this is what all who like like it.

How many things happen: Not any of a great many things do as well as more do not by that or which happen. It is just alike not that. Is it why they like what they wish. It is not often that they allow for or with wishes. All of which is made to stay. Not to increase or to inquire which for and then needed yesterday.

How can they be called English french or Finnish. By that.

Marguerite was awakened to yesterday and not yet.

Marguerite she could say that dogs dribble as they lay. Or on account of it.

What could her feelings be. If this is all of three or more often.

She may be used to recklessness but not at all not at all used or to be used to it or not at all to be used to recklessness or not at all to be used to it.

What is the name the character the surname and the occupation of Marguerite. Does it make any difference. Will she be known. Can she come again. Is it useful as well as necessary. Do they do not do as they like it. Or may she not be always there. What is her name. Marguerite is her name. What is her surname. What is her surname what difference is it what is her surname what difference does it make.

How could she be not frightened or not frightening or not

well.

Marguerite made carefully apart. Her name of Marguerite is a rare name.

It can be repeated it does will and can say that the name a name if a name to be that name is a rare name and so she is so kind and the best of which nearly which and only which it is.

Marguerite is her name was it given to her does she remember her mother her grandmother her uncle or what. Anyway it is her name. And she knows well which she knows that rarely which she knows.

Marguerite may feel afresh that it is twice as a life.

And they think thanks.

Was Marguerite known as not or was she in a care or was she be which and ever which makes it be all.

She could recover. And recover.

So that Marguerite is not toothless and fevered she is just pale and fair. And so it has been not only mine but mine. And Marguerite will not feel that there is any or an in occasionally. Not that she has pain. There is no pain in complain or in fair or in there. No explain in not here nor in not here nor in not here which is not there. It is better to be fearful than to be tremulous. Oh yes.

Marguerite found many hours. Or easily plain or easily past or easily why or easily gain. They hope not for better times often.

Marguerite was not born for ages. It is a common name. One has known a Marguerite just yes.

Marguerite which they are willing but then they could not always know one that has was adopted. But then northern northern people often adopt children. Children are not motherless. They are fatherless. They are not fatherless. Nor uncleless nor indeed a date in which they do not meet. They are always without change. Who can be in search of a father without a mother. Even if the grandmother had known that no one was dead. And so they were accounted for. It should be rarely that they do engage.

Marguerite was known to be often. That they were with their and on their account. Oh nicely now.

She was adopted and they dropped the name not she. It was rare. She was to be no dupe to fancy. She was to be known older she was to be which they can have if they fancy it. No one taught to be alike. It was just as plainly taught as when they mentioned. Marguerite can be so sweetly in a swoon.

All taught not only not but left to how so naturally to fill a swan with butter. Oh swoon.

This makes Marguerite complete but not how she was born.

She was born the children of more than one. And so more likely. It was more likely that she would like not it what is it that it made not be this as born.

She was born and so she away. Let alone. It is nice what they like with remain. She was adopted by them as could be not children. Children are known as such. She was not happy but very pleased. Very pleased and very well seen and played. And they could judge.

Will she be known. Not unless it may they it we they they we say. She is not here. So she came to be. Known to have the place and the pay oh yes to say. How kindly. They should frighten.

It is once in a while an occasion. More she can do.

Marguerite was adopted very nearly and she could leave very nearly and go very nearly when she did not come. There could be nothing. Done. By her known with her as her resolution.

She sneezed but not from pleasure but in spite of their refusal but this has nothing whatever to do with Marguerite.

Or like it quite as well.

She may be exercised by their thinking just as well of it.

And now Marguerite who will think well of wealth and a wreath.

Marguerite has been warned to be close not to be with them with these not to wonder when they will and when they were near nor which by which they mean leave it or leave it here.

Marguerite may be an instance of why they liked the name or which they had or why they smile or when they will or be or is it not or just the same. Marguerite is always made. Leave it to her to end the same as when she will and when she will and will and can.

She thinks very well of why she is selfish. Who has hopes of in the end of the spring. She has not because she knows if she has known they will leave him and it will be most nefarious. Or will she just yet. Suit it. She may be thought to be obliged and in their way. They may not be alike. All of which she knows now.

Marguerite has almost forgotten adoption but not yet. She has almost forgotten that they might. But not yet. She has almost forgotten all one day. She has almost forgotten all one day but not yet. She has almost but not yet forgotten that it is not whichever they are for. And so the hours crowd.

She would be so sweet soon if she were known at noon.

Is it not best for Marguerite to say. She has been well reconciled to be abruptly at noon. Seen. They may care not to scare but she has forgotten that is not forgotten in between. And this leads to so much.

Marguerite was born a Finn that is to say on the border which is near the Russian border and they thought or ordered that she was not there when she was adopted because she was adopted as is common in northern countries but she might have known.

On account of which they may be often more than all alike on account of which they are not.

If she went away if she came to stay she was Finnish.

After a while it is an example that she looked like this. It is easy to understand. They may account for more than in and noon.

Should they challenge Finland to be England.

Marguerite was born in Finland not in England. She was in England not in Finland. She was in France.

Just when she was to be sure that she would do if they understood that she was not to be thought hurried as she was not through just then she was by no means not alone.

Why is why yes.

She had not been adopted by distress. She had not been adopted not again not when. Oh yes she knew who were how many how many who were through.

She knew they were fresh in pleasure but not in there. She knew that they could leave and learn and pay and fasten but not in there. She knew that they were kind and careful and all and she but not in there. All the rest of it she knew. How did she know. She knew. She had left home adopted when she was young and now there was some time since then. All this she knew. They were there to arrange. May be not. May be they do. May be they call. May be they have printed what was not known. May be not.

She may be said to be thoroughly content to see more which is why it is nobody's fault that she does not love what they do not say for them presently.

Think of how Marguerite was not willing to be famous, it was why she went that she knew that she came and she would not ease or release what is not that no one is which it is that they remember in which they do not manage to blame.

Why this when that is perfect.

Marguerite was born in Finland near the border of Russian and she was well when she had but she not only knew but could not remember. After she was as is frequent in northern countries adopted by a married couple she was adopted for the sake of the mother who did not care for her.

This can happen when in Finland which is a northern country they adopt some one which again is not only not often but quite often done in such a northern country. Finland is a northern country just as often.

After the death of the mother which was sure to happen later she left the father which was what will be nearly earlier. After which just alike.

This is England. Who told any one that England was across the water. Who told any one that any England was anywhere across wherever there was water. She likes England better than french and why. Because she knows why.

Marguerite could be born it is not a cup which is forlorn nor a cup measured it is not a cup measured nor may she make a mistake since which it is all read. She knows that if it is said so she finds it not only there but there.

Marguerite what will become of any one adopted. Marguerite what will become of any one adopted.

Marguerite has not this to answer oh no she has not this to answer.

Marguerite what will become of any one who has been adopted and is now not one who has been adopted. Marguerite has not this to answer either.

Marguerite will not settle anything because there is no waiting in adopting. If one is adopted one is not waiting and so they realise that ice which is cold is welcome to believe that she makes it be good with them alone that they like what they admire. Often one says does she know. Can no one who is told be waiting with which they come to wish which for a dish. It is easy to say no I do not like it if it is so. Nor indeed do they collect publicly more than once for once. She may be often with and without a wish. All of which they could reconcile more abundantly. Just why they are. All is my best.

It is often that they end before.

She might be why with all of which.

Are and are not is not are they otherwise like it in

possession. After which I like it green. This is not only because of whys but because of yes. And she was nearly in no case. It is often that nobody knows how.

All which she likes because all which she may they think he said it like that.

Marguerite was afraid of a rose.

Or was she why she came.

Oh dear Marguerite was afraid she could be taught with which she came.

May be she be lawful.

It was well to adopt. Could it.

It was well that they knew did not know that she could not be seen waiting. Nobody can be seen waiting sometime. For this they like it for that.

Marguerite was born in Finland.

Why are they there when they are born. Or may be they will feel well and be well until which they may not at all very careful. All should be thought.

Will she feel well if she agrees with them or is with them or is agrees with them.

Marguerite was not strong she preferred kneeling to standing or not sitting or standing or not kneeling or kneeling and not waiting. This might be because she was made to be believe it of her that she will not be.

May they account that for her.

Marguerite was never married. She could keep it as if she were not so or not in any sense likely at all likely. Could those who have been adopted marry.

Once when her hair was fine she was one at a time and always.

Oh think so well of it and wishes.

Marguerite had not fair hair it was fair but she was dark in Finland not dark in England not dark in France.

North east south west home is best that is what she hears them say.

Marguerite shall be not known not to be placed where they do whatever they do like. She is not anxious not to hear something that is not only all not to her credit but very likely more often than not at all doubly likely.

She was never disagreeable in thought.

How can they reasonably feel better without it ever not only not having been bought.

Will they remember that yesterday it could if she did say that not any one properly could be necessary to go not only not away but not their way.

If she was adopted which does not differ from if she were adopted she would not then be after more often more than any other after all.

It is often not so and not so often and not only not so but not so soon and not sewn nor as soothing to be adopted and which is a difference between next to and next to this. She is adopted and she is not interested in any one. And so they make her be careful to be fatigued that is she reminds herself.

To be so sorry not to have after all been there which is the same as remarkable.

How can there be an exercise of adoption with and without question which she may if she dies like.

In northern countries they do adopt. Children.

Marguerite could cry and not to love to die. Marguerite could cry and often enough to pull through not likely to not need it to not to be without it as she had not been through without it not it without for you. She having been adopted and not leaving for not left could be all so nicely faded to not a ground. A ground is plainly what they like often while they think what they do like. She is not known instantly that they make it do sooner.

It is very well to be an advantage or just as likely.

What could Marguerite do if everybody was anxious.

They should be thought to be always well when thay came after as they might cause it.

Marguerite was born in Finland and admired Sweden. She was born nearly where they had been but she was not only not used to it.

All of which they feel like it.

She was adopted by a husband and wife but they did not remember alike. It was of no use not to be well and selfish and she never minded it. She could hear it at all. And they were liked. After she left before that they were not there not only not as needing but in which case. She left Finland for England where she learned English. She learned English and left England and she came to France but although she tried she did not learn french.

She said to say it to have it to be she said she had none and she had some.

It was not by asking after anxious wishes that she was obliged to be back.

She could be nearer to it or not.

She would be better to be or not.

This is how they could wait.

Every day Marguerite waited she waited to see if she were not going and so they could not abandon waiting.

Because by the time that she cherished all or more readily what she not only knew she was made often not that she did not know that is allow that she had sent it away. By this. Could they in some country ask them this.

Marguerite earned money in Finland in England and in France. She liked England she sent money to Finland and she stayed in France.

Always when I am through she is not only through but not commenced.

Marguerite says that in Finland she floated upon ice.

All which is made to pull a praise for progress.

Let me hear you say that Marguerite is usual every day.

This is a history of her day.

She wakes up in the morning and nearly. Always ought

to.

After she accepts not only not a wedding but effectively to repeat all which is bought. For this they do not call her early nor does she come with not forever running. It is quite quietly that she said yes.

Marguerite has been a privilege and a pleasure in the beginning and often that sameness has become inconstant. Does she love. She says but that may be because by that she passes France and England because by that she repasses Finland. Because by that no hope of pleasure makes any thing this there this delight. It is awfully often all. She can be caught with dated pleasure. Every little once in a while a pause. She recounts. How many hours before to-day may make two an afternoon. Her life is reasonable without economy. By which means she remains fortunately there or theirs alone.

A very likely home is Finland. Marguerite was born in Finland near the borders of Russia and there she came to France but neither directly or even not more placed as a departure carefully. She came again. It is often as exciting not to pray as to stay.

She might be thought to be cross because she opened the name not on the same day.

Or with it inclined.

It is past that they understood.

This is a history of her life she could be even ever if she cried.

The fortunes and misfortunes of Marguerite. Marguerite had no misfortunes. The misfortunes and fortunes of Marguerite. Marguerite had no fortunes. And why had she no fortunes. Why had she not any misfortunes.

Marguerite was born in Finland and she was not often mistaken by that. She had been engaged to England and there she was praiseworthy. She had been recalled to France that is just as well she had never been there before. After that any one could not be very fortunate for their belief. She believed she would as she was not known once. It is very easy not to be deceitful.

There is not any home for Marguerite a home town means something but not something else.

It is by which by me that Marguerite can see that she can say that when she looks and it is a pleasure that she can say not only not yesterday.

Marguerite was employed to be all of which they knew she was employed scarcely as to blame.

This was her unhappy experience.

Now let us think woefully of nationality. A nationality is this she does not know how not to receive more knowledge that not as bliss that not not only not and not to miss which she knew she knew that she could be blamed and payed for as if in defence not only of herself but many and more kind. Who could know that she would not say so say that she knew that they could come never to come. She refused to see them.

Was she known to have a dream without danger. Or was she not known.

Marguerite she suggests not Marguerite because marguerites although not attractive not only attractive are smaller as well as faithful they are not because there has been some mistake only in names.

Now this is telling it truly. She was born in Finland and not as many might think not truly of her mother which is her father because she does not care to know. She always thinks of it of which it is so.

She might keep it not only from not being so. Every time it is said it is always the same even when it is added. She was born in Finland and this is near the Russian border which she thinks is exactly her name. Her name is now not any different at any one time. She was born and the name is the name of her grandmother but this she knows but is not certain which.

Marguerite has not come back again when she has been or not.

Marguerite could be in imagination not born in Finland not either or not. It is not.

She was been born in Finland which she admires she admires the country by way of which she made England for a change. Nobody sought for her.

She was born in Finland when she was old enough after having lived in Finland she went to England. In Finland she had been old enough so that afer England she came to France. This is where she is now. All sorts of differences do not matter nor can they make it which it is not known for which it is not known or really better it does not matter.

She left Finland for England and she left England for France not to be in England not to be in France not yet or rather not to have not been in Finland not in England not in France.

She could be meant to be born in Finland when she says good by to France. In saying all this she does not miss one country.

This is what they like to do.

Marguerite was adopted as is the custom in a northern country. She was not less than all of which. She may be fortunate or fought more but not as likely as that they were never more around than when she was alone which after all was not right there not only with it. It was why she was born not for it really she could know but she had not wanted not only not to know but without doubt. How very much and also how very often.

She was born in Finland. She left Finland and went to England. She was often in England after she had been in Finland and not back again. It is not very likely that they were often there.

She was waiting for no dog. She had been left not by them but by leaving. She would be often found in tears not without reason.

Marguerite was often happily better.

What is it. She was born in Finland and in Finland they do not thank that is in England they thank and also not only in France.

She had been born with care. She had come away from there and had been adopted by a man and woman that she called mother and father naturally and not unfortunately. She was not unfortunate either. By which she meant nothing.

Do do be sure that she is here.

Many things that have happened in her life are these. She would not say. What is it when you ask. She was not born in vain in Finland nor did she in vain go to England nor in a way in vain did she come to France. All these succeeded one another. And oftentimes she would not be conscious that this was past. Because quite naturally these countries were there in a way to her they might since without calculation there is no prostration they might not only follow it alone. She who was not blind because she had that beauty thoughtfully could be not known. I have often said I will not mention her.

In every likelihood nobody can do harm. She was born in the country where she had not visited nor had she failed very likely.

I will now tell why she came. She could not do otherwise nor could she leave it as a reason moreover formerly there is no such pleasure as a touch.

It is very often true that no one in Finland was born in England. This may not be carried away. And now I ask. Will she furnish us.

And so no one is silent in her presence not even as much so.

She was not only in England and in France. Very likely they are thoroughly better than any commencement immediately.

The great question is can any one very immediately stay away.

At least no one is blamed.

She is often always there. On no account. But which will gradually know its worth.

It is not often that not as well she spoke she called it the dog she called him the man she called her the woman and they were each and all not averse not to be welcome which she is if wishes. And derived.

And so they may. She was born in Finland near Russia and England and France and she may without that difference. Having blamed others or not now. And so they need never please her either. But she need not leave it for this nevertheless.

I can no longer remember how she says what she says.

Finis.

Or who will be carried better nearer.

Finis

By Gertrude Stein

Advertisements

I was winsome. Dishonored. And a kingdom. I was not a republic. I was an island and land. I was early to bed. I was a character sodden agreeable perfectly constrained and not artificial. I was relieved by contact. I said good-morning, good evening, hour by hour. I said one had power. I said I was frequently troubled. I can be fanciful. They have liberal ideas. They have dislikes. I dread smoke. Where are there many children. Where are there many children. We have an account. We count daisy. Daisy is a daughter. Her name is Antonia. She is pleased to say what will you have. Horns and horns. Nicholas is not a stranger. Neither is Monica. No one is a stranger. We refuse to greet any one. We like Genevieve to satisfy us. I do not like what I am saying.

How can you describe a trip. It is so boastful.

He said definitely that they would. They have. It's a little late. I hope the other things will be as he states them. I have confidence. I have not eaten peaches. Yes I have. I apologize. I did not want to say the other word that was red. You know what I mean.

Why can I read it if I know page to page what is coming if I have not read it before. Why can I read it. I do.

I didn't.

Let me see. I wish to tell about the door. The door opens before the kitchen. The kitchen is closed. The other door is open and that makes a draft. This is very pleasant in summer. We did not expect the weather to change so suddenly. There seem to be more mosquitoes than ever. I don't understand why I like narrative so much to read. I do like it. I see no necessity for disclosing particularity I am mightily disturbed by a name such as an English home. An English home is beautiful. So are the times.

A dog does not bark when he hears other dogs bark. He sleeps carefully he does not know about it. I am not pained.

This is the narrative. In watching a balloon, a kite, a boat, steps and watches, any kind of a call is remarkable remarkably attuned. A resemblance to Lloyd George, bequeathing prayers, saying there is no hope, having a french meeting. Jenny said that she said that she did not believe in her country. Any one who does not believe in her country speaks the truth. How dare you hurt the other with canes. I hope he killed him. Read it. I believe Bulgaria. I have pledges. I have relief.

I AM NOT PATIENT

I am interested. In that table. I like washing gates with a mixture. We get it by bringing up melons. White melons have a delicious flavor.

I am not patient. I get angry at a dog. I do not wish to hear a noise. I did not mind the noise which the client made. I wished to see the pearls. How easily we ask for what we are going to have. By this we are pleased and excited.

The hope there is is that we will hear the news. We are all elated. Did you see her reading the paper. I cannot help wanting to write a story.

A woman who had children and called to them making them hear singing is a match for the man who has one child and does not tell him to play there with children. Heaps of them are gambling. They tell about stitches. Stitches are easily made in hot weather and vegetation. Tube roses are famous.

I could be so pleased. It would please me if Van would

mention it. Why is an index dear to him. He has thousands of gesticulations. He can breathe.

White and be a Briton. This means a woman from the north of France. They are very religious. They say blue is not a water color. It should be a bay. We are pleased with her. She washes her hair very often.

Do not tremble. If she had an institution it is the one excluding her mother. Her native land is not beautiful. She likes the poet to mutter. He does. The olive.

We had that impression. Do speak. Have they been able to arrange matters with the proprietor.

I will not please play. I will adorn the station. It has extraordinarily comfortable seats.

TO OPEN

Not too long for leading, not opening his mouth and sitting. Not bequeathing butter. Butter comes from Brittany. In the summer it smells rancid. We do not like it. We have ceased use of it. We find that oil does as well. We can mix oil with butter but we have lard. We use lard altogether. We prefer it to butter. We use the butter in winter. We have not been using it before the winter. We mix lard and oil. We will use butter.

DO LET US BE FAITHFUL AND TRUE

I do not wish to see I do not wish to see Harry I do not wish to see Harry Brackett I do not wish to see Harry Brackett.

A GRAPE CURE

What did we have for dinner we had a melon lobster chicken then beet salad and fruit. How can you tell a melon. You tell it by weight and pressing it. You do not make mistakes. We are pleased with it. Do we like a large dog. Not at all.

BATTLE

Battle creek. I was wet. All the doors showed light. It is strange how Brittany is not attractive as Mallorca and yet butter does make a difference. We are perfect creatures. What is a festival. Saturday to some. Not to be dishonored. Not to be tall and dishonored they usually aren't but some are, some are tall and dishonored. By this I mean that coming down the mountain faces which are shining are reflecting the waving of the boat which is there now. I distrust everybody. Do sleep well. Everywhere there is a cat. We will leave by boat. I am not pleased with this. I will get so that I can write a story.

FASTENING TUBE ROSES

I understand perfectly well how to fix an electric fan. Of course it makes sparks but when the two black pieces that do not come together are used up you get this. I do it without any bother. I am not certain I could learn it. It is not difficult. We do not find that it does away with mosquitoes. We use it in the night. Sundays there is no electricity.

THEY DO IT BETTER THAN I DO

I can. I can be irritated. I hate lizards when you call them crocodile. She screamed. She screamed. I do not know why I am irritated.

IT IS A NATURAL THING

Do not do that again. I do not like it. Please give it away. We will not take it to Paris. I do not want the gas stove. It has a round oven. It does not bake. We use coal by preference. It is very difficult not to bathe in rain water. Rain water is so delicious. It is boiled. We boil it.

LOUD LETTERS

Look up and not down.
Look right and not left.
And lend a hand.
We were so pleased with the Mallorcans and the wind and the party. They were so good to offer us ice-cream. They do not know the french names.

Isn't it peculiar that those that fear a thunder storm are willing to drink water again and again, boiled water because it is healthy. All the water is in cisterns rain water. There are no vegetables that is to say no peas. There are plenty of beets. I like them so much. So do I melons I was so glad that this evening William came and ate some. It would not go back as if it hadn't been good.

PLEASURES IN SINCERE WISHES

I wish you to enjoy these cigarettes. They are a change from those others. I understand that you had some very good ones. You are not able to get these any more. I have tried to get them. They tell me that they cannot say when they will come. They do not know that about them. We sleep easily. We are awakened by the same noise. It is so disagreeable.

AN EXHIBITION

I do not quite succeed in making an exhibition. Please place me where there is air. I like to be free. I like to be sure that the dogs will not be worried. I don't see how they can avoid crickets. They come in. They are so bothersome. We must ask Polybe to wish.

THE BOAT

I was so disappointed in the boat. It was larger than the other. It did not have more accommodation. It made the noise which was disagreeable. I feel that I would have been willing to say that I liked it very well if I had not seen it when it was painted. It is well never to deceive me.

THREADNEEDLE STREET

I am going to conquer. I am going to be flourishing. I am going to be industrious. Please forgive me everything.

PRESENT

This is a ceremonial. When you are bashful you do not think. When a present is offered you accept it you accept the bracelet worn by the nun so that it rusted. You do not know what to do with it. You describe its qualities. It is a pleasure to have it. You will give it. You are steadily tender. You say the beginning is best. Why do you say Englishman. You say Englishman because he wished it. Do not hurry.

EVIAN WATER

Evian water is very good. Sometimes I am not sure it is put up by them at least now when there is a war. I say it is fresh. When I do not like a bottle I throw it away. I throw the water away.

By Gertrude Stein

Pink Melon Joy

(excerpt)

My dear what is meat.
I certainly regret visiting.
My dear what does it matter.
Leaning.
Maintaining maintaining checkers.
I left a leaf and I meant it.
Splintering and hams.
I caught a cold.

                              Bessie
They are dirty.
Not polite.
Not steel.
Not fireless.
Not bewildered.
Not a present.
Why do I give old boats.
Theresa.

                Exchange in bicycles.
   It happened that in the aggregate and they did not hear
then, it happened in the aggregate that they were alone.
   It is funny. When examples are borrowing and little
pleasures are seeking after not exactly a box then comes the

time for drilling. Left left or left. Not up. Really believe me it is sheltered oaks that matter. It is they who are sighing. It really is.

Not when I hear it.

I go on.

This is not a dear noise. It is so distressing. Why was he angry. Did he mean to be laughing.

I was astonished besides. Oh do go on.

He was a ruffian.

Especially made. Why does she satisfy it.

It was a beautiful hat anyway it looked like that or by the way what was the handkerchief. Good.

Now I neglected him.

I made mention of an occasion. I made mention of a syllable. I mentioned that. I was reasonably considerate. I undertook nothing.

Why were birds.

When I decided not to look twice I felt that all three were made of the only distinct changeable brown. I did not mean foxes. This is why I shall not visit. Do go gladly. Do be willing.

What an accident.

What a horrid thought.

What a decent ribbon.

That is why I answered.

No please don't be wakened. Do think it over. Do mind what I say. Do breathe when you can. Explain whites for eggs. Examine every time. Do not deceive a brother. What is perfect instigation. I make I go across.

Instances.

Violences.

Not any whirl.

Not by all means.
Don't you think so.

Fourteen days.
I meant to be closeted.
I should have been thin.
I was aching.
I saw all the rose. I do mostly think that there is politeness. All of it on leather. Not it. I shall speak of it. I so mean to be dried. In the retracting glory there is more choice. There is what was threaded. I don't mean permitting.

Webster.
Little reinforced Susan.
Actual.
Actual believe me.
I see it all.
Why shouldn't I.
Lizzie Make Us.
I believe it.
Why shall I polite it. Pilot it.
Eleven o'clock.

Pillow.
I meant to say.
Saturday.
Not polite.
Do satisfy me.
This is to say that baby is all well. That baby is baby. That baby is all well. That there is a piano. That baby is all well. This is to say that baby is all well. This is to say that baby is all well.

Selling.
She has always said she was comfortable.

Was the water hot.

Hymns.

Look here let us think about hospitality. There is more said and kindness. There are words of praise. There is a wonderful salad. There can be excellent excellent arrangements. There can be excellent arrangements. Suddenly I saw that. I rushed in. I was wise.

We were right. We meant pale. We were wonderfully shattered. Why are we shattered. Only by an arrest of thought. I don't make it out. Hope there. Hope not. I didn't mean it. Please do be silly. I have forgotten the height of the table.

That was a good answer.

I have been going on in a little while.

I am going to take it along. Lena says that there is a chance.

I don't mean to deny it.

That's right.

I shall be very tired I shall be extraordinarily pleased, I shall settle it all presently.

Very likely.

I have to look at her all the time. I never see fruit now unless I pick it in my garden. Put it in my garden. Don't put too many. Because it's so much looser. All right. Oh no. I haven't. Chalk. Great Portland Street. I'll mention it. I have resisted. I have resisted that excellently well. I have resisted that I have resisted that excellently. Not a disappointment.

I don't understand, why hasn't she been there before. I know why. I will not have a selection again. It is too many horribly. Is it any use.

I do want to meet pearly. Now I am forgetting I will begin.
She had a jewel. She was in that set.

It meant so much.

I wish I had a little celebration.

It meant so much.

The wise presentation comes from saying north, the best
one comes a little way, it comes because she wanted to try
breads. Why are pansies so stringy, why do they have heaps
of resemblance. I said she was anaemic. I meant to coincide.
I did certainly. It was so. Not in Paris.

Not is Paris very likely.

I do not mention that for a name. I mention it for a place.
I mention it for a please do not consider me. I mention it for
that.

Did she mind my saying that I was disappointed. I was not
in that way out in that way. I was not in that way a
circumstance which counted for it. She did not meet me. She
did not observe clouds. She did not say that we were in the
window. She did not like it before it was mentioned.

Come in.

I don't mean to antagonize the present aged parent. That
is a strong present leaf.

Line.

Line line line away.
Line
Lining.

I don't care what she mentions
It will be very funny when I don't mean to say it.
I can forgive that is to say chopping.
Not any more.
Will I be surprisded with Jane Singleton. I will not if I meet
her. I will say not yet. I will say that. I am determined. It is so

much. Good bye.

I did do it then.
Come back to me Fanny.

Oh dear.
Come back to me Fanny.

That's a picture.
When I remembered how surprised I was at certain places which were nearly in the way I cannot doubt that more accumulation is needed. I cannot doubt it.

All recovering.
James Death is a nice name.
I am breaking down I suppose he said when he arrived.
Forbade any communication with him.
He did say when he arrived I suppose.
It was a bright warm spring Sunday morning.
This egg for instance.
She was dressed in dark blue set off by red ribbons.
Except that of custom perhaps.
If you prefer it I will go.
The only lady who had been saved.
He was not hungry and he knew that there would be nothing to eat.
He was aware of a desire to eat and drink now that it was quite impossible for him to obtain anything.
Thanks I chew.
Jakins thinks me a fool I know sometime maybe I'll be able to prove I'm not.
You're busy.
His excitement was gone.
With mouth and muscle.
When used for male voices substitute bless for kiss.

Shall rest.
Shall rest more.
Shall in horror.
Shall rest.
Shall rest more then.

This is it mentioning.
Why do richness make the best heights.
Why do richness make the best heights.

Enough to leave him for ever and to live in another country
I don't see anything any more do I. Yes you do.
Are you pleased with them darling.

I meant to guess later.
I do not please.
Thanks so much.
Yes.
Yes.
Yes.
Please remember that I have said I will not be patient.
Please remember that which I have said.

Do not put in a hot water bottle. Thanks so much.

Feeling mounting.
What did she do. She did not sit she was standing. She was standing and filling with a pepper thing and she had a collar not on her head but because she was shining. She was shining with gloves. This is a new destination. I never was surprised before.

What is the matter with it.
Nothing is the matter with it.

I mean to cough.

She said it was a wish.

You are not angry with me.

It's infamous. To put a cold water bottle in a bed. It is steering.

I meant to mention it and it is astonishing that there is a sentence.

Silence is southern.

I will not especially engage to be sick. I will not especially engage to be sick.

Why is Ellen so attractive.

Willing.

Willing, willing.

Willing willing, I met a kind of a clock. It was deepened.

I am not pleased. I am not satisfied and pleased. I am not pleased and certainly I am not more pleased. I am so repressed and I can state it. I can say. It was bitter.

I do not like her.

Fancy a miserable person. Repeat flowers.

A section.

Breathing.

Polite.

Politeness.

Absolutely.

Not a curl.

I come to say.

Winding.

Place

Wheat.

Or not.

Come in.
Splashes splashes of jelly splashes of jelly.

Weather.
Whether he was presented.
I meant to stay.
Easy or blocks.
Do not be held by the enemy.
All the time.

Now line or them.
That's an established belt or tooth. Really not. I didn't mean to bellow. I won't be a table. I regret it. I shall be very likely to be walking. I shall introduce myself fairly. I do mind it.

Not again.
I do say not again.
I mean to be heavy.
It stands up against as much as it stands up for. That's what I object to. I don't want to be unflattering to us but I think it has been entirely forgotten.

Furs.
Perhaps you will. Then she wrote a very warm letter and sent these furs.

Shall ill.
I don't like it and in neglecting cherishing songs I am so pleased with all and by settling chalk. I am satisfied. We are neglected immensely. Not resting.
Shall it be continuous the liberty of sobriety. The dear thing. Little tremors. I ask the question.

With a wide piano.

Come.

Neglecting cherishing says shall I mistake pleases.

In mistakes there is a salutary secretion. What. I said it.

Now and then.

War is Saturday and let us have peace.

Peace is refreshing, let us bear let us be or not by that mine.

Mended.

Now I come to stay away.

Answer.

I shook a darling.

Not eating Oh it was so timely.

Why should pitchers be triumphant. Does it proclaim that eleven, eleven, eleven, come across, speak it, satisfy a man, be neat, leave off oxes, shine flies, call spoken shouting call it back call it by little dotted voices and do be sweet, remember the accoutrement. No I will not pay away.

What a system in voices, what a system in voices.

I met a regular believe me it is not for the pleasure in it that I do it. I met a regular army. I was not certain of that, I was not certain of paper. I knew I was safe. And so he was. Shall I believe it.

I can't help mentioning that I was earnest. In that way there was a reason. I can destroy wetter wetter soaps. I can destroy wetter soaps.

I do.

I do not.

Leave it in there for me.

Leave it in an especial place. Do not make that face. Show it by the indication. I do mean to spell. I am. Believe me.

Pink Melon Joy.
II.

It please me very much.

Little swimming on the water.

I meant to mention pugilism. Pugilism leaning. Leaning and thinking. Thinking.

I meant to mention pugilism. Pugilism and leaning. Leaning and thinking. I think.

I meant to mention that it was a resemblance that was not by way of exceeding the kind thought.

Pugilism. Pugilism and leaning.

I saw a door not that exactly, I saw a lamp shade. Certainly that. I will not stir. Pugilism and leaning.

Leaning.

Pugilism and leaning.

The reason I mention what is happening is not by way of concealing that I have babies. I don't mean to leave so and I shall speak in silence. What is a baby.

Now I know what I say.

I had loads of stationary.

Not pink melon joy. Pink melon joy. Pink melon joy.

I had loads of stationary.

Pugilism and leaning.

The little keys trembling. Why do they spoil a part. They were noisy.

Go to Mudie's first.

Go slowly and carefully and love your dearest.

That's a good idea.

Reconcile is a plain case of wretched pencils.

I cannot see what I shall a bit.

My one idea is to place cloth where there is cloth and to paper where I have hotter water, to place paper where I have hotter water.

I don't determine selfishness. I point it so that always I

can always I do, I do always mean to get about.

Shall I be splendid.

Baby mine baby mine I am learning letters I am learning that to be sent baby mine baby mine I arranged it fairly early.

Complete cause for handles.

Complete cause for not tightening that.

I won't say it again.

This is the place to water horses.

I like to be excellently seized.

I made a mistake.

I like to be excellently seizing.

North north I went around and went in that minute.

I like to be excellently searching.

I like to be excellently chimes.

Chiming.

It isn't very good.

Deep set trustworthy eyes dark like his hair

Lips close fitting and without flew.

Blue should have dark eyes.

Light brown flesh color amber shades black nose, ears, legs, good sized feet rather.

Color dark blue, blue and tan, tan and liver, sandy, sandy and tan.

Height about fifteen to sixteen inches.

He wondered if she had ever thought of him as she sat in the chair or walked on the floor.

Islands.

I came to say that I like some things better.

Actual likenesses.

Of course I need large plates.

Standing alone.

She doesn't like it.
She likes to walk on the floor.
She might as well be pretty.
I don't blame Carrie.

No

What do I see when I like to be tall.
I see when there is a platter.
I was not mistaken with violets.
It was no pleasure.
Can you believe me.
Can you not be thoughtful.
Can you be aghast.
I mention most things regularly.
I do not wish whispers.
This makes mining such a loud noise.
I do not forget a war.
It isn't easy to please everybody.
Teeth are perfect.

No.

There is no influence.

Scattered.

Nine times twenty.
Crowded.
Crowded in.
Cups white.
I am solemn.
All taste.
Do you excuse me.
It was a stir.
Please state it please deny it please mean to be right. I am
intending.

Able to mingle pennies.
A penny is not a cent.

Why do I see sisters.
It's rice.

Wheat.
I couldn't imagine gladder or more perfect shapes, I couldn't imagine others.
He was really interested in the fluttering deftness of her twinkling hands.
I don't care too.
Likely.
I meant pearls.
Shall I be pleased.
Wire cakes.

In time or.
Not so far back.

Please.
When I came to stay.
Old places.
When a girl speaks.
Shall you.

Not pleasing.
It is a time for that.
Formidable.
Amiable.
Amiable baby.
Fan.

Fanning.
There is no way of stretching.

Plan.

It is a good pitcher it is a good pitcher and a black pitcher.

It is a circle.

It is a circular.

I beg of you not to.

Bring in the fruit.

She was very comforting.

I wonder what he is doing. If he saw, well he couldn't see him because he is not here, if he saw him he would not ask him any questions, he would beg him to give him all the pictures and in any case he would ask him to arrange it.

What is a splendid horse. A splendid horse is one that is spread and really makes a lot of noise really makes an agreeable sound and a hoarse. This in not an interchange of rapid places by means of tubs.

I know you don't know what the pins are. I know you suspect much more. I know that anything is a great pleasure. I know esquimaux babies, that is to say tender.

I know what I am hearing. I am hearing accents. Not by any means placarded. Not by any means placarded. So that I met everybody.

What is the meaning of photographs.

Yes I mean it.

I believe that when there is a collection and tall pieces are missed and guided, I could have said it.

Let us take boats.

Boats are ships.

We will not take ships.

Ships are doors.

That's the way to be perfect.

I sell hats.

That's a kindness.

Please powder faces.

I have little chickens.

That doesn't mean anything.

When I said water I meant Sunday. Dear me it was Monday. No Tuesday. I don't care I shall please neatness. Then I calculated I did not see arithmetic I saw feathers, any two of them are thicker. What was the principle coughing, it went by way of dishes.

To be binding is to mean Sunday Saturday and eight o'clock. To be eight o'clock oh how heavenly singing. Leave Leave Leave oh my leaving and say why say, say I say say say go away go away I say. I say yes.

Plans.

I was able to state that I believed that if targets if targets not if targets.

Shall I be restless.

I could not eat buttons. I could not eat bundles. I couldn't, I might be why was I seen to be determined. I was surprising. Wasn't I silly.

Please miss me.

Not spider.

I saw a spider there.

Where.

I saw another.

Where.

I saw another and there I saw a pleasing sight.

I saw a waiter.

A spider.

Yes.

Not by left out.

Will you be faithful, will you be so glad that I left any way. Will you be delighted Saturday. Do you understand colors. It was my sister.

Why.

I cannot mention what I have.

I have.
Guess it.
I have a real sight. This is so critical.
Alice.

                              Put it in.
Put it in.
Nestles.
I wish I was a flower.
Were.
Were when.
Towers.

                              That is.
That is astonishing.

                              Mother.
I meant it.
When the moon.
I don't like it.
A million and ten.
Ten million and ten.
Ten and ten million.
Oh leave it to me.

                              Brutes.
I said whisper.

                    Anyway Pink melon or joy.
Is that the same.
Pink melon and enjoy.
Pink melon by joy.
Is that in him.
Is that in.
Positive.

Section Two

BOOK TWO

By Judy Grahn

Exiled to the Center of the World

A Woman in Her Life

Gertrude Stein is often made fun of for her "self centered-
ness." She often discusses the process of her writing in the
middle of whatever else she is talking about, and she often
discusses the matter of "being a genius," why her brother Leo
was not and she was, what it means to be a genius, and so
on. About "self-centeredness," it is clear to most artists, I
think, that a small "self" does our daily lives, our social lives,
careers and fears, while a much larger "Self," sometimes
called "muse," gives us the work itself.

I have two things that I think about the idea "genius"; one
is that being a genius means literally, listening to one's
geniis, or higher-minded voices—the ones outside our socialized human selves, accessed through creative meditation
and by asking them to speak to us. Stein did a great deal of
this kind of listening, much more than nearly anyone, and is
simply accurately describing it when she calls herself "genius." Secondly, I think it is not appropriate for Lesbian poets
to be modest (or any poets for that matter). It doesn't run true
to the Lesbian tradition, as Sappho herself said in 600 B.C.
that she would not be forgotten, and that words, although
they are only air, are immortal. Poets rule the world because
poets rule the word.

It is important to realize that some of Gertrude Stein's
style(s) must have come from the extraordinary and contra-

dictory pressure she was under to write from the immediate presence of her own life and mind, as poets do, connecting her inner world with the worlds of objective, and social, realities—while simultaneously having a personal life whose every overt definition—Jewish, Lesbian, female, artist, financially independent woman—was seen as alien, dangerous, forbidden, exotic or vile by much of Western civilization.

Since she certainly was self-centered, (which is not at all the same as self-obsessed, a state of lacking one's own center) it seems vital to examine some of the stuff of her life to see just what she was centered *in*, and how that gives value to what she wrote.

In the still brawley and physically growing American West coast where they grew up in the fourth quarter of the nineteenth century, the brother and sister Leo and Gertrude Stein wandered Oakland's beautiful tree-laden hills together. Closest companions as the youngest of five children of German Jewish immigrants from middleclass Vienna, the two found with each other an ecstasy of intellectual camaraderie otherwise missing in the American atmosphere; they devoured the libraries on both sides of the Bay. Leo knew all the botanical names of plants; Gertrude read everything and would go on reading throughout her life until she had absorbed the entire tradition in English.

Their mother was bedridden and then dead of cancer by the time Gertrude was fourteen and their father died when she was eighteen. When Leo went to Harvard in the east she followed to the Harvard annex for women, and then entered medical school at Johns Hopkins only to drop out in the last year, of boredom. She was drawn to the science, not the practical application of medical skill.

When Leo went back to the Europe of their early childhood, she followed again, and the two wandered Italy as much the eccentric intellectual outsiders in young adulthood as they had been as children. They wore sandals and monkish robes to distinguish their outsider status, their incipient Bohemianism with its secular/sacred aspects.

America, she would later write, had no place for artistic intellectual oddities such as she and Leo were, in the context of post Civil War expansion, massive tree cutting for elegant workingclass housing, continuing gold fever, and building, building, building. Yet her sensitivity and expressiveness were not dainty or limp wristed. She maintained a sturdy body and enthusiastic appetites.

No one, apparently, and fortunately, ever told Gertrude she would have to restrict herself in order to be a "girl," so at college when she wanted to lose a few pounds she hired a boy to give her boxing lessons. As Jennifer Stone has pointed out in her essay,[1] Gertrude thought of herself as a man, in the 17th century use of the word "man" as applicable to both sexes.

I feel indebted to the oldest Stein brother, Michael, for he made money with the development of San Francisco's cable cars and endowed his brothers and sisters with modest but crucial lifelong stipends after their parents died. Because of Michael, Gertrude could find in Paris a place cheap enough to live comfortably and metropolitan enough to support her habits of writing, talking, thinking, and knowing other artists.

Her self-imposed exile positioned her in the center of what became, for Western civilization, the center of the world of intellectual and artistic foment. And by operating a salon frequented by active people, artists, writers, intellectuals of all kinds in the generic grouping "Bohemian," she herself was a center of the center.

In 1907 she was joined by her lifelong lover and "wifely" companion, Alice B. Toklas, who moved in with her; shortly afterward Leo moved out. Leo, as Gertrude developed her writing, publicly and privately criticized it; Alice did the opposite, not only loving and appreciating the writing, but helping with its transcription and editing and the endless discussions and evaluations that accompanied its existence.

Alice Toklas had little money, and technically speaking she really was Gertrude's "wife." There was no satisfactory term for Lesbian lovers other than husband and wife until the surge of women into the work force and into business with each other in the seventies made "partner" the conjugal term of choice, a business term that is economically descriptive of the independent incomes of two equal people.

Stein and Toklas lived modestly in a country and at a time when good food, good wine and good company were abundant, and when servants were extremely cheap—and so they had a cook and set a fine table in their Paris apartment on the Rue de Fleurus. Stein once chose between buying a chair and buying a painting and the artists and writers in their early days sometimes traded their arts with each other for goods, including food. The two women never owned a house, though after they had lived together for a while they rented a place in the country at Bilignin with a fine garden, but they did not have electricity until 1927 nor a telephone until 1930. By no stretch of the imagination were they wealthy in the money sense; what Michael's stipend allowed them to have were their own minds, with independence of spirit, and of course, each other; and Gertrude could write as many days of her life as she chose. In this, and in their spirited participation in their times, they were wealthy.

Their friends and colleagues have reported that Stein was a warm, locquacious person, at times a nonstop talker, and especially trusted and loved by dogs and children. By contrast Toklas was more sharp tongued, withheld, more gossipy, very judgmental—by reputation. When guests came they were careful with Alice, for she could and often did make sure they were never invited back. Of course these are stories from outside of them, and any love relationship is a secret dance known only to the dancers.

The late Robert Duncan, a California-based poet and student of H.D.'s, told me that Alice liked to dress in costume, loving especially everything Spanish. She would ride down in style in a carriage to Monterey to a favorite restaurant. Once, she invited several of her women friends to a special dinner there, and when they were long seated and wondering where she was, she appeared in a formal maid's costume to serve them the entire meal.

Alice B. Toklas grew up across the Bay from Stein's childhood Oakland, in San Francisco. She was scheduled to stay in the family home and care for her father and brother as cook and housekeeper, but she took the economic limitations of her life in her own hands at the age of thirty. Stepping away from the role so common to spinsters of the nineteenth century, she set out for Europe on her slender savings with her friend Harriet, to visit Sarah and Michael Stein, and from there met her love Gertrude and changed her destiny completely. She became a servant of literature rather than a servant of family, and while her decidedly wifely role may not be as satisfying to us to think of as if she had succeeded, say, with her own career in music, still her accomplishment is great and warrants our appreciation, and gratitude, as she helped Gertrude stand in her own center to the great enhancement of the work.

Toklas loved Stein's writing which primarily at that time consisted of manuscripts of *Three Lives* and *The Making of Americans*. *Q.E.D* was already shelved as impossible to publish because of its overt Lesbian content.

After Toklas entered Stein's life, her work immediately stretched out in breathtaking nonlinear directions with *Tender Buttons*, then on to an amazing independence of thought and an increasingly solid woman-centeredness with a collection called *Geography and Plays*, and another called *Useful Knowledge*, several more novels, including *Lucy Church Amiably*, *Ida A Novel* and *Mrs. Reynolds*, a multitude of plays, essays, articles, and metaphysical writings.

Given how little attention the bulk of Stein's work received during her lifetime (with the exception of *The Autobiography of Alice B. Toklas*) it is difficult to imagine that she could have maintained the steadfast idealism and optimistic belief in herself necessary to write it—without the continual and comprehensive devotion of Alice B. Toklas. It was Alice who first published it, Alice who made endless arrangements with it, Alice who protected it, Alice who accompanied Gertrude on her tour of America after the autobiography hit best seller lists in America. It is Alice in the photographs, and appropriately so.

Alice is often present in photographs of Gertrude, as she is often present in the writing and most people who know of Gertrude also know of Alice. This is distinctly different from the spouses of Gertrude's fellow artists and modernist thinkers: few people can name Picasso's mistress or Hemingway's wife.

The portrait "Ada" is a description of how Alice went about breaking away from her father and what must have felt like heavy family obligation, in order to stay in Europe with her heart's love.

In the first third of this century we might easily have thought it was Lesbians, both part-time and full-time Lesbians according to the course of their lives, who ruled the world of words, so prominent were they in the burgeoning of twentieth century literature.

From England, Radclyffe Hall, Virginia Wolfe, the novelist Bryher, and the classical Greek scholar, Jane Ellen Harrison; from France, Violette Le Duc, Colette, and Adrienne Monnier; from the U.S., Natalie Barney, Djuna Barnes, Margaret Anderson, Jane Heap, Amy Lowell, H.D., Sylvia Beach, and of course Gertrude Stein.

In addition to writing, research and new philosophical

stances, Lesbians busied themselves, sometimes very daringly, on the cusp of the turn toward the period that would come to be called "modernism," as publishers of journals, reviews and presses that presented radical new material, much of it controversial, and as owners of bookstores featuring work by William Carlos Williams, T.S. Elliot, ee cummings, James Joyce, Thornton Wilder, Marianne Moore, Ernest Hemingway, Ezra Pound, Richard Wright, as well as the Lesbian writers listed above.

Yet for all this activity, Lesbians, except for Natalie Barney, who wrote in French, and Radclyffe Hall with her very overt novel on what was at that time politely, and medically, called "inversion," *The Well of Loneliness*, and a few obscure references hidden in poems by H.D. and Amy Lowell, did *not* write explicitly of their lives as Lesbians—as, say, Hemingway wrote of explicit heterosexual relations in novel after novel, without anyone giving it a second thought. Hall's book is an impassioned plea for social understanding of the "sad life of the invert," and even so raised a storm of controversy, a court trial and subsequent ban on "pornographic" grounds, although the book is distinctly unsexual, being a description of some social aspects of Gay life, and of cross dressing.

In concert with the courts, as late as the 1960's American publishers demanded that all stories with Lesbian content have sad endings, preferably suicide or at least a renouncing of "the life" and marriage to a man. Editors stipulated these conditions in response to any manuscripts with positive images of Lesbians; and in psychology and literature the steadfastly false portrait of the "miserable, pathetic invert" paralleled the equally false stereotype of the "happy go lucky" lowerclass and/or Negro person.

Consequently Gertrude Stein's first novel, *Q.E.D.*, was shelved by her as unpublishable. Finished in 1903, the book was not printed until nearly fifty years later, in 1950, in a limited edition of 516 copies, with editorial changes and with the title *Things As They Are*. A paperbound edition by Liverwright Press appeared in 1973 when a more receptive audience existed.

Q.E.D. is a Lesbian "coming out story," painful and self-examinatory, especially of power relationships in a love affair involving three people. The coming out story is a form so indigenous to Lesbian literature that the first major Lesbian anthology after the political/publishing activity of the early 1970's was *The Coming Out Stories.*[2]

Stein was clearly using her sense of scientific observation (*Q.E.D.*, *Quod Erat Demonstrandum*, literally "What can be demonstrated") in this autobiographical scrutiny of a common event in Lesbian relationships: the attraction of a young woman (Adele, a portrait of young Stein) who has not yet established a sexual relationship to one member of a longterm female couple.

The repercussions of this unfulfilled yet vital and extremely common attraction, the power relations among the three, which hinge on a stasis of entranced interest coupled with the force exerted by whoever can be most controlled, are explored in minute detail. The novel also brings up the (to date) otherwise untouched subject of how internal Lesbian relationships go about maintaining sexual interest over the years, in the absence of any reflecting or acknowledgment of the partnership from the world at large. *Q.E.D.* is more than fifty, closer to ninety or a hundred years ahead of its time.

In the first third of the century, there was an enormous and in some places public Gay presence in Europe, numbering in the millions, with a network of artists and publishers who overlapped with Bohemians and other cultural networks of prime movers especially in Berlin and Paris.

During and following World War II the Gay presence in the Western world was shoved into a very pinched closet of denial. Except in a few urban centers, the high international

Gay culture of the earlier part of the century was forgotten. Along with Sappho and Oscar Wilde, Gertrude and Alice were the few remembered Gay models, our carefully treasured center in a world which increasingly limited Gay public portraits to cruel representations in psychology textbooks that reduced our entire culture and history to a pathology, a blight on human culture. The symbolic value of Gertrude and Alice as a well known pair of Lesbians, obviously married to and utterly loyal to each other, obviously accepted and even revered by others, cannot be exaggerated.

When I ask people how tall they think Gertrude Stein and Alice Toklas were they often answer, "Oh very tall—over 5'10". I myself believed in their stature for a long while, a metaphor of the elegant giant lesbians, Gertrude and Alice, posed in their Mom and Pop stances through the twenties and thirties in big flowered hats, and accompanied by an immense poodle. Their stature is a trick of the mind they affected, and a trick of photography. By our standards they were physically tiny, Alice at 4'11", petite and beautiful as a young woman with her well defined features and creamy complexion. Gertrude was heavy set and just topped an inch over 5 feet.

The story probably most dear to romantic hearts was that Alice had become a Catholic after Gertrude's death, for the stated purpose of being able to see her love again, since Catholicism teaches an afterlife whereas Orthodox Judaism denies it. For some people dead is dead and for some people dead is not dead, as Gertrude Stein said, being herself a nonpracticing Orthodox Jew.

Yes, Gertrude and Alice were a romantic couple. At the same time we have lost a centering on Gertrude because of our ideas about Alice. The pair of them have blended in our minds into a mask that often prevents us seeing what mattered most for them, and ultimately for us: Gertrude Stein's writing. Alice herself feared that if she told too much to biographers, only their lives would be seen, and not the work itself.

The popular portrait of Gertrude that has been presented on stage in impersonation,[3] and on screen, seems largely drawn from one book, *The Autobiography of Alice B. Toklas.* Stein's only popular work, it was written when she was nearing sixty, and under pressure from Alice to make some money at her writing by telling about the people they had known twenty and thirty years before, who by now had become famous. The storytelling style, the motive and the subjects of the book, were all Alice's.

The "trick" of the "autobiography" is that it is ostensibly all about Gertrude as seen by Alice. The terrible ironical "trick" (on them) is that everyone has assumed that the persona of the book is "really" Stein. However, she was so good at seeing from another point of view, the persona really *is* Alice, with qualities such as her anecdotal interests and her love of famous personalities, and name dropping, and artful gossip—as well as her devotion to Stein's work. As Virgil Thomson describes: "This book is in every way except actual authorship Alice Toklas's book; it reflects her mind, her language, her private view of Gertrude, also her unique narrative powers. Every story in it is told as Alice herself had always told it." And: "Every story that ever came into the house eventually got told in Alice's way, and this was its definitive version."[4]

It is very important to distinguish between the two women, as otherwise we might try to read the bulk of Stein's work as if it is literary gossip, is arch, or snide, is sarcasm or wit, which it is not. She is an extremely sincere writer, just the opposite of arch; she is so completely literal and exacting in what she is saying that sometimes we don't get it because we just don't believe that anyone could be that deliberate. Most important of all, most of her writing came from her largest Self, the large, sweeping mind of a major language philosopher using metaphoric principles in an age of science.

But by writing a slick, popular book full of famous, arty, cafe society names and observations from her lover's point of view, quite inadvertently she created a mask, named Alice B. Toklas, behind which we have exiled her in her smaller self. We have decentralized Stein, un-self-centered her, and hence ourselves, away from the work itself.

This is an example of Alice's own writing in *What Is Remembered*, published in 1963:

> Rousseau took his violin out of its case and commenced to play endless dull music. Leo, who was sitting next to him, protected him from the exuberance of the guests. Marie Laurencin sang her songs. Appollinaire asked Harriet and me if we would sing the national song of the Red Indians. He was shocked and unhappy when we told him we did not think that they had one.
>
> When it was quite late we went into Salmon's studio to get our hats and coats. My hat, of which I had been so proud, had been divested of its yellow feather trimming. Salmon had eaten it and a telegram and a box of matches. He seemed unaware of our presence.

This is an example of Stein portraying Alice in *The Autobiography of Alice B. Toklas*:

> In these days Gertrude Stein wore a brown corduroy suit, jacket and skirt, a small straw cap, always crocheted for her by a woman in Fiesole, sandals, and she often carried a cane. That summer the head of the cane was of amber. It is more or less this costume without the cap and the cane that Picasso has painted in his portrait of her. This costume was ideal for

Spain, they all thought of her as belonging to some religious order and we were always treated with the most absolute respect. I remember that once a nun was showing us the treasures in a convent church in Toledo. We were near the steps of the altar. All of a sudden there was a crash, Gertrude Stein had dropped her cane. The nun paled, the worshippers startled. Gertrude Stein picked up her cane and turning to the frightened nun said reassuringly, no it is not broken.

This is an example of Stein being more typically Stein, in a later book, *Everybody's Autobiography*:

> We were very quiet that is were living in the country and that is very occupying. Madame Pierlot says that in the country you do not have to get ready to go out, in the city if you want to go out you have to get ready to go out but in the country if you go out you are out and you do not have to get ready. For some weeks nothing happened and then Janet Scudder announced that she was coming with a friend and that they would stay a few days. Janet always has a friend anybody always has a friend. As the earth is covered all over with people and they all do the same thing in the same way anybody can and does have a friend....
> The Polish woman cook did not look as happy as she had hoped to look and everybody went to bed.

Even trying to imagine a "typical" example of Stein is misleading, as her voice differs so greatly depending on whether it is poetry, one of her many plays or novels, or an expository essay that is being quoted.

However from these examples I hope we can see Toklas's mind trucking along in the linear anecdotal fashion of most people when they tell stories on themselves and their friends and beloveds, stories on the order of snapshots, meaningful to those showing them, or showing them off if they are of "famous" people (hence, "known" to all); not meaningful otherwise.

In the second example, Stein's interpretation of Toklas' perspective retains her lover's linear story telling style but adds deeper meaning in the selection of details, as with the description of the costume being perfect for Spain because it casts Stein in the guise of a holy person, (thus suggesting also the profoundness of her vision as understood by both lovers) and a similar and equally light hearted description of the utter self-centered confidence of Gertrude in thinking the nun was worried about the (sacred) cane breaking, rather than the church's holy objects.

In the third example Stein opens the meaning out still further, "As the earth is covered all over with people, etc," expanding a small anecdote out to include all the world's people and then jumping, in point of view, from inside her own head to inside the cook's head in a rapid telescoping of perspective between extremely objective and extremely subjective.

While trying to decipher "what she really meant" is one of the most frustrating and ultimately trivializing methods of understanding Stein's ideas, let alone acquiring for oneself a bit of the incredible sweep of the woman's mind, I myself gained much insight gradually over thirty years, and sometimes to my own deep embarrassment at my own naivete, by unravelling a literal interpretation of one short piece, first published in 1922: "Miss Furr and Miss Skeene."

The story is an excellent example of how she used techniques centralizing the essence of a character or event, coupled with her idea of value, harmonizing the vocabulary and thus giving the events value in and of themselves by using a language outside the traditional mode of judgment toward behavior. In this manner she was able to write a story that in any other vocabulary would have been considered immoral, decadent, pathetic, subnatural, and obscene. And she got it published in an era that would not have published a literal version.

Yet "Miss Furr and Miss Skeene" was done so perfectly, as to be included in a standard High School English literature textbook, where I first read it. The axis of the story is the fact that the word "Gay" in English has two distinctly different meanings—the first is the above ground "nice" meaning of festive, or exceedingly, almost giddily, happy. This was the only meaning my small-town, 1956 high school English class or its teacher, understood. We read the story as a peculiar example of Stein's mindless repetition, and our somewhat impatient and intermittent delight with it was limited by our understanding (or belief) that she was an eccentric, plotless and somewhat air headed writer who got away with something because of the vastness of her ego, and the uniqueness of her craziness.

Two years later my first lover told me the second, subterranean meaning of "Gay" as "participating in homosexual love and homosexual culture," and I looked at the story again, wondering if my high school teacher also knew the secret meaning. I am sure she did not. More amazingly, I was, in that repressed age, also sure that Gertrude Stein did not either, that she had naively used a word that, later, and in modern America, had come to mean a description of her own life. I thought this coincidence was funny.

Still later, in my early thirties when I began researching the homosexual word "Gay" I looked at "Miss Furr and Miss Skeen" again, and had the wild idea that the modern idiom had come from the story....because it looked more and more like a coming out story. I still could not understand all of it, the presence of the men was puzzling, and I thought they must surely be boy friends of the two women. I could not understand the ending very well. And meanwhile a whole aboveground Gay movement was growing up, instigated by me and others like me, taking to the streets and parks, the political, social and cultural arenas of America and other countries.

As I became even more conscious of the reality of Gay life, what it looked like, how it sounded in story form, Stein's little story came more and more into focus. Contemporary women told each other their own coming out stories, and some were published.

And finally, going into the 1980's, the antiquity of Gay culture completely surfaced into my consciousness. From my own research I could no longer believe that Lesbians of the past were naive or isolated, nor that Alice and Gertrude were lovers in a sea of heterosexual artists and had no contact with Gay people and the Gay underground that has sustained us all, century upon century. Rather, a large matrix of their world was Gay.

Reading the story when I am in my forties I am embarrassed by my protection of the two ladies, de-sexing them into hand-holding spinsters who held themselves apart from the stuff of life. Now I see the story as the literal, step by step telling of a complete first-love story between two women, of Helen Furr leaving her parents' home where although they were very pleasant people who kept a very pleasant home, nevertheless she could not come out. She chose to go to a sophisticated city where she could come out and begin being Gay, with her first lover, Georgine Skeene. Both of them had voices that they were cultivating, that is, they were artists, and of the two Georgine Skeene had the voice most worth cultivating. Georgine Skeene also liked best to travel, while Helen Furr preferred to stay in one place "and be gay there."

There in an urban center they set up housekeeping and had sex everyday, and learned quite a bit from each other about being Lesbians, and about being young intellectual women in a big world, but still there was much they did not know about being Gay.

They went to visit Helen Furr's parents, where she found it impossible to be Gay, and she told them so, and they were not worried or upset by this information.

Georgine Skeene went to visit her brother, who had some prominence, and every few years they visited their families, separately and together. Then once after such a visit they began making friends with, and sitting in public or private places with some Gay men, and after that they learned quite a few more things about being Gay that were of use to them, that is they absorbed the cultural dimensions of their love for each other.

Then Georgine Skeene went to visit her brother for two months, and Helen did not go see her own parents, instead she began to have affairs with another woman or perhaps more than one. She did not feel any need of Georgine then, and was very satisfied with her increasing Gay method of living. Georgine moved out, and then Helen moved also and she began telling other people how to go about being Gay, and she was living very well then.

The story as Stein spun it out is about six book pages in length, filled out rhythmically so it takes the same space and time that anyone would take to tell the same story. Yet it is done with a vocabulary of about thirty words, and in such a way that millions of people could read it with some kind of enjoyment and without the least idea of what it is about, and yet if you know what it is about it is completely simple and comprehensible.

How did she accomplish this feat of social illusion? The word "gay" occurs in the story a hundred and thirty six times. The word that the story is about is the exact center of the story. Perhaps that is the answer, complete centrality. Instead of avoiding the subject out of fear of its taboo nature, she centered on it, taking advantage of its natural above-ground camouflage as a "nice" word, which one would apply as a matter of course to "nice young ladies". Yet the story is a coming out story that includes sexual behavior, told with no moral judgment, no implications of social disapproval or righteousness on any possible side of any possible argument.

I don't consider the Lesbian content of her work as being more important than her many other contents, but deciphering "Miss Furr and Miss Skeene" allowed me entry where I hadn't gone before. I believe that we americans will reach a point of interstanding, at more than one level, all of her work, as our own consciousness grows, and as we become able to apply the subjective and the objective simultaneously. For what is most apparent to me now about the story is its utterly, completely literal honesty. Nothing is deliberately hidden except in our own minds. My own mind caused me to reject the obvious meaning because I had never attempted to examine or relate my life exactly and precisely as I had experienced it, and as a completely positive experience. As soon as I did, and others did, her story became clear.

In future time I believe that all her stories will come clear to us as we modern people stand more nearly in the center of who we are.

Like Miss Furr and Miss Skeene, Gertrude Stein did not try to hide who she was, not her Lesbianism, not her Jewishness, not her enormous female intellect. The Gay pop novelist and English professor Sam Steward, then a young Gay man in the late thirties, spent two weeks with Alice and Gertrude and later became a longtime friend of Alice's, especially after Gertrude's death in 1946. He documented conversations with Stein; on one occasion she asked him directly if he thought she and Alice were Lesbians, and if he cared about that, and if he himself were "queer or gay or different or 'of it' as the French say."

Of her own Lesbianism she said to Steward, "It bothers a

lot of people, but like you said, it's nobody's business, it
(homophobia) came from the Judeo-Christian ethos, especially Saint Paul the bastard, but he was complaining about
youngsters who were not really that way, they did it for
money, everybody suspects us or knows but nobody says
anything about it." She went on to describe her shelving of
the Q.E.D. manuscript and her embarrassment at having
written it so early in the century, when "everything was
puritanical and so it was too soon, maybe not if we were
Greek but Greek we weren't..."

By centering herself exactly in who she was, Gertrude
Stein acted neither out of fear nor from attempt to curry favor.
When Steward talked of being considered inferior in England, Stein asked if he had any British blood. "I'm part Scot,"
Steward said. "There you have it," Gertrude replied, "If you
have a single drop of British blood in you, you're thought
inferior (in the English class system)...Now I, I am a Jew,
orthodox background, and I never make any bones about it.
So in England I had a wonderful time when I went for the
Cambridge lectures because no one expected me to be
anything but a Jew and I could say what I pleased, even
before I was I."⁵

And in *Everybody's Autobiography* (1937) she wrote: "...I
dislike it when instead of saying Jew they say Hebrew or
Israelite or Semite, I do not like it and why should a Negro
want to be called colored. Why should he want to lose being
a Negro...I have stated that a noun to me is a stupid thing, if
you know a thing and its name why bother about it but you
have to know its name to talk about it. Well its name is Negro
if it is a Negro and Jew if it is a Jew and both of them are nice
strong solid names and so let us keep them."

Speaking as a non-Jew, the elements in Stein I associate
with her Jewishness overlap some with her middleclass
German-American upbringing as well, and the values of her
very proper Vienna-based family. Politically she was a 19th

Century Republican, in her manners and manner of speech she was Victorian, socially she was more liberal than not, with strongly developed individualism coupled with democratic values based in pragmatism; thus at the opening of the German occupation of France she favored the collaborative Vichy government, but by the end she did not, having witnessed firsthand the hardship it brought to the peasants. She had social ease with the "common folk" in Paris and the countryside around Bilignin where she and Alice spent their summers, and the years of World War II. At the same time they mostly had servants, especially a cook to help Alice in the kitchen. Gertrude gardened and walked the countryside visiting with whoever she met, sometimes for as much as six hours a day, as a method of meditation.

During World War I she participated by driving an ambulance and during World War II by helping the local underground French resistance, the Maquis, in the neighborhood of Bilignin, and at the close of the war members of the resistance gave her an award of appreciation. The character Constance in "Yes Is for a Very Young Man," her play about collaboration and resistance, is, like herself, an expatriate American.

Stein has a concern with numbers that is reminiscent of Jewish mysticism of earlier centuries, I am thinking particularly of kabbalism with its use of numerology, and especially in the sense that numbers have *qualities* beyond flatfootedly practical linear counting. Since most modern Jews had put away mysticism as the superstition of an earlier age, Stein's uses of it and her open advocacy of things metaphysical differentiates her from the materialist thinking held so dear in modern times.

Stein devoted nearly as much scrutinizing evaluation toward numbers as a part of language as she devoted to commas and prepositions. In some of her work numbers become characters, and in some of her plays they become "acts." This reminds me of computer musical programs in which every note is assigned numerical values and is also called an "event." She said that the difference between humans and animals is counting, using numbers, nor was she condescending to animal intelligence in saying this, crediting them with all other forms of thinking except the use of counting.

Like the other major Jewish thinkers who have so greatly influenced Western civilization (at least) in this century— Albert Einstein, Sigmund Freud, Karl Marx—Stein incorporated principles of modern science, especially of scientific observation, into her work. Like Einstein, she mixed her science with a sensibility that also took into account her higher mind, a kind of channelling method of intuitively knowing, of gathering information from meditations connecting her to the cosmos.

I cannot resist considering it particularly Jewish of her that she refused so utterly to use "graven images," that is, very little of stock imagery or full-blown characters from mythology or much of the usual authorly prerogative of describing a character by external appearances. This decision alone would have distinguished her work, as it presses the reader always into current thought and currents of thought rather than remembered and visual thought.

Stein's ability to remain centered in her own Self enabled her to let her characters and her work do the same. One of her first well developed characters is Melanctha, a portrait of a person very different from Stein.

By displaying her in a field in which there is verbal equality, Stein is able to let Melanctha speak and in speaking reveal all we need to know about her internal self, her essence. Melanctha's speaking reveals herself, her femaleness, her youngness, her Negroness, her desires and passions and her lack of them. After the first halting page or two no outside eye examines her, judges, places her in any context outside of the one that her own voice engenders. She is herself as herself, not as a piece of sociology or history or even psychology. We are not pressed into what to think of her. We may think she is intriguing, sometimes boring, sometimes infuriating, sometimes endearing and what she is not is a Black or Negro character in relation to white people but rather in relation to herself and to the other characters, especially her lover, Jeff Campbell. The story that unfolds is more one of relationship than conflict, and what centers it are the essential natures of the characters.

Stein, writing in 1902, escaped none of the general framework of race and class of her turn of the century post-Civil War American education in her opening descriptions, which would rightfully be considered racist in a later, Civil Rights age: that Melanctha is "superior" to and "less lazy" than her friend Rose because of being half white, for instance.

However, as Stein centered herself within her African-descended characters this bias of the time falls away, growing into a remarkable portrait of a woman whose primary characteristics are her own psychology, her own internal desires and decisions. The accomplishment is extreme, a breakthrough in consciousness, brought about directly by Stein's use of equality and value in the landscape of the writing itself.

Among the more remarkable aspects of *Melanctha* is the "whole field" use of dialect in the text. Because the author has placed herself inside the characters, completely identifying with them from the inside out, their spoken language is used in the whole landscape of text, not distanced from it as is the usual case, not isolated inside quote marks indicating that this special (and hence, "inferior, ignorant") language, belongs only to the characters and not to the (hence, "superior, educated") author. The whole vocabulary has tonal *value*, and is synchronized from within itself. This technique destroys the class distance that is built into the usual style of treating regional or specialized dialects, or group languages. By creating a whole field of the language, a commonality in which the author and the characters have common purpose and common dignity, Melanctha and Jeff are centered in themselves.

Stein's very particular Self-centeredness has been useful to other authors, as a deep well we visit to help us locate our selves—in ourselves. Black writer Richard Wright first became acquainted with her work in a Chicago library where he stumbled across *Melanctha*:

"As I read it, my ears really opened up for the first time in my life and I began to hear Negroes...Above all, I began to hear for the first time the pure, deep dialect of my grandmother. And from that moment on, in all my attempts at writing I was able to tap that vast resevoir of living speech that went on about me.

"Then soon after my delight with Stein was jolted; a political critic of the reddest persuasion condemned Stein in a newspaper article, calling her decadent, implying that she reclined upon a silken couch in Paris smoking hashish day and night and was a hopeless prey to hallucinations. I asked myself if I were wrong or crazy or decadent. Being simple minded, I decided upon a very practical way of determining the worth of the prose of Stein, a prose I had accepted without qualms or distress. I gathered a group of semi-illiterate Negro workers into a Chicago basement and read them *Melanctha* aloud. They were enthralled, interrupting me constantly to tell where and when they had met such a strange and melancholy gal. I was convinced and Miss Stein's book never bothered or frightened me after that. If Negro stockyard workers could understand the stuff when it was read aloud to them, then surely anybody else could if they wanted to read with their ears as well as their eyes. For the prose of Stein is but the repetitive contemporaneousness of our living speech woven into a grammarless form of narrative..."[6]

Wright used Stein to legitimize use of the language of his own group; to stand in the center of his own "world," as has many another author since.

If the world were shaped like a plate, "exile," "marginal" and "difference" would be words accurately descriptive of life at the edge of a single universe, "the *one* real world," "normalcy," "society." Our social groups, countries and plant and creature groupings are globe shaped, and interactive; the walls can intermingle without losing their integrity. Reality continually folds in and out of itself, with as many "worlds" as we have the ability and judgment to perceive, each with its own center.

In a many-centered multiverse, exiles from one place are first class citizens of another, margins of one "globe" are centers of another, "marginality" itself becomes a ribbon of road, of continual and vital interaction shaping and reshaping whatever lies within borders, and "difference" is so essentially common (and Self-centered) that it is duplication that is the oddity. It is a matter of perspective, of metaphor: to seek not what is "universal," rather to seek what has commonality, what overlaps with others without losing its own center.

By having so much outsiderness to view everything through, Stein became the ultimate insider. Centered in her largest possible Self, she created moving centers, continually shifting centers, spelling the idea out in the structure of her very sentences.

The perception of many overlapping worlds has only slowly entered into social or biospheric relations, though it is certainly present in science, psychology, anthropology. Stein's work is rooted firmly in many-centered viewpoints, at the level of language itself, which means at the level of our basic understandings of the self itself. To be Self-centered is to be appropriately placed, in balance with space and time, and with other beings. Gertrude Stein lived this, and in her work has left us a model for thinking it, that to be centered fully in one's Self is also to be in the center of "the world."

Essential Clues For Really Reading Her:

1. Pay attention to the idea that she has ideas while you are reading her.

For instance, while reading Stein (preferably aloud) notice what happens to point of view, where does she go with it, and where does this take you inside/outside yourself. Notice the ways she continually recentralizes her subjects. Try applying this shifting point of view to other events and characters during your day.

2. Use her to help find your own center.

Stein has an uncanny ability to let us feel silly, at times. She has taken on the profound clown function of not letting us take ourselves too seriously. Take select paragraphs of her work into special life situations that take themselves very seriously, are heavily weighted, fearsome and claustrophobic, such as really rigid bureaucratic buildings, hospitals, waiting lines, police stations, army barracks. Think of her as a grounding reminder that life doesn't have to be tedious or difficult. I find when I use her in these ways, alone or in conjunction with a friend, my own power in the situation becomes much more evident.

Even paraphrasing her can work, provided you understand the essential principle. I once dreamed a healing and centering mantra that is a paraphrase of Stein's continuous present: "Having been one with a whole being, I am becoming one with a whole being; being one with a whole being, I am one with a whole being." This works because it does not contain a past when the disease or accident happened, nor is it seeking healing in the future; instead the eternally present wholeness, or wellness, is entered.

3. Hold a Gertrude Stein party.

Pick one of her shorter playable plays, such as "Three Sisters Who Are Not Sisters" or even a longer one such as "Dr. Faustus Lights the Lights" or "Yes Is For a Very Young Man." Make a photocopy for each person you invite for a reading of the play. You will need to assign the parts and narrate the action. These and dozens more of her plays are high fun, though remember to keep the pace moving fast so the humor and drama stay evident. Anyone can participate and the plays provoke reaction without anyone needing to lead a stifling (glurg) *literary* discussion.

Notes

1. J. Stone, *Stone's Throw*, Selected Essays, "Gertrude Stein in Circles," North Atlantic Books, Berkeley, California, 1988.

2. J. Penelope and S. J. Wolfe, *The Original Coming Out Stories*, The Crossing Press, Freedom, California, 1989.

3. See M. Perloff, "Impersonating Gertrude Stein," in *Gertrude Stein and the Making of Literature*, Boston, Northeastern University Press, 1988. She describes the phenomenon of a false Gertrude Stein presented in stage impersonations and though there are a couple of errors, her analysis is very interesting.

4. V. Thomson, "A Portrait of Gertrude Stein," in *An Autobiography of Virgil Thomson*, pp. 176-177.

5. See *Dear Sammy: Letters from Gertrude Stein and Alice B. Toklas*, edited and with a memoir by Samuel M. Steward, Boston, Houghton Mifflin Company, 1977.

6. R. Wright, rough draft of a review of *Wars I Have Seen*, "Gertrude Stein's Story is Drenched in Hitler's Horrors," 1946, Beinecke Library, Yale Collection of American Literature, Beinecke Rare Book and Manuscript Library, Yale University.

By Gertrude Stein

Miss Furr and Miss Skeene

Helen Furr had quite a pleasant home. Mrs. Furr was quite a pleasant woman. Mr. Furr was quite a pleasant man. Helen Furr had quite a pleasant voice a voice quite worth cultivating. She did not mind working. She worked to cultivate her voice. She did not find it gay living in the same place where she had always been living. She went to a place where some were cultivating something, voices and other things needing cultivating. She met Georgine Skeene there who was cultivating her voice which some thought was quite a pleasant one. Helen Furr and Georgine Skeene lived together then. Georgine Skeene liked travelling. Helen Furr did not care about travelling, she liked to stay in one place and be gay there. They were together then and travelled to another place and stayed there and were gay there.

They stayed there and were gay were, not very gay there, just gay there. They were both gay there, they were regularly working there both of them cultivating their voices there, they were both gay there. Georgine Skeene was gay there and she was regular, regular in being gay, regular in not being gay, regular in being a gay one who was one not being gay longer than was needed to be one being quite a gay one. They were both gay then there and both working there then.

They were in a way both gay there where there were many cultivating something. They were both regular in being gay there. Helen Furr was gay there, she was gayer and gayer there and really she was just gay there, she was gayer and gayer there, that is to say she found ways of being gay there that she was using in being gay there. She was gay there, not gayer and gayer, just gay there, that is to say she was not gayer by using the things she found there that were gay things, she was gay there, always she was gay there.

They were quite regularly gay there, Helen Furr and Georgine Skeene, they were regularly gay there where they were gay. They were very regularly gay.

To be regularly gay was to do every day the gay thing that they did every day. To be regularly gay was to end every day at the same time after they had been regularly gay. They were regularly gay. They were gay every day. They ended every day in the same way, at the same time, and they had been every day regularly gay.

The voice Helen Furr was cultivating was quite a pleasant one. The voice Georgine Skeene was cultivating was, some said, a better one. The voice Helen Furr was cultivating she cultivated and it was quite completely a pleasant enough one then, a cultivated enough one then. The voice Georgine Skeene was cultivating she did not cultivate too much. She cultivated it quite some. She cultivated and she would sometime go on cultivating it and it was not then an unpleasant one, it would not be then an unpleasant one, it would be a quite richly enough cultivated one, it would be quite richly enough to be a pleasant enough one.

They were gay where there were many cultivating something. The two were gay there, were regularly gay there. Georgine Skeene would have liked to do more travelling. They did some travelling, not very much travelling, Georgine Skeene would have liked to do more travelling, Helen Furr did not care about doing travelling, she liked to stay in a place and be gay there.

They stayed in a place and were gay there, both of them stayed there, they stayed together there, they were gay there, they were regularly gay there.

They went quite often, not very often, but they did go back to where Helen Furr had a pleasant enough home and then Georgine Skeene went to a place where her brother had quite some distinction. They both went, every few years, went visiting to where Helen Furr had quite a pleasant home. Certainly Helen Furr would not find it gay to stay, she did not find it gay, she said she would not stay, she said she did not find it gay, she said she would not stay where she did not find it gay, she said she found it gay where she did stay and she did stay there where very many were cultivating something. She did stay there. She always did find it gay there.

She went to see them where she had always been living and where she did not find it gay. She had a pleasant home there, Mrs. Furr was a pleasant enough woman, Mr. Furr was a pleasant enough man, Helen told them and they were not worrying, that she did not find it gay living where she had always been living.

Georgine Skeene and Helen Furr were living where they were both cultivating their voices and they were gay there. They visited where Helen Furr had come from and then they went to where they were living where they were then regularly living.

There were some dark and heavy men there then. There were some who were not so heavy and some who were not so dark. Helen Furr and Georgine Skeene sat regularly with them. They sat regularly with the ones who were dark and heavy. They sat regularly with the ones who were not so dark. They sat regularly with the ones that were not so heavy. They sat with them regularly, sat with some of them. They went with them regularly went with them. They were regular then, they were gay then, they were where they wanted to be then where it was gay to be then, they were regularly gay then. There were men there then who were dark and heavy and they sat with them with Helen Furr and Georgine Skeene and they went with them with Miss Furr and Miss Skeene, and they went with the heavy and dark men Miss Furr and Miss Skeene went with them, and they sat with them, Miss Furr and Miss Skeene sat with them, and there were other men, some were not heavy men and they sat with Miss Furr and Miss Skeene and Miss Furr and Miss Skeene sat with them, and there were other men who were not dark men and they sat with Miss Furr and Miss Skeene and Miss Furr and Miss Skeene sat with them. Miss Furr and Miss Skeene went with them and they went with Miss Furr and Miss Skeene, some who were not heavy men, some who were not dark men. Miss Furr and Miss Skeene sat regularly, they sat with some men. Miss Furr and Miss Skeene went and there were some men with them. There were men and Miss Furr and Miss Skeene went with them, went somewhere with them, went with some of them.

Helen Furr and Georgine Skeene were regularly living where very many were living and cultivating in themselves something. Helen Furr and Georgine Skeene were living very regularly then, being very regular then in being gay then. They did then learn many ways to be gay and they were then being gay being quite regular in being gay, being gay and they were learning little things, little things in ways of being gay, they were very regular then, they were learning very many little things in ways of being gay, they were being gay and using these little things they were learning to have to be gay with regularly gay with then and they were gay the same amount they had been gay. They were quite gay, they were quite regular, they were learning little things, gay little things, they were gay inside them the same amount they had been gay, they were gay the same length of time they had been gay every day.

They were regular in being gay, they learned little things that are things in being gay, they learned many little things that are things in being gay, they were gay every day, they were regular, they were gay, they were gay the same length of time every day, they were gay, they were quite regularly gay.

Georgine Skeene went away to stay two months with her brother. Helen Furr did not go then to stay with her father and her mother. Helen Furr stayed there where they had been regularly living the two of them and she would then certainly not be lonesome, she would go on being gay. She did go on being gay. She was not any more gay but she was gay longer every day than they had been being gay when they were together being gay. She was gay then quite exactly the same way. She learned a few more little ways of being in being gay. She was quite gay and in the same way, the same way she had been gay and she was gay a little longer in the day, more of each day she was gay. She was gay longer every day than when the two of them had been being gay. She was gay quite in the way they had been gay, quite in the same way.

She was not lonesome then, she was not at all feeling any need of having Georgine Skeene. She was not astonished at this thing. She would have been a little astonished by this thing but she knew she was not astonished at anything and so she was not astonished at this thing not astonished at not feeling any need of having Georgine Skeene.

Helen Furr had quite a completely pleasant voice and it was quite well enough cultivated and she could use it and she did use it but then there was not any way of working at cultivating a completely pleasant voice when it has become a quite completely well enough cultivated one, and there was not much use in using it when one was not wanting it to be helping to make one a gay one. Helen Furr was not needing using her voice to be a gay one. She was gay then and sometimes she used her voice and she was not using it very often. It was quite completely enough cultivated and it was quite completely a pleasant one and she did not use it very often. She was then, she was quite exactly as gay as she had been, she was gay a little longer in the day than she had been.

She was gay exactly the same way. She was never tired of being gay that way. She had learned very many little ways to use in being gay. Very many were telling about using other ways in being gay. She was gay enough, she was always gay exactly the same way, she was always learning little things to use in being gay, she was telling about using other ways in being gay, she was telling about learning other ways in being gay, she was learning other ways in being gay, she would be using other ways in being gay, she would always be gay in the same way, when Georgine Skeene was there not so long each day as when Georgine Skeene was away.

She came to using many ways in being gay, she came to use every way in being gay. She went on living where many were cultivating something and she was gay, she had used every way to be gay.

They did not live together then Helen Furr and Georgine Skeene. Helen Furr lived there the longer where they had been living regularly together. Then neither of them were living there any longer. Helen Furr was living somewhere else then and telling some about being gay and she was gay then and she was living quite regularly then. She was regularly gay then. She was quite regular in being gay then. She remembered all the little ways of being gay. She used all the little ways of being gay. She was quite regularly gay. She told many then the way of being gay, she taught very many then little ways they could use in being gay. She was living very well, she was gay then, she went on living then, she was regular in being gay, she always was living very well and was gay very well and was telling about little ways one could be learning to use in being gay, and later was telling them quite often, telling them again and again.

By Gertrude Stein

Book 2: Mabel Neathe

from Q.E.D.

1

Mabel Neathe's room fully met the habit of many hours of unaggressive lounging. She had command of an exceptional talent for atmosphere. The room with its very good shape, dark walls but mediocre furnishings and decorations was more than successfully unobtrusive, it had perfect quality. It had always just the amount of light necessary to make mutual observation pleasant and yet to leave the decorations in obscurity or rather to inspire a faith in their being good.

It is true of rooms as of human beings that they are bound to have one good feature and as a Frenchwoman dresses to that feature in such fashion that the observer must see that and notice nothing else, so Mabel Neathe had arranged her room so that one enjoyed one's companions and observed consciously only the pleasant fire-place.

But the important element in the success of the room as atmosphere consisted in Mabel's personality. The average guest expressed it in the simple comment that she was a perfect hostess, but the more sympathetic observers put it that it was not that she had the manners of a perfect hostess but the more unobtrusive good manners of a gentleman.

The chosen and they were a few individuals rather than a set found this statement inadequate although it was abundantly difficult for them to explain their feeling. Such an

Italian type frustrated by its setting in an unimpassioned and moral community was of necessity misinterpreted although its charm was valued. Mabel's ancestry did not supply any explanation of her character. Her kinship with decadent Italy was purely spiritual.

The capacity for composing herself with her room in unaccented and perfect values was the most complete attribute of that kinship that her modern environment had developed. As for the rest it after all amounted to failure, failure as power, failure as an individual. Her passions in spite of their intensity failed to take effective hold on the objects of her desire. The subtlety and impersonality of her atmosphere which in a position of recognised power would have had compelling attraction, here in a community of equals where there could be no mystery as the seeker had complete liberty in seeking she lacked the vital force necessary to win. Although she was unscrupulous the weapons she used were too brittle, they could always be broken in pieces by a vigorous guard.

Modern situations never endure for a long enough time to allow subtle and elaborate methods to succeed. By the time they are beginning to bring about results the incident is forgotten. Subtlety moreover in order to command efficient power must be realised as dangerous and the modern world is a difficult place in which to be subtly dangerous, the risks are too great. Mabel might now compel by inspiring pity, she could never in her world compel by inspiring fear.

Adele had been for some time one of Mabel's selected few. Her enjoyment of ease and her habit of infinite leisure, combined with her vigorous personality and a capacity for endless and picturesque analysis of all things human had established a claim which her instinct for intimacy without familiarity and her ready adjustment to the necessary impersonality which a relation with Mabel demanded, had confirmed.

"It's more or less of a bore getting back for we are all agreed that Baltimore isn't much of a town to live in, but this old habit is certainly very pleasant" she remarked as she stretched herself comfortably on the couch "and after all, it is much more possible to cultivate such joys when a town isn't wildly exciting. No my tea isn't quite right" she continued. "It's worth while making a fuss you know when there is a possibility of obtaining perfection, otherwise any old tea is good enough. Anyhow what's the use of anything as long as it isn't Spain? You must really go there some time." They continued to make the most of their recent experiences in this their first meeting.

"Did you stay long in New York after you landed?" Mabel finally asked. "Only a few days" Adele replied. "I suppose Helen wrote you that I saw her for a little while. We lunched together before I took my train," she added with a consciousness of the embarrassment that that meeting had caused her. "You didn't expect to like her so much, did you?" Mabel suggested. "I remember you used to say that she impressed you as almost coarse and rather decadent and that you didn't even find her interesting. And you know" she added "how much you dislike decadence."

Adele met her with frank bravado. "Of course I said that and as yet I don't retract it. I am far from sure that she is not both coarse and decadent and I don't approve of either of those qualities. I do grant you however that she is interesting, at least as a character, her talk interests me no more than it ever did" and then facing the game more boldly, she continued "but you know I really know very little about her except that she dislikes her parents and goes in for society a good deal. What else is there?"

Mabel drew a very unpleasant picture of that parentage. Her description of the father a successful lawyer and judge, and an excessively brutal and at the same time small-minded man who exercised great ingenuity in making himself unpleasant was not alluring, nor that of the mother who was very religious and spent most of her time mourning that it was not Helen that had been taken instead of the others a girl and boy whom she remembered as sweet gentle children.

One day when Helen was a young girl she heard her mother say to the father "Isn't it sad that Helen should have been the one to be left."

Mabel described their attempts to break Helen's spirit and their anger at their lack of success. "And now" Mabel went on "they object to everything that she does, to her friends and to everything she is interested in. Mrs. T. always sides with her husband. Of course they are proud of her good looks, her cleverness and social success but she won't get married and she doesn't care to please the people her mother wants her to belong to. They don't dare to say anything to her now because she is so much better able to say things that hurt than they are."

"I suppose there is very litle doubt that Helen can be uncommonly nasty when she wants to be," laughed Adele, "and if she isn't sensitive to other people's pain, a talent for being successful in bitter repartee might become a habit that would make her a most uncomfortable daughter. I believe I might condole with the elders if they were to confide their sorrows to me. By the way doesn't Helen address them the way children commonly do their parents, she always speaks of them as Mr. and Mrs. T." "Oh yes" Mabel explained, "they observe the usual forms."

"It's a queer game," Adele commented, "coming as I do from a community where all no matter how much they may quarrel and disagree have strong family affection and great respect for the ties of blood, I find it difficult to realise." "Yes there you come in with your middle-class ideals again" retorted Mabel.

She then lauded Helen's courage and daring. "Whenever there is any difficulty with the horses or anything dangerous

to be done they always call in Helen. Her father is also very
small-minded in money matters. He gives her so little and
whenever anything happens to the carriage if she is out in it,
he makes her pay and she has to get the money as best she
can. Her courage never fails and that is what makes her
father so bitter, that she never gives any signs of yielding and
if she decides to do a thing she is perfectly reckless, nothing
stops her."

"That sounds very awful" mocked Adele "not being myself
of an heroic breed, I don't somehow realise that type much
outside of story-books. That sort of person in real life doesn't
seem very real, but I guess it's alright. Helen has courage I
don't doubt that."

Mabel then described Helen's remarkable endurance of
pain. She fell from a haystack one day and broke her arm.
After she got home, her father was so angry that he wouldn't
for some time have it attended to and she faced him boldly to
the end. "She never winces or complains no matter how much
she is hurt," Mabel concluded. "Yes I can believe that" Adele
answered thoughtfully.

Throughout the whole of Mabel's talk of Helen, there was
an implication of ownership that Adele found singularly
irritating. She supposed that Mabel had a right to it but in
that thought she found little comfort.

As the winter advanced, Adele took frequent trips to New
York. She always spent some of her time with Helen. For
some undefined reason a convention of secrecy governed
their relations. They seemed in this way to emphasise their
intention of working the thing out completely between them.
To Adele's consciousness the necessity of this secrecy was
only apparent when they were together. She felt no obligation
to conceal this relation from her friends.

They arranged their meetings in the museums or in the
park and sometimes they varied it by lunching together and

taking interminable walks in the long straight streets. Adele was always staying with relatives and friends and although there was no reason why Helen should not have come to see her there, something seemed somehow to serve as one. As for Helen's house it seemed tacitly agreed between them that they should not complicate the situation by any relations with Helen's family and so they continued their homeless wanderings.

Adele spent much of their time together in announcing with great interest the result of her endless meditations. She would criticise and examine herself and her ideas with tireless interest. "Helen," she said one day, "I always had an impression that you talked a great deal but apparently you are a most silent being. What is it? Do I talk so hopelessly much that you get discouraged with it as a habit?" "No," answered Helen, "although I admit one might look upon you in the light of a warning, but really I am very silent when I know people well. I only talk when I am with superficial acquaintances." Adele laughed. "I am tempted to say for the sake of picturesque effect, that in that respect I am your complete opposite, but honesty compels me to admit in myself an admirable consistency. I don't know that the quantity is much affected by any conditions in which I find myself, but really Helen why don't you talk more to me?" "Because you know well enough that you are not interested in my ideas, in fact that they bore you. It's always been very evident. You know" Helen continued affectionately, "that you haven't much talent for concealing your feelings and impressions." Adele smiled, "Yes you are certainly right about most of your talk, it does bore me," she admitted. "But that is because it's about stuff that you are not really interested in. You don't really care about general ideas and art values and musical development and surgical operations and Heaven knows what all and naturally your talk about those things doesn't interest me. No talking is interesting that one hasn't hammered out oneself. I know I always bore myself unutterably when I talk the thoughts that I hammered out some time ago and that are no longer meaningful to me, for quoting even oneself lacks a flavor of reality, but you, you always make me feel that at no period did you ever have the thoughts that you converse with. Surely one has to hit you awfully hard to shake your realler things to the surface."

These meetings soon became impossible. It was getting cold and unpleasant and it obviously wouldn't do to continue in that fashion and yet neither of them undertook to break the convention of silence which they had so completely adopted concerning the conditions of their relation.

One day after they had been lunching together they both felt strongly that restaurants had ceased to be amusing. They didn't want to stay there any longer but outside there was an unpleasant wet snow-storm, it was dark and gloomy and the streets were slushy. Helen had a sudden inspiration. "Let us go and see Jane Fairfield," she said, "you don't know her of course but that makes no difference. She is queer and will interest you and you are queer and will interest her. Oh! I don't want to listen to your protests, you are queer and interesting even if you don't know it and you like queer and interesting people even if you think you don't and you are not a bit bashful in spite of your convictions to the contrary, so come along." Adele laughed and agreed.

They wandered up to the very top of an interminable New York apartment house. It was one of the variety made up apparently of an endless number of unfinished boxes of all sizes piled up in a great oblong leaving an elevator shaft in the centre. There is a strange effect of bare wood and uncovered nails about these houses and no amount of upholstery really seems to cover their hollow nakedness.

Jane Fairfield was not at home but the elevator boy trustingly let them in to wait. They looked out of the windows at the city all gloomy and wet and white stretching down to the river, and they watched the long tracks of the elevated making such wonderful perspective that it never really seemed to disappear, it just infinitely met.

Finally they sat down on the couch to give their hostess just another quarter of an hour in which to return, and then for the first time in Adele's experience something happened in which she had no definite consciousness of beginnings. She found herself at the end of a passionate embrace.

Some weeks after when Adele came again to New York they agreed to meet at Helen's house. It had been arranged quite as a matter of course as if no objection to such a proceeding had ever been entertained. Adele laughed to herself as she thought of it. "Why we didn't before and why we do now are to me equally mysterious" she said shrugging her shoulders. "Great is Allah, Mohammed is no Shodah! though I dimly suspect that sometimes he is."

When the time came for keeping her engagement Adele for some time delayed going and remained lying on her friend's couch begging to be detained. She realised that her certain hold on her own frank joyousness and happy serenity was weakened. She almost longed to back out, she did so dread emotional complexities. "Oh for peace and a quiet life!" she groaned as she rang Helen's doorbell.

In Helen's room she found a note explaining that being worried as it was so much past the hour of appointment, she had gone to the Museum as Adele had perhaps misunderstood the arrangement. If she came in she was to wait. "It was very bad of me to fool around so long" Adele said to herself gravely and then sat down very peacefully to read.

"I am awfully sorry" Adele greeted Helen as she came into the room somewhat intensely, "it never occurred to me that you would be bothered, it was just dilatoriness on my part," and then they sat down. After a while Helen came and sat on the arm of Adele's chair. She took her head between tense arms and sent deep into her eyes a long straight look of concentrated question. "Haven't you anything to say to me?" she asked at last. "Why no, nothing in particular," Adele answered slowly. She met Helen's glance for a moment, returned it with simple friendliness and then withdrew from it.

"You are very chivalrous," Helen said with sad self-defiance. "You realise that there ought to be shame some-where between us and as I have none, you generously undertake it all." "No I am not chivalrous" Adele answered, "but I realise my deficiencies. I know that I always take an everlasting time to arrive anywhere really and that the rapidity of my superficial observation keeps it from being realised. It is certainly all my fault. I am so very deceptive. I arouse false expectations. You see," she continued meeting her again with pleasant friendliness, "you haven't yet learned that I am at once impetuous and slow-minded."

Time passed and they renewed their habit of desultory meetings at public places, but these were not the same as before. There was between them now a consciousness of strain, a sense of new adjustments, of uncertain standards and of changing values.

Helen was patient but occasionally moved to trenchant criticism, Adele was irritable and discursive but always ended with a frank almost bald apology for her inadequacy.

In the course of time they again arranged to meet in Helen's room. It was a wet rainy, sleety day and Adele felt chilly and unresponsive. Throwing off her hat and coat, she sat down after a cursory greeting and looked meditatively into the fire. "How completely we exemplify entirely different types" she began at last without looking at her companion. "You are a blooming Anglo-Saxon. You know what you want and you go and get it without spending your days and nights changing backwards and forwards from yes to no. If you want to stick a knife into a man you just naturally go and stick straight and hard. You would probably kill him but it would soon be over while I, I would have so many compunctions and considerations that I would cut up all his surface anatomy and make it a long drawn agony but unless he should bleed to death quite by accident, I wouldn't do him any serious injury. No you are the very brave man, passionate but not emotional, capable of great sacrifice but not tender-hearted.

"And then you really want things badly enough to go out and get them and that seems to me very strange. I want things too but only in order to understand them and I never go and get them. I am a hopeless coward, I hate to risk hurting myself or anybody else. All I want to do is to meditate endlessly and think and talk. I know you object because you believe it necessary to feel something to think about and you contend that I don't give myself time to find it. I recognise the justice of that criticism and I am doing my best these days to let it come."

She relapsed into silence and sat there smiling ironically into the fire. The silence grew longer and her smile turned into a look almost of disgust. Finally she wearily drew breath, shook her head and got up. "Ah! don't go," came from Helen in quick appeal. Adele answered the words. "No I am not going. I just want to look at these books." She wandered about a little. Finally she stopped by Helen's side and stood looking down at her with a gentle irony that wavered on the edge of scorn.

"Do you know" she began in her usual tone of dispassionate inquiry "you are a wonderful example of double personality. The you that I used to know and didn't like, and the occasional you that when I do catch a glimpse of it seems to me so very wonderful, haven't any possible connection with each other. It isn't as if my conception of you had gradually changed because it hasn't. I realise always one whole you consisting of a laugh so hard that it rattles, a voice that suggests a certain brutal coarseness and a point of view that is aggressively unsympathetic, and all that is one whole you and it alternates with another you that possesses a purity and intensity of feeling that leaves me quite awestruck and a gentleness of voice and manner and an infinitely tender patience that entirely overmasters me. Now the question is which is really you because these two don't seem to have any connections. Perhaps when I really know something about you, the whole will come together but at present it is always either the one or the other and I haven't the least idea which is reallest. You certainly are one too many for me." She shrugged her shoulders, threw out her hands helplessly and sat down again before the fire. She roused at last and became conscious that Helen was trembling bitterly. All hesitations were swept away by Adele's instant passionate sympathy for a creature obviously in pain and she took her into her arms with pure maternal tenderness. Helen gave way utterly. "I tried to be adequate to your experiments" she said at last "but you had no mercy. You were not content until you had dissected out every nerve in my body and left it quite exposed and it was too much, too much. You should give your subjects occasional respite even in the ardor of research." She said it without bitterness. "Good God" cried Adele utterly dumbfounded "did you think that I was deliberately making you suffer in order to study results? Heavens and earth what do you take me for! Do you suppose that I for a moment realised that you were in pain. No! no! it is only my cursed habit of being concerned only with my own thoughts, and then you know I never for a moment believed that you really cared about me, that is one of the things that with all my conceit I never can believe. Helen how could you have had any use for me if you thought me capable of such wanton cruelty?" "I didn't know," she answered "I was willing that you should do what you liked if it interested you and I would stand it as well as I could." "Oh! Oh!" groaned Adele yearning over her with remorseful sympathy "surely dear you believe that I had no idea of your pain and that my brutality was due to ignorance and not intention." "Yes! yes! I know" whispered Helen, nestling to her. After a while she went on, "You know dear you mean so very much to me for with all your inveterate egotism you are the only person with whom I have ever come into close contact, whom I could continue to respect." "Faith" said Adele ruefully "I confess I can't see why. After all even at my best I am only tolerably decent. There are plenty of others, your experience has been unfortunate that's all, and then you know you have always shut yourself off by that fatal illusion of yours that you could stand completely alone." And then she chanted with tender mockery, "And the very strong man Kwasind and he was a very strong man" she went on "even if being an unconquerable solitary wasn't entirely a success."

2

All through the winter Helen at intervals spent a few days with Mabel Neathe in Baltimore. Adele was always more or less with them on these occasions. On the surface they preserved the same relations as had existed on the steamer. The only evidence that Mabel gave of a realisation of a difference was in never if she could avoid it leaving them alone together.

It was tacitly understood between them that on these rare occasions they should give each other no sign. As the time drew near when Adele was once more to leave for Europe this time for an extended absence, the tension of this self-imposed inhibition became unendurable and they as tacitly ceased to respect it.

Some weeks before her intended departure Adele was one afternoon as usual taking tea with Mabel. "You have never met Mr. and Mrs. T. have you?" Mabel asked quite out of the air. They had never definitely avoided talking of Helen but they had not spoken of her unnecessarily. "No" Adele answered, "I haven't wanted to. I don't like perfunctory civilities and I know that I belong to the number of Helen's friends of whom they do not approve." "You would not be burdened by their civility, they never take the trouble to be as amiable as that." "Are your experiences so very unpleasant when you are stopping there? I shouldn't think that you would care to do it often." "Sometimes I feel as if it couldn't be endured but if I didn't, Helen would leave them and I think she would regret that and so I don't want her to do it. I have only to say the word and she would leave them at once and sometimes I think she will do it anyway. If she once makes up her mind she won't reconsider it. Of course I wouldn't say such things to any one but you, you know." "I can quite believe that," said Adele rather grimly, "isn't there anything else that you would like to tell me just because I am I. If so don't let me get in your way." "I have never told you about our early relations," Mabel continued. "You know Helen cared for me long before I knew anything about it. We used to be together a great deal at College and every now and then she would disappear for a long time into the country and it wasn't until long afterwards that I found out the reason of it. You know Helen never gives way. You have no idea how wonderful she is. I have been so worried lately" she went on "lest she should think it necessary to leave home for my sake because it is so uncomfortable for me in the summer when I spend a month with her." "Well then why don't you make a noble sacrifice and stay away? Apparently Helen's heroism is great enough to carry her through the ordeal." Adele felt herself to be quite satisfactorily vulgar. Mabel accepted it literally. "Do you really advise it?" she asked. "Oh yes" said Adele "there is nothing so good for the soul as self-imposed periods of total abstinence." "Well, I will think about it" Mabel answered "it is such a comfort that you understand everything and one can speak to you openly about it all." "That's where you are entirely mistaken" Adele said decisively, "I understand nothing. But after all" she added, "it isn't any of my business anyway. Adios," and she left.

When she got home she saw a letter of Helen's on the table. She felt no impulse to read it. She put it well away. "Not that it is any of my business whether she is bound and if so how," she said to herself. "That is entirely for her to work out with her own conscience. For me it is only a question of what exists between us two. I owe Mabel nothing"; and she resolutely relegated it all quite to the background of her mind.

Mabel however did not allow the subject to rest. At the very next opportunity she again asked Adele for advice. "Oh hang it all" Adele broke out "what do I know about it? I understand nothing of the nature of the bond between you." "Don't you really?" Mabel was seriously incredulous. "No I don't." Adele answered with decision, and the subject dropped.

Adele communed with herself dismally. "I was strong-minded to put it out of my head once, but this time apparently it has come to stay. I can't deny that I do badly want to know and I know well enough that if I continue to want to know the only decent thing for me to do is to ask the information of Helen. But I do so hate to do that. Why? well I suppose because it would hurt so to hear her admit that she was bound. It would be infinitely pleasanter to have Mabel explain it but it certainly would be very contemptible of me to get it from her. Helen is right, it's not easy this business of really caring about people. I seem to be pretty deeply in it" and she smiled to herself "because now I don't regret the bother and the pain. I wonder if I am really beginning to care" and she lost herself in a revery.

Mabel's room was now for Adele always filled with the atmosphere of the unasked question. She could dismiss it when alone but Mabel was clothed with it as with a garment although nothing concerning it passed between them.

Adele now received a letter from Helen asking why she had not written, whether it was that faith had again failed her. Adele at first found it impossible to answer; finally she wrote a note at once ambiguous and bitter.

At last the tension snapped. "Tell me then" Adele said to Mabel abruptly one evening. Mabel made no attempt to misunderstand but she did attempt to delay. "Oh well if you want to go through the farce of a refusal and an insistance, why help yourself," Adele broke out harshly, "but supposing all that done, I say again tell me." Mabel was dismayed by Adele's hot directness and she vaguely fluttered about as if to escape. "Drop your intricate delicacy" Adele said sternly "you wanted to tell, now tell." Mabel was cowed. She sat down and explained.

The room grew large and portentous and to Mabel's eyes Adele's figure grew almost dreadful in its concentrated repulsion. There was a long silence that seemed to roar and menace and Mabel grew afraid. "Good-night" said Adele and left her.

Adele had now at last learned to stop thinking. She went home and lay motionless a long time. At last she got up and sat at her desk. "I guess I must really care a good deal about Helen" she said at last, "but oh Lord," she groaned and it was very bitter pain. Finally she roused herself. "Poor Mabel" she said "I could almost find it in my heart to be sorry for her. I must have looked very dreadful."

On the next few occasions nothing was said. Finally Mabel began again. "I really supposed Adele that you knew, or else I wouldn't have said anything about it at all and after I once mentioned it, you know you made me tell." "Oh yes I made you tell." Adele could admit it quite cheerfully; Mabel seemed so trivial. "And then you know," Mabel continued "I never would have mentioned it if I had not been so fond of you." Adele laughed, "Yes it's wonderful what an amount of devotion to me there is lying around the universe; but what will Helen think of the results of this devotion of yours?" "That is what worries me" Mabel admitted "I must tell her that I have told you and I am afraid she won't like it." "I rather suspect she won't" and Adele laughed again "but there is nothing like seizing an opportunity before your courage has a chance to ooze. Helen will be down next week, you know, and that will give you your chance but I guess now there has been enough said," and she definitely dismissed the matter.

Adele found it impossible to write to Helen, she felt too sore and bitter but even in spite of her intense revulsion of feeling, she realised that she did still believe in that other Helen that she had attempted once to describe to her. In spite of all evidence she was convinced that something real existed there, something that she was bound to reverence.

She spent a painful week struggling between revulsion and respect. Finally two days before Helen's visit, she heard from her. "I am afraid I can bear it no longer" Helen wrote. "As long as I believed there was a chance of your learning to be something more than your petty complacent self, I could willingly endure everything, but now you remind me of an ignorant mob. You trample everything ruthlessly under your feet without considering whether or not you kill something precious and without being changed or influenced by what you so brutally destroy. I am like Diogenes in quest of an honest man; I want so badly to find some one I can respect and I find them all worthy of nothing but contempt. You have done your best. I am sorry."

For some time Adele was wholly possessed by hot anger, but that changed to intense sympathy for Helen's pain. She realised the torment she might be enduring and so sat down at once to answer. "Perhaps though she really no longer cares" she thought to herself and hesitated. "Well whether she does or not makes no difference I will at least do my part."

"I can make no defence" she wrote "except only that in spite of all my variations there was grown within me steadily an increasing respect and devotion to you. I am not surprised at your bitterness but your conclusions from it are not justified. It is hardly to be expected that such a changed estimate of values, such a complete departure from established convictions as I have lately undergone could take place without many revulsions. That you have been very patient I fully realise but on the other hand you should recognise that I too have done my best and your word to the contrary notwithstanding that best has not been contemptible. So don't talk any more nonsense about mobs. If your endurance is not equal to this task, why admit it and have done with it; if it is I will try to be adequate."

Adele knew that Helen would receive her letter but there would not be time to answer it as she was to arrive in Baltimore the following evening. They were all three to meet at the opera that night so for a whole day Adele would be uncertain of Helen's feeling toward her. She spent all her strength throughout the day in endeavoring to prepare herself to find that Helen still held her in contempt. It had always been her habit to force herself to realise the worst that was likely to befall her and to submit herself before the event. She was never content with simply thinking that the worst might happen and having said it to still expect the best, but she had always accustomed herself to bring her mind again and again to this worst possibility until she had really mastered herself to bear it. She did this because she always doubted her own courage and distrusted her capacity to meet a difficulty if she had not inured herself to it beforehand.

All through this day she struggled for her accustomed definite resignation and the tremendous difficulty of accomplishment made her keenly realise how much she valued Helen's regard.

She did not arrive at the opera until after it had commenced. She knew how little command she had of her expression when deeply moved and she preferred that the first greeting should take place in the dark. She came in quietly to her place. Helen leaned across Mabel and greeted her. There was nothing in her manner to indicate anything and Adele realised by her sensation of sick disappointment that she had really not prepared herself at all. Now that the necessity was more imperative she struggled again for resignation and by the time the act was over she had pretty well gained it. She had at least mastered herself enough to entertain Mabel with elaborate discussion of music and knife fights. She avoided noticing Helen but that was comparatively simple as Mabel sat between them.

Carmen that night was to her at once the longest and the shortest performance that she had ever sat through. It was short because the end brought her nearer to hopeless certainty. It was long because she could only fill it with suspense.

The opera was at last or already over, Adele was uncertain which phrase expressed her feeling most accurately, and then they went for a little while to Mabel's room. Adele was by this time convinced that all her relation with Helen was at an end.

"You look very tired to-night, what's the matter?" Mabel asked her. "Oh!" she explained "there's been a lot of packing and arranging and good-bys to say and farewell lunches and dinners to eat. How I hate baked shad, it's a particular delicacy now and I have lunched and dined on it for three days running so I think it's quite reasonable for me to be worn out. Good-by no don't come downstairs with me. Hullo Helen has started down already to do the honors. Good-by I will see you again to-morrow." Mabel went back to her room and Helen was already lost in the darkness of the lower hall. Adele slowly descended the stairs impressing herself with the necessity of self-restraint.

"Can you forgive me?" and Helen held her close. "I haven't anything to forgive if you still care," Adele answered. They were silent together a long time. "We will certainly have earned our friendship when it is finally accomplished," Adele said at last.

"Well good-by," Mabel began as the next day Adele was leaving for good. "Oh! before you go I want to tell you that it's alright. Helen was angry but it's alright now. You will be in New York for a few days before you sail" she continued. "I know you won't be gone for a whole year, you will be certain to come back to us before long. I will think of your advice" she concluded. "You know it carries so much weight coming from you." "Oh of course" answered Adele and though to herself, "What sort of a fool does Mabel take me for anyway."

Adele was in Helen's room the eve of her departure. They had been together a long time. Adele was sitting on the floor her head resting against Helen's knee. She looked up at Helen and then broke the silence with some effort. "Before I go" she said "I want to tell you myself what I suppose you know already, that Mabel has told me of the relations existing between you." Helen's arms dropped away. "No I didn't know." She was very still. "Mabel didn't tell you then?" Adele asked. "No" replied Helen. There was a sombre silence. "If you were not wholly selfish, you would have exercised self-restraint enough to spare me this," Helen said. Adele hardly heard the words, but the power of the mood that possessed Helen awed her. She broke through it at last and began with slow resolution.

"I do not admit" she said, "that I was wrong in wanting to know. I suppose one might in a spirit of quixotic generosity deny oneself such a right but as a reasonable being, I feel that I had a right to know. I realise perfectly that it was hopelessly wrong to learn it from Mabel instead of from you. I admit I was a coward, I was simply afraid to ask you." Helen laughed harshly. "You need not have been," she said "I would have told you nothing." "I think you are wrong, I am quite sure that you would have told me and I wanted to spare myself that pain, perhaps spare you it too, I don't know. I repeat I cannot believe that I was wrong in wanting to know."

They remained there together in an unyielding silence. When an irresistible force meets an immovable body what happens? Nothing. The shadow of a long struggle inevitable as their different natures lay drearily upon them. This incident however decided was only the beginning. All that had gone before was only a preliminary. They had just gotten into position.

The silence was not oppressive but it lasted a long time. "I am very fond of you Adele" Helen said at last with a deep embrace.

It was an hour later when Adele drew a deep breath of resolution, "What foolish people those poets are who say that parting is such sweet sorrow. Although it isn't for ever I can't find a bit of sweetness in it not one tiny little speck. Helen I don't like at all this business of leaving you." "And I" Helen exclaimed "when in you I seem to be taking farewell of parents, brothers sisters my own child, everything at once. No dear you are quite right there is nothing pleasant in it."

"Then why do they put it into the books?" Adele asked with dismal petulance. "Oh dear! but at least it's some comfort to have found out that they are wrong. It's one fact discovered anyway. Dear we are neither of us sorry that we know enough to find it out, are we?" "No," Helen answered "we are neither of us sorry."

On the steamer Adele received a note of farewell from Mabel in which she again explained that nothing but her great regard for Adele would have made it possible for her to speak as she had done. Adele lost her temper. "I am willing to fight in any way that Mabel likes" she said to herself "underhand or overhand, in the dark, or in the light, in a room or out of doors but at this I protest. She unquestionably did that for a purpose even if the game was not successful. I don't blame her for the game, a weak man must fight with such weapons as he can hold but I don't owe it to her to endure the hypocrisy of a special affection. I can't under the circumstances be very straight but I'll not be unnecessarily crooked. I'll make it clear to her but I'll complicate it in the fashion that she loves."

"My dear Mabel" she wrote, "either you are duller than I would like to think you or you give me credit for more good-natured stupidity than I possess. If the first supposition is correct then you have nothing to say and I need say nothing; if the second then nothing that you would say would carry weight so it is equally unnecessary for you to say anything. If you don't understand what I am talking about then I am talking about nothing and it makes no difference, if you do then there's enough said." Mabel did not answer for several months and then began again to write friendly letters.

It seemed incredible to Adele this summer that it was only one year ago that she had seemed to herself so simple and all morality so easily reducible to formula. In these long lazy Italian days she did not discuss these matters with herself. She realised that at present morally and mentally she was too complex, and that complexity too much astir. It would take much time and strength to make it all settle again. It might, she thought, be eventually understood, it might even in a great deal of time again become simple but at present it gave little promise.

She poured herself out fully and freely to Helen in their ardent correspondence. At first she had had some hesitation about this. She knew that Helen and Mabel were to be together the greater part of the summer and she thought it possible that both the quantity and the matter of the correspondence, if it should come to Mabel's notice would give Helen a great deal of bother. She hesitated a long time whether to suggest this to Helen and to let her decide as to the expediency of being more guarded.

There were many reasons for not mentioning the matter. She realised that not alone Helen but that she herself was still uncertain as to the fidelity of her own feeling. She could not as yet trust herself and hesitated to leave herself alone with a possible relapse.

"After all," she said to herself, "it is Helen's affair and not mine. I have undertaken to follow her lead even into very devious and underground ways but I don't know that it is necessary for me to warn her. She knows Mabel as well as I do. Perhaps she really won't be sorry if the thing is brought to a head."

She remembered the reluctance that Helen always showed to taking precautions or to making any explicit statement of conditions. She seemed to satisfy her conscience and keep herself from all sense of wrong-doing by never allowing herself to expect a difficulty. When it actually arrived the active necessity of using whatever deception was necessary to cover it, drowned her conscience in the violence of action. Adele did not as yet realise this quality definitely but she was vaguely aware that Helen would shut her mind to any explicit statement of probabilities, that she would take no precautions and would thus avoid all sense of guilt. In this fashion she could safeguard herself from her own conscience.

Adele recognised all this dimly. She did not formulate it but it aided to keep her from making any statement to Helen.

She herself could not so avoid her conscience, she simply had to admit a change in moral basis. She knew what she was doing, she realised what was likely to happen and the way in which the new developments would have to be met.

She acknowledged to herself that her own defence lay simply in the fact that she thought the game was worth the candle. "After all" she concluded, "there is still the most important reason for saying nothing. The stopping of the correspondence would make me very sad and lonely. In other words I simply don't want to stop it and so I guess I won't."

For several months the correspondence continued with vigor and ardour on both sides. Then there came a three weeks' interval and no word from Helen then a simple friendly letter and then another long silence.

Adele lying on the green earth on a sunny English hillside communed with herself on these matters day after day. She had no real misgiving but she was deeply unhappy. Her unhappiness was the unhappiness of loneliness not of doubt. She saved herself from intense misery only by realising that the sky was still so blue and the country-side so green and beautiful. The pain of passionate longing was very hard to bear. Again and again she would bury her face in the cool grass to recover the sense of life in the midst of her sick despondency.

"There are many possibilities but to me only one probability," she said to herself. "I am not a trustful person in spite of an optimistic temperament but I am absolutely certain in the face of all the facts that Helen is unchanged. Unquestionably there has been some complication. Mabel has gotten hold of some letters and there has been trouble. I can't blame Mabel much. The point of honor would be a difficult one to decide between the three of us."

As time passed she did not doubt Helen but she began to be much troubled about her responsibility in the matter. She felt uncertain as to the attitude she should take.

"As for Mabel" she said to herself "I admit quite completely that I simply don't care. I owe her nothing. She wanted me when it was pleasant to have me and so we are quits. She entered the fight and must be ready to bear the results. We were never bound to each other, we never trusted each other and so there has been no breach of faith. She would show me no mercy and I need grant her none, particularly as she would wholly misunderstand it. It is very strange how very different one's morality and one's temper are when one wants something really badly. Here I, who have always been hopelessly soft-hearted and good-natured and who have always really preferred letting the other man win, find myself quite cold-blooded and relentless. It's a lovely morality that in which we believe even in serious matters when we are not deeply stirred, it's so delightfully noble and gentle." She sighed and then laughed. "Well, I hope some day to find a morality that can stand the wear and tear of real desire to take the place of the nice one that I have lost, but morality or no morality the fact remains that I have no compunctions on the score of Mabel.

"About Helen that's a very different matter. I unquestionably do owe her a great deal but just how to pay it is the difficult point to discover. I can't forget that to me she can never be the first consideration as she is to Mabel for I have other claims that I would always recognise as more important. I have neither the inclination or the power to take Mabel's place and I feel therefore that I have no right to step in between them. On the other hand morally and mentally she is in urgent need of a strong comrade and such in spite of all evidence I believe myself to be. Some day if we continue she will in spite of herself be compelled to choose between us and what have I to offer? Nothing but an elevating influence.

"Bah! what is the use of an elevating influence if one hasn't bread and butter. Her possible want of butter if not of bread, considering her dubious relations with her family must be kept in mind. Mabel could and would always supply them and I neither can nor will. Alas for an unbuttered influence say I. What a grovelling human I am anyway. But I do have occasional sparkling glimpses of faith and those when they come I truly believe to be worth much bread and butter. Perhaps Helen also finds them more delectable. Well

I will state the case to her and abide by her decision."

She timed her letter to arrive when Helen would be once more at home alone. "I can say to you now" she wrote "what I found impossible in the early summer. I am now convinced and I think you are too that my feeling for you is genuine and loyal and whatever may be our future difficulties we are now at least on a basis of understanding and trust. I know therefore that you will not misunderstand when I beg you to consider carefully whether on the whole you had not better give me up. I can really amount to so little for you and yet will inevitably cause you so much trouble. That I dread your giving me up I do not deny but I dread more being the cause of serious annoyance to you. Please believe that this statement is sincere and is to be taken quite literally."

"Hush little one" Helen answered "oh you stupid child, don't you realise that you are the only thing in the world that makes anything seem real or worth while to me. I have had a dreadful time this summer. Mabel read a letter of mine to you and it upset her completely. She said that she found it but I can hardly believe that. She asked me if you cared for me and I told her that I didn't know and I really don't dearest. She did not ask me if I cared for you. The thing upset her completely and she was jealous of my every thought and I could not find a moment even to feel alone with you. But don't please don't say any more about giving you up. You are not any trouble to me if you will only not leave me. It's alright now with Mabel, she says that she will never be jealous again." "Oh Lord!" groaned Adele "well if she isn't she would be a hopeless fool. Anyhow I said I would abide by Helen's decision and I certainly will but how so proud a woman can permit such control is more than I can understand."

By Gertrude Stein

Ada

Barnes Colhard did not say he would not do it but he did not do it. He did it and then he did not do it, he did not ever think about it. He just thought some time he might do something.

His father Mr. Abram Colhard spoke about it to every one and very many of them spoke to Barnes Colhard about it and he always listened to them.

Then Barnes fell in love with a very nice girl and she would not marry him. He cried then, his father Mr. Abram Colhard comforted him and they took a trip and Barnes promised he would do what his father wanted him to be doing. He did not do the thing, he thought he would do another thing, he did not do the other thing, his father Mr. Colhard did not want him to do the other thing. He really did not do anything then. When he was a good deal older he married a very rich girl. He had thought perhaps he would not propose to her but his sister wrote to him that it would be a good thing. He married the rich girl and she thought he was the most wonderful man and one who knew everything. Barnes never spent more than the income of the fortune he and his wife had then, that is to say they did not spend more than the income and this was a surprise to very many who knew about him and about his marrying the girl who had such a large fortune. He had a happy life while he was living and after he was dead his wife and children remembered him.

He had a sister who also was successful enough in being one being living. His sister was one who came to be happier than most people come to be in living. She came to be a completely happy one. She was twice as old as her brother. She had been a very good daughter to her mother. She and her mother had always told very pretty stories to each other. Many old men loved to hear her tell these stories to her mother. Every one who ever knew her mother liked her mother. Many were sorry later that not every one liked the daughter. Many did like the daughter but not every one as every one had liked the mother. The daughter was charming inside in her, it did not show outside in her to every one, it certainly did to some. She did sometimes think her mother would be pleased with a story that did not please her mother, when her mother later was sicker the daughter knew that there were some stories she could tell her that would not please her mother. Her mother died and really mostly altogether the mother and the daughter had told each other stories very happily together.

The daughter then kept house for her father and took care of her brother. There were many relations who lived with them. The daughter did not like them to live with them and she did not like them to die with them. The daughter, Ada they had called her after her grandmother who had delightful ways of smelling flowers and eating dates and sugar, did not like it at all then as she did not like so much dying and she did not like any of the living she was doing then. Every now and then some old gentlemen told delightful stories to her. Mostly then there were not nice stories told by any one then in her living. She told her father Mr. Abram Colhard that she did not like it at all being one being living then. He never said anything. She was afraid then, she was one needing charming stories and happy telling of them and not having that thing she was always trembling. Then every one who could live with them were dead and there were then the father and the son a young man then and the daughter coming to be that one then. Her grandfather had left some money to them each one of them. Ada said she was going to use it to go away from them. The father said nothing then, then he said something and she said nothing then, then they both said nothing and then it was that she went away from them. The father was quite tender then, she was his daughter then. He wrote her tender letters then, she wrote him tender letters then, she never went back to live with him. He wanted her to come and she wrote him tender letters then. He liked the tender letters she wrote to him. He wanted her to live with him. She answered him by writing tender letters to him and telling very nice stories indeed in them. He wrote nothing and then he wrote again and there was some waiting and then he wrote tender letters again and again.

She came to be happier than anybody else who was living then. It is easy to believe this thing. She was telling some one, who was loving every story that was charming. Some one who was living was almost always listening. Some one who was loving was almost always listening. That one who was loving was almost always listening. That one who was loving was telling about being one then listening. That one being loving was then telling stories having a beginning and a middle and an ending. That one was then one always completely listening. Ada was then one and all her living then one completely telling stories that were charming, completely listening to stories having a beginning and a middle and an ending. Trembling was all living, living was all loving, some one was then the other one. Certainly this one was loving this Ada then. And certainly Ada all her living then was happier in living than any one else who ever could, who was, who is, who ever will be living.

By Gertrude Stein

Lifting Belly
(excerpt)

She is worthy of a queen.
Will she go as we do dream.
She will do satisfactorily.
And so will we.
Thank you so much.
Smiling to me.
Then we can see him.
Yes we can.
Can we always go.
I think so.
You will be secure.
We are secure.
Then we see.
We see the way.
This is very good for me.
In this way we play.
Then we are pleasing.
We are pleasing to him.
We have gone together.
We are in our Ford.
Please me please me.
We go then.
We go when.
In a minute.

Next week.
Yes indeed oh yes indeed.
I can tell you she is charming in a coat.
Yes and we are full of her praises.
Yes indeed.
This is the way to worry. Not it.
Can you smile.
Yes indeed oh yes indeed.
And so can I.
Can we think.
Wrist leading.
Wrist leading.
A kind of exercise.
A brilliant station.
Do you remember its name.
Yes Morlet.
Can you say wishes.
I can.
Winning baby.
Theoretically and practically.
Can we explain a season.
We can when we are right.
Two is too many.
To be right.
One is right and so we mount and have what we want.
We will remember.
Can you mix birthdays.
Certainly I can.
Then do so.
I do so.
Do I remember to write.
Can he paint.
Not after he has driven a car.
I can write.
There you are.

Lifting belly with me.
You inquire.
What you do then.
Pushing.
Thank you so much.
And lend a hand.
What is lifting belly now.
My baby.
Always sincerely.
Lifting belly says it there.
Thank you for the cream.
Lifting belly tenderly.
A remarkable piece of intuition.
I have forgotten all about it.
Have you forgotten all about it.
Little nature which is mine.
Fairy ham
Is a clam.
Of chowder
Kiss him Louder.
Can you be especially proud of me.
Lifting belly a queen.
In that way I can think.
Thank you so much.
I have,
Lifting belly for me.
I can not forget the name.
Lifting belly for me.
Lifting belly again.
Can you be proud of me.
I am.
Then we say it.
In miracles.
Can we say it and then sing. You mean drive.
I mean to drive.

We are full of pride.
Lifting belly is proud.
Lifting belly my queen.
Lifting belly happy.
Lifting belly see.
Lifting belly.
Lifting belly address.
Little washers.
Lifting belly how do you do.
Lifting belly is famous for recipes.
You mean Genevieve.
I mean I never ask for potatoes.
But you liked them then.
And now.
Now we know about water.
Lifting belly is a miracle.
And the Caesars.
The Caesars are docile.
Not more docile than is right.
No beautifully right.
And in relation to a cow.
And in relation to a cow.
Do believe me when I incline.
You mean obey.
I mean obey.
Obey me.
Husband obey your wife.
Lifting belly is so dear.
To me.
Lifting belly is smooth,
Tell lifting belly about matches.
Matches can be struck with the thumb.
Not by us.
No indeed.
What is it I say about letters.

Twenty six.
And counted.
And counted deliberately.
This is not as difficult as it seems.
Lifting belly is so strange
And quick.
Lifting belly in a minute.
Lifting belly in a minute now.
In a minute.
Not to-day.
No not to-day.
Can you swim.
Lifting belly can perform aquatics.
Lifting belly is astonishing.
Lifting belly for me.
Come together.
Lifting belly near.
I credit you with repetition.
Believe me I will not say it.
And retirement.
I celebrate something.
Do you.
Lifting belly extraordinarily in haste.
I am so sorry I said it.
Lifting belly is a credit. Do you care about poetry.
Lifting belly in spots.
Do you like ink.
Better than butter.
Better than anything.
Any letter is an alphabet.
When this you see you will kiss me.
Lifting belly is so generous.
Shoes.
Servant.
And Florence.

Then we can sing.
We do among.
I like among.
Lifting belly keeps.
Thank you in lifting belly.
Can you wonder that they don't make preserves.
We ask the question and they answer you give us help.
Lifting belly is so successful.
Is she indeed.
I wish you would not be disobliging.
In that way I am.
But in giving.
In giving you always win.
You mean in effect.
In mean in essence.
Thank you so much we are so much obliged.
This may be a case
Have no fear.
Then we can be indeed.
You are and you must.
Thank you so much.
In kindness you excel.
You have obliged me too.
I have done what is necessary.
Then can I say thank you may I say thank you very much.
Thank you again.
Because lifting belly is about baby.
Three eggs in lifting belly.
Eclair.
Think of it.
Think of that.
We think of that.
We produce music.
And in sleeping.
Noises.

Can that be she.
Lifting belly is so kind.
Darling wifie is so good.
Little husband would.
Be as good.
If he could.
This was said.
Now we know how to differ.
From that.
Certainly.
Now we say.
Little hubbie is good.
Every Day.
She did want a photograph.
Lifting belly changed her mind.
Lifting belly changed her mind.
Do I look fat.
Do I look fat and thin.
Blue eyes and windows.
You mean Vera.
Lifting belly can guess.
Quickly.
Lifting belly is so pleased.
Lifting belly seeks pleasure.
And she finds it altogether.
Lifting belly is my love.
Can you say meritorious.
Yes camellia.
Why do you complain.
Postal cards.
And then.
The Louvre.
After that.
After that Francine.
You don't mean by that name.

What is Spain.
Listen lightly.
But you do.
Don't tell me what you call me.
But he is pleased.
But he is pleased.
That is the way it sounds.
In the morning.
By that bright light.
Will you exchange purses.
You know I like to please you.
Lifting belly is so kind.
Then sign.
I sign the bulletin.
Do the boys remember that nicely
To-morrow we go there.
And the photographs
The photographs will come.
When
You will see.
Will it please me.
Not suddenly
But soon
Very soon.
But you will hear first.
That will take some time.
Not very long.
What do you mean by long.
A few days.
How few days.
One or two days.
Thank you for saying so.
Thank you so much.
Lifting belly waits splendidly.
For essence.

For essence too.
Can you assure me.
I can and do.
Very well it will come
And I will be happy.
You are happy.
And I will be
You always will be.
Lifting belly sings nicely.
Not nervously.
No not nervously.
Nicely and forcefully.
Lifting belly is so sweet.
Can you say you say.
In this thought.
I do think lifting belly.
Little love lifting
Little love light.
Little love heavy.
Lifting belly tight.
Thank you.
Can you turn over.
Rapidly.
Lifting belly so meaningly.
Yes indeed the dog.
He watches.
The little boys.
They whistle on their legs,
Little boys have meadows,
Then they are well.
Very well.
Please be the man.
I am the man.
Lifting belly praises.
And she gives

By Gertrude Stein

Melanctha

(excerpt)

One night Jeff Campbell was lying in his bed with his thinking, and night after night now he could not do any sleeping for his thinking. To-night suddenly he sat up in his bed, and it all came clear to him, and he pounded his pillow with his fist, and he almost shouted out alone there to him, "I ain't a brute the way Melanctha has been saying. It's all wrong the way I been worried thinking. We did begin fair, each not for the other but for ourselves, what we were wanting. Melanctha Herbert did it just like I did it, because she liked it bad enough to want to stand it. It's all wrong in me to think it any way except the way we really did it. I certainly don't know now whether she is now real and true in her loving. I ain't got any way ever to find out if she is real and true now always to me. All I know is I didn't ever make her to begin to be with me. Melanctha has got to stand for her own trouble, just like I got to stand for my own trouble. Each man has got to do it for himself when he is in real trouble. Melanctha, she certainly don't remember right when she says I made her begin and then I made her trouble. No by God, I ain't no coward nor a brute either ever to her. I been the way I felt it honest, and that certainly is all about it now between us, and everybody always has just got to stand for their own trouble. I certainly am right this time the way I see it." And Jeff lay down now, at last in comfort, and he slept, and he was free from his long doubting torment.

"You know Melanctha," Jeff Campbell began, the next time he was alone to talk a long time to Melanctha. "You know Melanctha, sometimes I think a whole lot about what you like to say so much about being game and never doing any hollering. Seems to me Melanctha, I certainly don't understand right what you mean by not hollering. Seems to me it certainly ain't only what comes right away when one is hit, that counts to be brave to be bearing, but all that comes later from your getting sick from the shock of being hurt once in a fight, and all that, and all the being taken care of for years after, and the suffering of your family, and all that, you certainly must stand and not holler, to be certainly really brave the way I understand it." "What you mean Jeff by your talking." "I mean, seems to me really not to holler, is to be strong not to show you ever have been hurt. Seems to me, to get your head hurt from your trouble and to show it, ain't certainly no braver than to say, oh, oh, how bad you hurt me, please don't hurt me mister. It just certainly seems to me, like many people think themselves so game just to stand what we all of us always just got to be standing, and everybody stands it, and we don't certainly none of us like it, and yet we don't ever most of us think we are so much being game, just because we got to stand it."

"I know what you mean now by what you are saying to me now Jeff Campbell. You make a fuss now to me, because I certainly just have stopped standing everything you like to be always doing so cruel to me. But that's just the way always with you Jeff Campbell, if you want to know it. You ain't got no kind of right feeling for all I always been forgiving to you." "I said it once for fun, Melanctha, but now I certainly do mean it, you think you got a right to go where you got no business, and you say, I am so brave nothing can hurt me, and then something, like always, it happens to hurt you, and you show your hurt always so everybody can see it, and you say, I am so brave nothing did hurt me except he certainly didn't have any right to, and see how bad I suffer, but you never hear me make a holler, though certainly anybody got any feeling, to see me suffer, would certainly never touch me except to take good care of me. Sometimes I certainly don't rightly see Melanctha, how much more game that is than just the ordinary kind of holler." "No, Jeff Campbell, and made the way you is you certainly ain't likely ever to be much more understanding." "No, Melanctha, nor you neither. You think always, you are the only one who ever can do any way to really suffer." "Well, and ain't I certainly always been the only person knows how to bear it. No, Jeff Campbell, I certainly be glad to love anybody really worthy, but I made so, I never seem to be able in this world to find him." "No, and your kind of way of thinking, you certainly Melanctha never going to any way be able ever to be finding of him. Can't you understand Melanctha, ever, how no man certainly ever really can hold your love for long times together. You certainly Melanctha, you ain't got down deep loyal feeling, true inside you, and when you ain't just that moment quick with feeling, then you certainly ain't ever got anything more there to keep you. You see Melanctha, it certainly is this way with you, it is, that you ain't ever got any way to remember right what you been doing, or anybody else that has been feeling with you. You certainly Melanctha, never can remember right, when it comes what you have done and what you think happens to you." "It certainly is all easy for you Jeff Campbell to be talking. You remember right, because you don't remember nothing till you get home with your thinking everything all over, but I certainly don't think much ever of that kind of way of remembering right, Jeff Campbell. I certainly do call it remembering right Jeff Campbell, to remember right just when it happens to you, so you have a right kind of feeling not to act the way you always been doing to me, and then you go home Jeff Campbell, and you begin with your thinking, and then it certainly is very easy for you to be good and forgiving with it. No, that ain't to me, the way of remembering Jeff Campbell, not as I can see it not to make people always suffer, waiting for you certainly to get to do it. Seems to me like Jeff Campbell, I never could feel so like a man was low and to be scorning of him, like that day in the summer, when you threw me off just because you got one of those fits of your remembering. No, Jeff Campbell, it's real feeling every moment when it's needed, that certainly does seem to me like real remembering. And that way, certainly, you don't never know nothing like what should be right Jeff Campbell. No Jeff, it's me that always certainly has had to bear it with you. It's always me that certainly has had to suffer, while you go home to remember. No you certainly ain't got no sense yet Jeff, what you need to make you really feeling. No, it certainly is me Jeff Campbell, that always has got to be remembering for us both, always. That's what's the true way with us Jeff Campbell, if you want to know what it is I am always thinking." "You is certainly real modest Melanctha, when you do this kind of talking, you sure is Melanctha," said Jeff Campbell laughing. "I think sometimes Melanctha I am certainly awful conceited, when I think sometimes I am all out doors, and I think I certainly am so bright, and better than most everybody I ever got anything now to do with, but when I hear you talk this way Melanctha, I certainly do think I am a real modest kind of fellow." "Modest!" said Melanctha, angry, "Modest, that certainly is a queer thing for you Jeff to be calling yourself even when you are laughing." "Well it certainly does depend a whole lot what you are thinking with," said Jeff Campbell. "I never did use to think I was so much on being real modest Melanctha, but now I know really I am, when I hear you talking. I see all the time there are many people living just as good as I am, though they are a little different to me. Now with you Melanctha if I understand you right what you are talking, you don't think that way of no other one that you are ever knowing." "I certainly could be real modest too, Jeff Campbell," said Melanctha, "If I could meet somebody once I could keep right on respecting when I got so I was really knowing with them. But I certainly never met anybody like that yet, Jeff Campbell, if you want to know it." "No, Melanctha, and with the way you got of thinking, it certainly don't look like as if you ever will Melanctha, with your never remembering anything only what you just then are feeling in you, and you not understanding what anyone else is ever feeling, if they don't holler just the way you are doing. No Melanctha, I certainly don't see any ways you are likely ever to meet one, so good as you are always thinking you be." "No, Jeff Campbell, it certainly ain't that way with me at all the way you say it. It's because I am always knowing what it is I am wanting, when I get it. I certainly don't never have to wait till I have it, and then throw away what I got in me, and then come back and say, that's a mistake I just been making, it ain't that never at all like I understood it, I want to have, bad, what I didn't think it was I wanted. It's that way of knowing right what I am wanting, makes me feel nobody can come right with me, when I am feeling things, Jeff Campbell. I certainly do say Jeff Campbell, I certainly don't think much of the way you always do it, always never knowing what it is you are ever really wanting and everybody always got to suffer. No Jeff, I don't certainly think there is much doubting which is better and the stronger with us two, Jeff Campbell."

"As you will, Melanctha Herbert," cried Jeff Campbell, and he rose up, and he thundered out a black oath, and he was fierce to leave her now forever, and then with the same movement, he took her in his arms and held her.

"What a silly goose boy you are, Jeff Campbell," Melanctha whispered to him fondly.

"Oh yes," said Jeff, very dreary. "I never could keep really mad with anybody, not when I was a little boy and playing. I used most to cry sometimes, I couldn't get real mad and

keep on a long time with it, the way everybody always did it.
It's certainly no use to me Melanctha, I certainly can't ever
keep mad with you Melanctha, my dear one. But don't you
ever be thinking it's because I think you right in what you
been just saying to me. I don't Melanctha really think it that
way, honest, though I certainly can't get mad the way I ought
to. No Melanctha, little girl, really truly, you ain't right the
way you think it. I certainly do know that Melanctha, honest.
You certainly don't do me right Melanctha, the way you say
you are thinking. Good-bye Melanctha, though you certainly
is my own little girl for always." And then they were very good
a little to each other, and then Jeff went away for that
evening, from her.

Melanctha had begun now once more to wander.
Melanctha did not yet always wander, but a little now she
needed to begin to look for others. Now Melanctha Herbert
began again to be with some of the better kind of black girls,
and with them she sometimes wandered. Melanctha had not
yet come again to need to be alone, when she wandered.

Jeff Campbell did not know that Melanctha had begun
again to wander. All Jeff knew, was that now he could not be
so often with her.

Jeff never knew how it had come to happen to him, but
now he never thought to go to see Melanctha Herbert, until
he had before, asked her if she could be going to have time
then to have him with her. Then Melanctha would think a
little, and then she would say to him, "Let me see Jeff, to-
morrow, you was just saying to me. I certainly am awful busy
you know Jeff just now. It certainly does seem to me this week
Jeff, I can't anyways fix it. Sure I want to see you soon Jeff.
I certainly Jeff got to do a little more now, I been giving so
much time, when I had no business, just to be with you when
you asked me. Now I guess Jeff, I certainly can't see you no
more this week Jeff, the way I got to do things. "All right
Melanctha," Jeff would answer and he would be very angry.

"I want to come only just certainly as you want me now Melanctha." "Now Jeff you know I certainly can't be neglecting always to be with everybody just to see you. You come see me next week Tuesday Jeff, you hear me. I don't think Jeff I certainly be so busy, Tuesday." Jeff Campbell would then go away and leave her, and he would be hurt and very angry, for it was hard for a man with a great pride in himself, like Jeff Campbell, to feel himself no better than a beggar. And yet he always came as she said he should, on the day she had fixed for him, and always Jeff Campbell was not sure yet that he really understood what it was Melanctha wanted. Always Melanctha said to him, yes she loved him, sure he knew that. Always Melanctha said to him, she certainly did love him just the same as always, only sure he knew now she certainly did seem to be right busy with all she certainly now had to be doing.

Jeff never knew what Melanctha had to do now, that made her always be so busy, but Jeff Campbell never cared to ask Melanctha such a question. Besides Jeff knew Melanctha Herbert would never, in such a matter, give him any kind of a real answer. Jeff did not know whether it was that Melanctha did not know how to give a simple answer. And then how could he, Jeff, know what was important to her. Jeff Campbell always felt strongly in him, he had no right to interfere with Melanctha in any practical kind of a matter. There they had always, never asked each other any kind of question. There they had felt always in each other, not any right to take care of one another. And Jeff Campbell now felt less than he had ever, any right to claim to know what Melanctha thought it right that she should do in any of her ways of living. All Jeff felt a right in himself to question, was her loving.

Jeff learned every day now, more and more, how much it was that he could really suffer. Sometimes it hurt so in him, when he was alone, it would force some slow tears from him.

But every day, now that Jeff Campbell knew more how it could hurt him, he lost his feeling of deep awe that he once always had had for Melanctha's feeling. Suffering was not so much after all, thought Jeff Campbell, if even he could feel it so it hurt him. It hurt him bad, just the way he knew he once had hurt Melanctha, and yet he too could have it and not make any kind of a loud holler with it.

In tender hearted natures, those that mostly never feel strong passion, suffering often comes to take them harder. When these do not know in themselves what it is to suffer, suffering is then very awful to them and they badly want to help everyone who ever has to suffer, and they have a deep reverence for anybody who knows really how to always suffer. But when it comes to them to really suffer, they soon begin to lose their fear and tenderness and wonder. Why it isn't so very much to suffer, when even I can bear to do it. It isn't very pleasant to be having all the time, to stand it, but they are not so much wiser after all, all the others just because they know too how to bear it.

Passionate natures who have always made themselves, to suffer, that is all the kind of people who have emotions that come to them as sharp as a sensation, they always get more tender-hearted when they suffer, and it always does them good to suffer. Tender-hearted, unpassionate, and comfortable natures always get much harder when they suffer, for so they lose the fear and reverence and wonder they once had for everybody who ever has to suffer, for now they know themselves what it is to suffer and it is not so awful any longer to them when they know too, just as well as all the others, how to have it.

And so it came in these days to Jeff Campbell. Jeff knew now always, way inside him, what it is to really suffer, and now every day with it, he knew how to understand Melanctha better. Jeff Campbell still loved Melanctha Herbert and he still had a real trust in her and he still had a little hope that some day they would once more get together, but slowly, every day, this hope in him would keep growing always weaker. They still were a good deal of time together, but now they never any more were really trusting with each other. In the days when they used to be together, Jeff had felt he did not know much what was inside Melanctha, but he knew very well, how very deep always was his trust in her; now he knew Melanctha Herbert better, but now he never felt a deep trust in her. Now Jeff never could be really honest with her. He never doubted yet, that she was steady only to him, but somehow he could not believe much really in Melanctha's loving.

Melanctha Herbert was a little angry now when Jeff asked her, "I never give nobody before Jeff, ever more than one chance with me and I certainly been giving you most a hundred Jeff, you hear me." "And why shouldn't you, Melanctha, give me a million, if you really love me!" Jeff flashed out very angry. "I certainly don't know as you deserve that anyways from me, Jeff Campbell." "It ain't deserving, I am ever talking about to you Melanctha. It's loving, and if you are really loving to me you won't certainly never any ways call them chances." "Deed Jeff, you certainly are getting awful wise Jeff now, ain't you, to me." "No I ain't Melanctha, and I ain't jealous either to you. I just am doubting from the way you are always acting to me." "Oh yes Jeff, that's what they all say, the same way, when they certainly got jealousy all through them. You ain't got no cause to be jealous with me Jeff, and I am awful tired of all this talking now, you hear me."

Jeff Campbell never asked Melanctha any more if she loved him. Now things were always getting worse between them. Now Jeff was always very silent with Melanctha. Now Jeff never wanted to be honest to her, and now Jeff never had much to say to her.

Now when they were together, it was Melanctha always did most of the talking. Now she often had other girls there with her. Melanctha was always kind to Jeff Campbell but she never seemed to need to be alone now with him. She always treated Jeff, like her best friend, and she always spoke so to him and yet she never seemed now to very often want to see him.

Every day it was getting harder for Jeff Campbell. It was as if now, when he had learned to really love Melanctha, she did not need any more to have him. Jeff began to know this very well inside him.

Jeff Campbell did not know yet that Melanctha had begun again to wander. Jeff was not very quick to suspect Melanctha. All Jeff knew was, that he did not trust her to be now really loving to him.

Jeff was no longer now in any doubt inside him. He knew very well now he really loved Melanctha. He knew now very well she was not any more a real religion to him. Jeff Campbell knew very well too now inside him, he did not really want Melanctha, now if he could no longer trust her, though he loved her hard and really knew now what it was to suffer.

Every day Melanctha Herbert was less and less near to him. She always was very pleasant in her talk and to be with him, but somehow now it never was any comfort to him.

By Gertrude Stein

The Mother of Us All

(excerpt)

ACT II, Scene V

Susan B.

Will they remember that it is true that neither they that neither you, will they marry will they carry, aloud, the right to know that even if they love them so, they are alone to live and die, they are alone to sink and swim they are alone to have what they own, to have no idea but that they are here, to struggle and thirst to do everything first, because until it is done there is no other one.

(Jo the Loiterer leads in Indiana Elliot in wedding attire, followed by John Adams and Constance Fletcher and followed by Daniel Webster and Angel More. All the other characters follow after. Anne and Jenny Reefer come and stand by Susan B. Ulysses S. Grant sits down in a chair right behind the procession)

Anne. Marriage.

Jenny Reefer. Marry marriage.

Susan B. I know I know and I have told you so,

	but if no one marries how can there be women to tell men, women to tell men.
Anne.	What
Jenny Reefer.	Women should not tell men.
Susan B.	Men can not count, they do not know that two and two make four if women do not tell them so. There is a devil creeps into men when their hands are strengthened. Men want to be half slave half free. Women want to be all slave or all free, therefore men govern and women know, and yet.
Anne.	Yet.
Jenny Reefer.	There is no yet in paradise.
Susan B.	Let them marry.

(The marrying commences)

Jo the Loiterer.	I tell her if she marries me do I marry her.
Indiana Elliot.	Listen to what he says so you can answer, have you the ring.
Jo the Loiterer.	You did not like the ring and mine is too large.
Indiana Elliot.	Hush.
Jo the Loiterer.	I wish my name was Adams.
Indiana Elliot.	Hush.
John Adams.	I never marry I have been twice divorced but I have never married, fair Constance Fletcher fair Constance Fletcher do you not admire me that I never can married be. I who have been twice divorced. Dear Constance Fletcher dear dear Constance Fletcher do you not admire

	me.
Constance Fletcher.	So beautiful. It is so beautiful to meet you here, so beautiful, so beautiful to meet you here dear, dear John Adams, so beautiful to meet you here.
Daniel Webster.	When I have joined and not having joined have separated and not having separated have led, and not having led have thundered, when I having thundered have provoked and having provoked have dominated, may I dear Angel More not kneel at your feet because I cannot kneel my knees are not kneeling knees but dear Angel More be my Angel More for evermore.
Angel More.	I join the choir that is visible, because the choir that is visible is as visible.
Daniel Webster.	As what Angel More.
Angel More.	As visible as visible, do you not hear me, as visible.
Daniel Webster.	You do not and I do not.
Angel More.	What.
Daniel Webster.	Separate marriage from marriage.
Angel More.	And why not.
Daniel Webster.	And.

(Just at this moment Ulysses S. Grant makes his chair pound on the floor)

Ulysses S. Grant.	As long as I sit I am sitting, silence again as you were, you were all silent, as long as I sit I am sitting.
All Together.	We are silent, as we were.
Susan B.	We are all here to celebrate the civil

and religious marriage of Jo the Loiterer and Indiana Elliot.

Jo the Loiterer. Who is civil and who is religious.

Anne. Who is, listen to Susan B. She knows.

The Brother of Indiana Elliot rushes in.

Nobody knows who I am but I forbid the marriage, do we know whether Jo the Loiterer is a bigamist or a grandfather or an uncle or a refugee. Do we know, no we do not know and I forbid the marriage, I forbid it, I am Indiana Elliot's brother and I forbid it, I am known as Herman Atlan and I forbid it, I am known as Anthony Comstock and I forbid it, I am Indiana Elliot's brother and I forbid it.

Jo the Loiterer. Well well well, I knew that ring of mine was too large, It could not fall off on account of my joints but I knew it was too large.

Indiana Elliot. I renounce my brother.

Jo the Loiterer. That's right my dear that's all right.

Susan B. What is marriage, is marriage protection or religion, is marriage renunciation or abundance, is marriage a stepping-stone or an end. What is marriage.

Anne. I will never marry.

Jenny Reefer. If I marry I will divorce but I will not marry because if I did marry, I would be married.

(Ulysses S. Grant pounds his chair)

Ulysses S. Grant. Didn't I say I do not like noise, I do not like cannon balls, I do not like storms, I do not like talking, I do not

	like noise. I like everything and everybody to be silent and what I like I have. Everybody be silent.
Jo the Loiterer.	I know I was silent, everybody can tell just by listening to me just how silent I am, dear General, dear General Ulysses, dear General Ulysses Simpson dear General Ulysses Simpson Grant, dear dear sir, am I not a perfect example of what you like, am I not silent.

(Ulysses S. Grant's chair pounds and he is silent)

Susan B.	I am not married and the reason why is that I have had to do what I have had to do, I have had to be what I have had to be, I could never be one of two I could never be two in one as married couples do and can, I am but one all one, one and all one, and so I have never been married to any one.
Anne.	But I I have been, I have been married to what you have been to that one.
Susan B.	No no, no, you may be married to the past one, the one that is not the present one, no one can be married to the present one, the one, the one, the present one.
Jenny Reefer.	I understand you undertake to overthrow their undertaking.
Susan B.	I love the sound of these, one over two, two under one, three under four, four over more.
Anne.	Dear Susan B. Anthony thank you.

John Adams.	All this time I have been lost in my thoughts in my thoughts of thee beautiful thee, Constance Fletcher, do you see, I have been lost in my thoughts of thee.
Constance Fletcher.	I am blind and therefore I dream.
Daniel Webster.	Dear Angel More, dear Angel More, there have been men who have stammered and stuttered but not, not I.
Angel More.	Speak louder.
Daniel Webster.	Not I.
The Chorus.	Why the hell don't you all get married, why don't you, we want to go home, why don't you.
Jo the Loiterer.	Why don't you.
Indiana Elliot.	Why don't you.
Indiana Elliot's Brother	Why don't you because I am here.

(The crowd remove him forcibly)

Susan B. Anthony suddenly.	They are married all married and their children women as well as men will have the vote, they will they will, they will have the vote.

Curtain

ACT II, Scene VI

(Susan B. doing her house-work in her house)

Enter Anne.	Susan B. they want you.
Susan B.	Do they
Anne.	Yes. You must go.
Susan B.	No.

Jenny Reefer
   comes in.   Oh yes they want to know if you are here.

Susan B.   Yes still alive. Painters paint and writers write and soldiers drink and fight and I I am still alive.

Anne.   They want you.

Susan B.   And when they have me.

Jenny Reefer.   Then they will want you again.

Susan B.   Yes I know, they love me so, they tell me so and they tell me so, but I, I do not tell them so because I know, they will not do what they could do and I I will be left alone to die but they will not have done what I need to have done to make it right that I live lived my life and fight.

Jo the Loiterer
   at the window.   Indiana Elliot wants to come in, she will not take my name she says it is not all the same, she says that she is Indiana Elliot and that I am Jo, and that she will not take my name and that she will always tell me so. Oh yes she is right of course she is right it is not all the same Indiana Elliot is her name, she is only married to me, but there is no difference that I can see, but all the same there she is and she will not change her name, yes it is all the same.

Susan B.   Let her in.

Indiana Elliot.   Oh Susan B. they want you they have to have you, can I tell them you are coming I have not changed my

	name can I tell them you are coming and that you will do everything.
Susan B.	No but there is no use in telling them so, they won't vote my laws, there is always a clause, there is always a pause, they won't vote my laws.

(Andrew Johnson puts his head in at the door)

Andrew Johnson.	Will the good lady come right along.
Thaddeus Stevens behind him.	We are waiting, will the good lady not keep us waiting, will the good lady not keep us waiting.
Susan B.	You you know so well that you will not vote my laws.
Stevens.	Dear lady remember humanity comes first.
Susan B.	You mean men come first, women, you will not vote my laws, how can you dare when you do not care, how can you dare, there is no humanity in humans, there is only law, and you will not because you know so well that there is no humanity there are only laws, you know it so well that you will not you will not vote my laws.

(Susan B. goes back to her housework.
All the characters crowd in)

Chorus.	Do come Susan B. Anthony do come nobody no nobody can make them come the way you make them come, do come do come Susan B. Anthony, it is your duty, Susan B. Anthony, you know you know your duty, you come, do come, come.

Susan B. Anthony. I suppose I will be coming, is it because you flatter me, is it because if I do not come you will forget me and never vote my laws, you will never vote my laws even if I do come but if I do not come you will never vote my laws, come or not come it always comes to the same thing it comes to their not voting my laws, not voting my laws, tell me all you men tell me you know you will never vote my laws.

All the Men. Dear kind lady we count on you, and as we count on you so can you count on us.

Susan B. Anthony. Yes but I work for you I do, I say never again, never again, never never, and yet I know I do say no but I do not mean no, I know I always hope that if I go that if I go and go and go, perhaps then you men will vote my laws but I know how well I know, a little this way a little that way you steal away, you steal a piece away you steal yourselves away, you do not intend to stay and vote my laws, and still when you call I go, I go, I go, I say no, no, no, and I go, but no, this time no, this time you have to do more than promise, you must write it down that you will vote my laws, but no, you will pay no attention to what is written, well then swear by my hearth, as you hope to have a home and hearth, swear after I work for you swear that you will vote my laws, but no, no oaths, no thoughts, no decisions, no intentions, no gratitude, no convictions, no nothing will make you pass my laws. Tell me can any of you be honest now, and say you will not pass my laws.

Jo the Loiterer. I can I can be honest I can say I will not pass your laws, because you see I have no vote, no loiterer has a vote so it is easy Susan B. Anthony easy for one man among all these men to be honest and to say I will not pass your laws. Anyway Susan B. Anthony what are your laws. Would it really be all right to pass them, if you say so it is all right with me. I have no vote myself but I'll make them as long as I don't have to change my name don't have to don't have to change my name.

T. Stevens. Thanks dear Susan B. Anthony, thanks we all know that whatever happens we all can depend upon you to do your best for any cause which is a cause, and any cause is a cause and because any cause is a cause therefore you will always do your best for any cause, and now you will be doing your best for this cause our cause the cause.

Susan B. Because. Very well is it snowing.
Chorus. Not just now.
Susan B. Anthony. Is it cold.
Chorus. A little.

Susan B. Anthony.	I am not well
Chorus.	But you look so well and once started it will be all right.
Susan B. Anthony.	All right

Curtain

ACT II, Scene VII

(Susan B. Anthony busy with her housework)

Anne comes in.	Oh it was wonderful, wonderful, they listen to nobody the way they listen to you.
Susan B.	Yes it is wonderful as the result of my work for the first time the word male has been written into the constitution of the United States concerning suffrage. Yes it is wonderful.
Anne.	But
Susan B.	Yes but, what is man, what are men, what are they. I do not say that they haven't kind hearts, if I fall down in a faint, they will rush to pick me up, if my house is on fire, they will rush in to put the fire out and help me, yes they have kind hearts but they are afraid, afraid, they are afraid, they are afraid. They fear women, they fear each other, they fear their neighbor, they fear other countries and then they hearten themselves in their fear by crowding together and fol-

lowing each other, and when they crowd together and follow each other they are brutes, like animals who stampede, and so they have written in the name male into the United States constitution, because they are afraid of black men because they are afraid of women, because they are afraid afraid. Men are afraid.

Anne timidly.

And women.

Susan B.

Ah women often have not any sense of danger, after all a hen screams pitifully when she sees an eagle but she is only afraid for her children, men are afraid for themselves, that is the real difference between men and women.

Anne.

But Susan B. why do you not say these things out loud.

Susan B.

Why not, because if I did they would not listen they not alone would not listen they would revenge themselves. Men have kind hearts when they are not afraid but they are afraid afraid afraid. I say they are afraid, but if I were to tell them so their kindness would turn to hate. Yes the Quakers are right, they are not afraid because they do not fight, they do not fight.

Anne.

But Susan B. you fight and you are not afraid.

Susan B.

I fight and I am not afraid, I fight but I am not afraid.

Anne.

And you will win.

Susan B.	Win what, win what.
Anne.	Win the vote for women.
Susan B.	Yes some day some day the women will vote and by that time.
Anne.	By that time oh wonderful time.
Susan B.	By that time it will do them no good because having the vote they will become like men, they will be afraid, having the vote will make them afraid, oh I know it, but I will fight for the right, for the right to vote for them even though they become like men, become afraid like men, become like men.

(Anne bursts into tears. Jenny Reefer rushes in)

Jenny Reefer.	I have just converted Lillian Russell to the cause of woman's suffrage, I have converted her, she will give all herself and all she earns oh wonderful day I know you will say, here she comes isn't she beautiful.

(Lillian Russell comes in followed by all the women in the chorus. Women crowding around, Constance Fletcher in the background)

Lillian Russell.	Dear friends, it is so beautiful to meet you all, so beautiful, so beautiful to meet you all.

(John Adams comes in and sees Constance Fletcher)

John Adams.	Dear friend beautiful friend, there is no beauty where you are not.
Constance Fletcher.	Yes dear friend but look look at real beauty look at Lillian Russell look at real beauty.
John Adams.	Real beauty real beauty is all there is of beauty and why should my eye

wander where no eye can look without having looked before. Dear friend I kneel to you because dear friend each time I see you I have never looked before, dear friend you are an open door.

(Daniel Webster strides in, the women separate)

Daniel Webster.   What what is it, what is it, what is the false and the true and I say to you you Susan B. Anthony, you know the false from the true and yet you will not wait you will not wait, I say you will you will wait. When my eyes, and I have eyes when my eyes, beyond that I seek not to penetrate the veil, why should you want what you have chosen, when mine eyes, why do you want that the curtain may rise, why when mine eyes, why should the vision be opened to what lies behind, why, Susan B. Anthony fight the fight that is the fight, that any fight may be a fight for the right. I hear that you say that the word male should not be written into the constitution of the United States of America, but I say, I say, that so long that the gorgeous ensign of the republic, still full high advanced, its arms and trophies streaming in their original luster not a stripe erased or polluted not a single star obscured.

Jo the Loiterer.   She has decided to change her name.

Indiana Elliot.   Not because it is his name but it is such a pretty name, Indiana Loiterer is such a pretty name I think all the same he will have to change his name, he must be Jo Elliot, yes he must, it is what he has to do, he has to be Jo Elliot and I am going to be Indiana Loiterer, dear friends, all friends is it not a lovely name, Indiana Loiterer all the same.

Jo the Loiterer. All right I never fight, nobody will know it's men, but what can I do, if I am not she and I am not me, what can I do, if a name is not true, what can I do but do as she tells me.

All the Chorus. She is quite right, Indiana Loiterer is so harmonious, so harmonious, Indiana Loiterer is so harmonious.

All the Men Come In. What did she say.

Jo. I was talking not she but nobody no nobody ever wants to listen to me.

All the Chorus
Men and Women. Susan B. Anthony was very successful we are all very grateful to Susan B. Anthony because she was so successful, she worked for the votes for women and she worked for the vote for colored men and she was so successful, they wrote the word male into the constitution of the United States of America, dear Susan B. Anthony. Dear Susan B., whenever she wants to be and she always wants to be she is always so successful so very successful.

Susan B. So successful.
Curtain

ACT II, Scene VIII

(The Congressional Hall, the replica of the statue of Susan
   B. Anthony and her comrades in the suffrage fight)
Anne alone in front
    of the statuary.   The Vote. Women have the vote.
                         They have it each and every one, it is
                         glorious glorious glorious.
Susan B. Anthony
    behind the statue.   Yes women have the vote, all my long
                         life of strength and strife, all my long
                         life, women have it, they can vote,
                         every man and every woman have
                         the vote, the word male is not there
                         any more, that is to say, that is to
                         say.
(Silence. Virgil T. comes in very nicely, he looks around
              and sees Anne)
Virgil T.   Very well indeed, very well indeed,
                         you are looking very well indeed,
                         have you a chair anywhere, very well
                         indeed, as we sit, we sit, some day
                         very soon some day they will vote
                         sitting and that will be a very suc-
                         cessful day any day, every day.
(Henry B. comes in. He looks all around at the statue and
              then he sighs)
Henry B.   Does it really mean that women are
                         as white and cold as marble does it
                         really mean that.
(Angel More comes in and bows gracefully to the sculp-
              tured group)
Angel More.   I can always think of dear Daniel
                         Webster daily.
(John Adams comes in and looks around, and then

carefully examines the statue)

John Adams. I think that they might have added dear delicate Constance Fletcher I do think they might have added her wonderful profile, I do think they might have, I do, I really do.

(Andrew Johnson shuffles in)

Andrew Johnson. I have no hope in black or white in white or black in black or white or white, no hope.

(Thaddeus Stevens comes in, he does not address any-body, he stands before the statue and frowns)

Thaddeus S. Rob the cradle, rob it, rob the rob-ber, rob him, rob whatever there is to be taken, rob, rob the cradle, rob it.

Daniel Webster (he sees nothing else).

Angel More, more more Angel More, did you hear me, can you hear shall you hear me, when they come and they do come, when they go and they do go, Angel More can you will you shall you may you might you would you hear me, when they have lost and won, when they have won and lost, when words are bitter and snow is white, Angel More come to me and we will leave together.

Angel More. Dear sir, not leave, stay.

Henrietta M. I have never been mentioned again. (She curtseys)

Constance Fletcher. Here I am, I am almost blind but here I am, dear dear here I am, I cannot see what is so white, here I am.

John Adams (kissing her hand).

> Here you are, blind as a bat and beautiful as a bird, here you are, white and cold as marble, beautiful as marble, yes that is marble but you you are the living marble dear Constance Fletcher, you are.

Constance Fletcher.

> Thank you yes I am here, blind as a bat, I am here.

Indiana Elliot.

> I am sorry to interrupt so sorry to interrupt but I have a great deal to say about marriage, either one or the other married must be economical, either one or the other, if either one or the other of a married couple are economical then a marriage is successful, if not not, I have a great deal to say about marriage, and dear Susan B. Anthony was never married, how wonderful it is to be never married how wonderful. I have a great deal to say about marriage.

Susan B. Anthony
voice from behind
the statue.

> It is a puzzle, I am not puzzled but it is a puzzle, if there are no children there are no men and women, and if there are men and women, it is rather horrible, and if it is rather horrible, then there are children, I am not puzzled but it is very puzzling, women and men vote and children, I am not puzzled but it is very puzzling.

Gloster Heming.

> I have only been a man who has a

very fine name, and it must be said I made it up yes I did, so many do why not I, so many do, so many do, and why not two, when anybody might, and you can vote and you can dote with any name. Thank you.

Isabel Wentworth. They looked for me and they found me, I like to talk about it. It is very nearly necessary not to be noisy not to be noisy and hope, hope and hop, no use in enjoying men and women no use, I wonder why we are all happy, yes.

Annie Hope. There is another Anne and she believes, I am hopey hope and I do not believe I have been in California and Kalamazoo, and I do not believe I burst into tears and I do not believe.

(They all crowd closer together and Lillian Russell who comes in stands quite alone)

Lillian Russell. I can act so drunk that I never drink, I can drink so drunk that I never act, I have a curl I was a girl and I am old and fat but very handsome for all that.

(Anthony Comstock comes in and glares at her)

Anthony Comstock. I have heard that they have thought that they would wish that one like you could vote a vote and help to let the ones who want do what they like, I have heard that even you, and I am through, I cannot hope that there is dope, oh yes a horrid word. I have never heard, short.

Jenny Reefer. I have hope and faith, not charity no

	not charity, I have hope and faith, no not, not charity, no not charity.
Ulysses S. Grant.	Women are women, soldiers are soldiers, men are not men, lies are not lies, do, and then a dog barks, listen to him and then a dog barks, a dog barks a dog barks any dog barks, listen to him any dog barks. (he sits down)
Herman Atlan.	I am not loved any more, I was loved oh yes I was loved but I am not loved any more, I am not, was I not, I knew I would refuse what a woman would choose and so I am not loved any more, not loved any more.
Donald Gallup.	Last but not least, first and not best, I am tall as a man, I am firm as a clam, and I never change, from day to day.

(Jo the Loiterer and Chris a Citizen)

Jo the Loiterer.	Let us dance and sing, Chrissy Chris, wet and not in debt, I am a married man and I know how I show I am a married man. She votes, she changes her name and she votes.

(They all crowd together in front of the statue, there is a moment of silence and then a chorus)

Chorus.	To vote the vote, the vote we vote, can vote do vote will vote could vote, the vote the vote.
Jo the Loiterer.	I am the only one who cannot vote, no loiterer can vote.
Indiana Elliot.	I am a loiterer Indiana Loiterer and I can vote.
Jo the Loiterer.	You only have the name, you have

	not got the game.
Chorus.	The vote the vote we will have the vote.
Lillian Russell.	It is so beautiful to meet you all here so beautiful.
Ulysses S. Grant.	Vote the vote, the army does not vote, the general generals, there is no vote, bah vote.
The Chorus.	The vote we vote we note the vote.

(They all bow and smile to the statue. Suddenly Susan B.'s voice is heard)

| Susan B.'s voice. | We cannot retrace our steps, going forward may be the same as going backwards. We cannot retrace our steps, retrace our steps. All my long life, all my life, we do not retrace our steps, all my long life, but. |

(A silence a long silence)

But—we do not retrace our steps, all my long life, and here, here we are here, in marble and gold, did I say gold, yes I said gold, in marble and gold and where—

(A silence)

Where is where. In my long life of effort and strife, dear life, life is strife, in my long life, it will not come and go, I tell you so, it will stay it will pay but

(A long silence)

But do I want what we have got, has it not gone, what made it live, has it not gone because now it is had, in my long life in my long life

(Silence)

Life is strife, I was a martyr all my life
not to what I won but to what was
done.
    (Silence)
Do you know because I tell you so, or
do you know, do you know.
    (Silence)
My long life, my long life.

Curtain

By Gertrude Stein

Yes Is For A Very Young Man

(excerpt)

ANNOUNCER. Attention, attention, attention, Paris is free. Attention, attention, Paris is free.

CONSTANCE. I don't care what Henry says, that is the reward of my work.

(OLYMPE *and* CLOTHILDE *enter the room*)

CLOTHILDE. Oh Mademoiselle, is it true, is it, is it true that Paris is free.

OLYMPE. Georges Poupet just called out that Paris is free.

CONSTANCE. (*Kissing them on both cheeks*) Yes, my dears, it is true, where is Georges, I want to kiss him, Georges.

GEORGES. (*Coming in*) Yes, Mademoiselle, it is true, Paris is free and we are free, we have just shot fifty Boches that were left in the marshes, shot them like rabbits, they are like rabbits, when they do not win they run like rabbits and we shoot them like rabbits. I shot five. Shot them dead, all five of them.

CLOTHILDE. Of course you did, you good brave Georges.

OLYMPE. We heard you shoot them.

CLOTHILDE. When we remember how they occupied this house in forty and how they slept in the house.

OLYMPE. And took sunbaths all naked on the lawn.

CLOTHILDE. And then the day of the Armistice, the beasts.

OLYMPE. We were just two sad lonely old women.

CLOTHILDE. And they put their phonograph in front of our

kitchen door and it blared out all their horrible German songs.

OLYMPE. And each one would come into the kitchen and call out-

CLOTHILDE. France Kaput. And we just wouldn't cry in front of them.

OLYMPE. No we just wouldn't.

CLOTHILDE. And they broke open our trunks and they stole all our shoes and stockings.

OLYMPE. All we had.

CLOTHILDE. Oh the dirty beasts, Germany Kaput.

OLYMPE. Germany Kaput.

CLOTHILDE. Oh Georges.

OLYMPE. Oh Mademoiselle.

(*They both fall weeping*)

Yes, now we can cry, now they are gone, gone forever.

CLOTHILDE. Yes, now we can cry, now we can.

CONSTANCE. (*Patting them both*) Now pull yourselves together, we have to make flags, French flags and American flags and English flags and Russian flags.

GEORGES. No use in making them, Mademoiselle, you can buy them, and American and French flag ribbon.

CONSTANCE. From whom?

GEORGES. (*Laughing*) From the bazaar, the biggest collabo in this town, the one who said everybody should send their sons to Germany to help the Germans and he was consistent enough, he sent his. He has his store full of flags. French flags, English flags and ribbons, no, no Russian flags. Everybody is in there buying them, he is just coining money.

CONSTANCE. Will I ever understand? But Georges, where did he get them?

GEORGES. Get them, he always had them, he was sure the Germans were going to win but he kept them all, well he always keeps everything. I suppose some of them were left over from the last war and now he is as pleased as anything to have them and to sell them and everybody is as pleased as anything to buy them.

CONSTANCE. But Georges, how is it that the Germans did not find them?

GEORGES. Because he had them put away, hid them if you like, but what difference would it make. The Germans, bah, the Germans, they never found anything.

CONSTANCE. Well all of you go to that collabo and buy a lot of them and we will cover the house with them and lots of ribbon for the children.

(*They all go out.* DENISE *comes rushing in*)

DENISE. Hello Constance.

CONSTANCE. Are you pleased, Denise, pleased that Paris is free?

DENISE. Of course, of course, well yes, of course, although, well yes, of course, do you know Constance, Achille is joining the army, he says that he will help the Americans beat Japan.

CONSTANCE. He does say that does he. Well you can tell him from me, that the Americans don't want him, they won't have him. You can tell him that from me.

DENISE. What do you mean, won't have him? They have to have him, the French army wants him, of course they want him, he has written to his old captain to tell him he is ready to join him. My gracious not want an aviator who has brought down six enemy planes. Of course they will want him.

CONSTANCE. (*Angrily*) I tell you they don't want him and they won't have him. The French army can take him if they want him, we don't. But anyway Denise, what does he want to fight for now, why doesn't he stick to his opinions?

DENISE. Of course you don't understand, you never understand. As long as the Marshal was at the head of the government, he obeyed the Marshal, any good soldier would and now that the Marshal is not any longer at the head of the government, why naturally Achille obeys the man who is at present at the head of the government and so he joins the army. Anybody ought to be able to understand that.

CONSTANCE. So Achille is just like a dog, when you tell him to come to heel he comes to heel and when you tell him to fight, he fights. What's the use of being a man if you are going to be like that, what is the use? Well I can tell you the American army does not want anybody like that fighting with them. I don't much think the French army does either.

DENISE. You are just jealous, you don't know anybody who has ever brought down six airplanes.

CONSTANCE. And did not wear his decorations because he was so modest although everybody knew about it.

DENISE. You are horrible, I always hated you but when America was not successful I did not care so much but now that America is successful, that she has gotten rid of the dear Marshal, that she has opened the door to Bolshevism, that she hates the aristocracy, I tell you Constance, I just hate you, hate you and all Americans, I hate you.

CONSTANCE. And still Achille wants to fight side by side with them.

DENISE. Well, if he does it is because he does because as a soldier he does.

CONSTANCE. There is no use talking, Denise, they won't have him. Nothing could make me believe the French army would have him. No I don't believe they would have him in spite of his six airplanes. No, all this time, well we did not say much, but now France is free we tell each other what we really think. No the French army does not want Achille.

DENISE. You beast, if they don't take him I know it will be your fault, the fault of those awful Americans, and it will break my mother's heart and it will disappoint Achille, and never, never, never, no never will I speak to you again, no never.

(*She rushes out.* CONSTANCE *sits down heavily*)

CONSTANCE. Oh, my gracious.

(OLYMPE *and* CLOTHILDE *come in with arms full of flags*)

CLOTHILDE. Oh, Mademoiselle, just think there are lots of little children in this town who have never seen any flag.

OLYMPE. Not any kind of a flag, not even a Boche flag.

CLOTHILDE. You know they never carried flags, we don't know why but they never did and little children who are now five and six years old have never seen a flag.

OLYMPE. And certainly never seen a French flag. You should have seen, they touched the flags so timidly.

CLOTHILDE. And one little one wanted to know what it was.

OLYMPE. And we knew you would like it and we pinned pieces of American ribbon on each one and then we made them stand up in front of the French flag and say, "Vive la France."

CLOTHILDE. "Honor to the Marquis."

OLYMPE. And the darlings, they all said it.

CLOTHILDE. And we were so happy and they are so happy and it is all so wonderful.

OLYMPE. We are free and everybody's eyes are all smiling.

CLOTHILDE. Oh dear me.

(*They both begin to cry*)

OLYMPE. Yes.

(*They both begin to laugh*)

CLOTHILDE. We can cry now all we want.

OLYMPE. Yes, Mademoiselle, we can.

(HENRY *enters*)

HENRY. Hello you old dears, my gracious, you have gotten flags, has the old collabo any left now that you have bought out the collection. Well, hang them out, hang them out.

(OLYMPE *and* CLOTHILDE *exit with flags*)

CONSTANCE. Henry, I have just had a dreadful quarrel with Denise, a really dreadful quarrel.

HENRY. (*Pouring himself a drink*) Did you? Well one does and one does not but one mostly does, did you?

CONSTANCE. Yes, Henry and this time really this time we probably will never speak to each other again.

HENRY. Well, perhaps not and then perhaps you will. You never can tell.

CONSTANCE. Henry, don't be so unfeeling.

HENRY. Unfeeling and I have just come from a wonderful family scene, Denise was not there, she was busy quarreling with you but all the rest of them were there.

CONSTANCE. And Achille.

HENRY. Achille, my gracious, poor Achille, he is holding his head and surrounded with papers he must sign to get back into the army. But in every one there is the question, what did you do for the resistance. No, they don't say, what did you do in the great war, daddy, but what did you do for the resistance. And, oh my goodness, Achille, what did he.

CONSTANCE. Well then he won't be taken into the army.

HENRY. Not unless he finds out that he did do something for the resistance. You never can tell perhaps he will find out that he did something for the resistance, perhaps he will.

CONSTANCE. Oh Henry, it is so awful now we are all so happy and we are all quarreling. Oh Henry it is awful.

HENRY. Why not, if not why not. Oh you ought to see them. You see now of course, now there is going to be communism, anyway that is the way they feel about it and they think, the old mother thinks, of course the old father never thinks anything, the old mother thinks she better divide up the property among the children so the communists won't notice as they might if it was all together, but she hates to let go. How she hates to let go.

CONSTANCE. And what do you get, Henry?

HENRY. Well, as the most unpopular son-in-law I only get a duck pond with the meadow around it. My, it's funny. Hello, if there isn't Ferdinand. Come in, Ferdinand, well, well.

CONSTANCE. Ferdinand.

HENRY. Yes, there he is.

(FERDINAND *comes in*)

FERDINAND. Paris is free.

HENRY. As if we didn't know it. Yes, Paris is free. Have you said goodbye up at the house, Ferdinand?

FERDINAND. Yes, I have said goodbye.

HENRY. Well, so long, old man.

FERDINAND. So long.

(HENRY *embraces* FERDINAND *and goes*)

CONSTANCE. Why are you saying goodbyes up at the house?

FERDINAND. Because goodbyes have to be said.

CONSTANCE. Ferdinand, you know I have had a dreadful quarrel with Denise and I do not really think that we will ever speak to each other again.

FERDINAND. Does that really matter, Constance?

CONSTANCE. Ferdinand, what do you mean?

FERDINAND. Why should it matter, it's all over. You will never see any of us again, you won't see Henry. Henry loves his wife and adores his little girl and it's all over and that is all there is when it's all over.

CONSTANCE. Is it really all over?

FERDINAND. Yes, really all over. You will go back to the quays of Paris and sooner or later to roasted chickens.

CONSTANCE. And you, Ferdinand?

FERDINAND. Ah, this time I do disappear.

CONSTANCE. Disappear, where to?

FERDINAND. Hush, you did say that yes is for a very young man. You must not ask but I'll tell you just the same, to Germany. No I do not go back there to work, but I am being sent to organize my fellow countrymen.

CONSTANCE. Ferdinand.

FERDINAND. Yes, Constance, this is our war, you have done your share, your countrymen will fight some more, but this is our war, our war, and we will fight it and we will win.

CONSTANCE. Yes, I know, and so it is all over.

FERDINAND. Yes, look facts in the face, Constance, for you it is all over, for Henry it is all over, but for me it is just beginning, yes is for a very young man.

CONSTANCE. Yes, Ferdinand, yes Ferdinand.

FERDINAND. I won't have time to think so I won't think about you and the quays of Paris and the roast chickens and Henry and Denise and the little girl who looks like me, no I won't have time to think. Goodbye, Constance.

CONSTANCE. (*Extending her hand*) Goodbye Ferdinand.

  (FERDINAND *shakes her hand, then kisses it and leaves*)

Curtain

By Gertrude Stein

The Making of Americans

(excerpt)

This is then complete disillusionment in living, the complete realisation that no one can believe as you do about anything, so not really any single one and to some as I am saying this is a sad thing, to mostly every one it is sometime a shocking thing, sometimes a shocking thing, sometime a real shock to them, to mostly every one a thing that only very slowly with constant repetition is really a complete certain thing inside to give to them the being that is no longer in them really young being. This is then the real meaning of not being any longer a young one in living, the complete realising that not any one really can believe what any other one is believing and some there are, enough of them, who never have completely such a realisation, they are always hoping to find her or him, they are always changing her or him to fit them, they are always looking, they are always forgetting failing or explaining it by something, they are always going on and on in trying. There are a very great many of them who are this way to their ending. There are a very great many who are this way almost to their very ending, there are a great many men and women who have sometime in them in their living complete disillusion.

This is then a very little description of feeling disillusionment in living. There is this thing then there is the moment and a very complete moment to those that have had it when something they have bought or made or loved or are is a thing that they are afraid, almost certain, very fearful that no one will think it a nice thing and then some one likes that thing and this then is a very wonderful feeling to know that some one really appreciates the thing. This is a very wonderful thing, this is a thing which I will now be illustrating.

Disillusionment in living is the finding out nobody agrees with you not those that are and were fighting with you. Disillusionment in living is the finding out nobody agrees with you not those that are fighting for you. Complete disillusionment is when you realise that no one can for they can't change. The amount they agree is important to you until the amount they do not agree with you is completely realised by you. Then you say you will write for yourself and strangers, you will be for yourself and strangers and this then makes an old man or an old woman of you.

It is a very strange feeling when one is loving a clock that is to every one of your class of living an ugly and a foolish one and one really likes such a thing and likes it very much and liking it is a serious thing, or one likes a colored handkerchief that is very gay and every one of your kind of living thinks it a very ugly or a foolish thing and thinks you like it because it is a funny thing to like it and you like it with a serious feeling, or you like eating something and liking it is a childish thing to every one or you like something that is a dirty thing and no one can really like that thing or you write a book and while you write it you are ashamed for every one must think you are a silly or a crazy one and yet you write it and you are ashamed, you know you will be laughed at or pitied by every one and you have a queer feeling and you are not very certain and you go on writing. Then some one says yes to it, to something you are liking, or doing or making and then never again can you have completely such a feeling of being afraid and ashamed that you had then when you were writing or liking the thing and not any one had said yes about the thing. In a way it is a very difficult thing to like anything, to do anything. You can never have again either about something you have done or about something any one else has done the same complete feeling if some one else besides the first one sees it, some other one if you have made it, yourself if you have understood something, you can never again have the complete feeling of recognition that you have then. You can have very many kinds of feelings you can only alone and with the first one have the perfect feeling of not being almost completely filled with being ashamed and afraid to show something to like something with a really serious feeling.

It is a very queer thing this not agreeing with any one. It would seem that where we are each of us always telling and repeating and explaining and doing it again and again that some one would really understand what the other one is always repeating. But in loving, in working, in everything it is always the same thing. In loving some one is jealous, really jealous and it would seem an impossible thing to the one not understanding that the other one could have about such a thing a jealous feeling and they have it and they suffer and they weep and sorrow in it and the other one cannot believe it, they cannot believe the other one can really mean it and sometime the other one perhaps comes to realise it that the other one can really suffer in it and then later that one tries to reassure the other one the one that is then suffering about that thing and the other one the one that is receiving such reassuring says then, did you think I ever could believe this thing, no I have no fear of such a thing, and it is all puzzling, to have one kind of feeling, a jealous feeling, and not have a fear in them that the other one does not want them, it is a very mixing thing and over and over again when you are certain it is a whole one some one, one must begin again and again and the only thing that is a help to one is that there is really so little fundamental changing in any one and always every one is repeating big pieces of them and so sometime perhaps some one will know something and I certainly would like very much to be that one and so now to begin.

It happens very often that a man has it in him, that a man does something, that he does it very often that he does many things, when he is a young man when he is an old man, when he is an older man. Some kind of young men do things because they are so good then they want every one to be wise enough to take care of themselves and so they do some things to them. This is very common and these then are very often good enough kind of young men who are very good men in their living. There will soon be a little description of one of them. There are then very many men and there is then from the generalised virtue and concrete action that is from the nature of them that might make one think they were hypocrites in living but they are not although certainly there are in living some men wanting to deceive other men but this is not true of this kind of them. One of such of these kind of them had a little boy and this one, the little son wanted to make a collection of butterflies and beetles and it was all exciting to him and it was all arranged then and then the father said to the son you are certain this is not a cruel thing that you are wanting to be doing, killing things to make collections of them, and the son was very disturbed then and they talked about it together the two of them and more and more they talked about it then and then at last the boy was convinced it was a cruel thing and he said he would not do it and his father said the little boy was a noble boy to give up pleasure when it was a cruel one. The boy went to bed then and then the father when he got up in the early morning saw a wonderfully beautiful moth in the room and he caught him and he killed him and he pinned him and he woke up his son then and showed it to him and said to him "see what a good father I am to have caught and killed this one," the boy was all mixed up inside him and then he said he would go on with his collecting and that was all there was then of discussing and this is a little description of something that happened once and it is very interesting.

It happens very often that a man has it in him, that he does things, that he does something, that he does many things when he is a young man and an older man and an old man, that he feels always in a way about everything, that he is a good enough man in living, that he is a very good man.

The thing that is the important thing now in this part of the long history of a family's being is the kind of being in Alfred Hersland and in Mr. Henry Dehning. The thing that is the important thing to be understanding is being good in being and in living. To begin then now about being a good one, about all the kinds of ways of being a good one men and women have in them, all the kinds of ways I can think about them now in writing and the funny ways it can come out of many of them.

Being good in living is something, it is in some way mostly in every one, it is a very peculiar thing sometimes, and sometimes not a very peculiar thing. Being good in living is certainly a very important thing, it is in some way mostly in every one, in some way in very many women and in very many men it makes them what they are in living, it makes very many what they are to every one and to themselves in all their living. Being in some ways a good one is very common, it is a very common thing, it is in some way in very many men and in very many women.

There are many then believing thinking knowing feeling doing things, mostly every one is feeling knowing thinking doing something, doing feeling believing knowing thinking a very great many things that if any one really knew it about them any one knowing them would be thinking that one a crazy one, would be afraid of such a one, and no one knowing that one is thinking such a one really a seriously crazy one and that is because mostly every one does not really believe any other one really believes thinks knows feels does the thing, the many things that one really does do, think, feel, believe, know in living. Sometimes it is a funny thing to know it about some one the things they really can know and feel and believe and do and think in them, sometimes it is a very puzzling sometimes it is a very frightening thing, sometimes it is an impossible thing and mostly every one is contenting themselves with feeling that that other one is not really feeling thinking doing knowing believing the thing the things they are doing knowing believing or thinking that they never did have such things in them that they are just talking that it is really all different in them. One once who was a very intelligent active bright well-read fairly well experienced woman thought that what happens every month to all women, she thought it only happened to Plymouth Brethren, women having that religion. She was a child of Plymouth Brethren and had only known very intimately Plymouth Brethren women. She had known other women but it had not happened to her to have known about this thing. She was a child of Plymouth Brethren and she thought that what happens to all women every month only happened to Plymouth Brethren women, women having that religion, she was twenty eight years old when she learned that it happened to every kind of women. This is not an astonishing thing that she should have believed this thing. Every one mostly always is thinking feeling believing knowing something that is to every one else when they know it about them a thing no one that was not a crazy one would be thinking feeling believing or knowing. Mostly every one can be content with being certain that the other one never did believe that thing.

There are a very great men and women and they are very well educated intelligent ones who are very certain that a river can not flow north because water can never be going up hill in a natural way of flowing. They are very certain of this thing and when one understands it about them, some of them, it is astonishing that they can really be thinking such a thing and sometimes it takes almost a quarrelling to make them realise that a river can flow north and that north is not going up hill. They are knowing then that north is not going up hill when they think of it as travelling, they think of north as up hill when they think of it as water flowing and this is very common. Such things then are very common, every kind of way there ever can be of thinking feeling believing knowing doing is common and the way mostly every one has it in them the way one has it in them of knowing feeling, believing thinking doing is a thing that every one knowing that one if they really thought that one was really believing feeling thinking knowing doing as that one really is, was and will be thinking feeling doing believing knowing would be thinking that one a crazy one, that one a fool, that one a liar and a bad one, would be afraid or hating or despising or pitying that one or completely puzzled by that one. Mostly then no one really is ever believing any other one really can be believing feeling thinking doing knowing, the things the other one really is feeling believing thinking doing knowing.

Kinds of being in women and in men is a peculiar thing, that there are always the same kinds of them existing is a peculiar thing. That there are so very many always existing of each kind of them is a peculiar thing. That there are so very many always existing of every kind of them is a peculiar thing. When one sees a very great many of any thing, if it is jewels, or exotic fruits or old furniture or any precious thing in any place then always one is thinking they must be cheap there, they have so many of them it must be that they are selling them cheap they have so many of them and one mostly always has this feeling and this is the kind of feeling very many men and women have about men and women, there are so many they must be cheap things and one can use them any way one can be wanting them without any thinking about them and this is a very natural thing and then when it is a store and one wants to buy the rare thing or something

where they have so many of them and then one finds out one
has to pay them the same as in the stores where there are only
a few of these things that they have for selling and that is
always astonishing, that is to some always a certain shock to
them and this is now beginning to be very true of men and
women everywhere where men and women are living, they
come just as high where there are a great many of them as
where there are a few of them. But this is another thing,
always to my feeling there are a very great many men and
women always existing, always to my feeling there are a very
great many of each kind of them always existing, always to
my feeling each one of them is an expensive thing to be
learning to be understanding and now I begin again.

There are a very great many then that have as a concrete
realisation always in them that dead is dead, that things are
as they see them, that they are doing things when they are
doing them and these then can have it in them that they
realise as a generalisation that to be dead is not to be so very
really dead, that things are not perhaps what they are to
them, that they are living with other men around them who
have it in them to have religion in them which is certain that
to be dead is not to be a really dead one and these then have
it in them to equilibrate themselves to this opinion, the
opinion the conviction of being not dead when they are dead
of having virtue in them when they are not doing any good
thing of never doing anything any good man cannot be doing
when really they are doing that thing very often and this is a
generalised sense in them all through their living and always
then they are really living the dead is dead living as a concrete
living. To some having this equilibrating, this generalised
conception is only sentimental in them, in some it is a way of
being important to themselves inside them to make it strongly
in them this generalised equilibration in them, to very many
it is a very simple thing of being like every one for every one
to mostly any one is like this in their living is being of a con-

viction that dead is not really dead, that good is progressing, that every one is a good one in some way of endeavoring. This is a very common thing then and always and always it will in its simple in its complicated forms will be interesting, will be illuminating in the being and the living of Alfred Hersland and Mr. Herman Dehning and his son George Dehning.

There are many ways of being and of loving and of winning and of losing, and having honor in them, and horror of something, and religion in them and virtuous feeling being believing and thinking in them from the nature of them when this is strong enough in them to make their own in men and women. Sometimes some one to every one is strong enough to make his own or her own living thinking feeling being loving, horror, working and religion and virtuous feeling and this is not then true of that one, this one is one having anticipating suggestion and then being like a resounding board to the suggestion they were anticipating and so giving it forth then so that to themselves then and mostly to every one they are strong to do their own living, to make their own opinion and virtue and working and thinking and loving and religion and this will soon now be some description of such a one. Some then can make their own honor, and virtue and work and thinking and loving and religion. Some can make their own horror, some their own loving, some their own religion, some are weak and can do one thing their own, some are strong enough and all of it is some one else's thinking, feeling, doing, religion, virtue in them, they are strong enough men and women. There are some can just resist and not make their own anything. Some out of their own virtue make a god who sometimes later is a nuisance to them, a terror perhaps to them, a difficult thing to be forgetting. Some are controlled by other's virtue and religion and that scares them, it is a superstition to them and always after it is a scared part of them. Some like religion, some forget it, some are it, some have a prejudice against it. There are many who love themselves enough to not want to lose themselves from living, to not want other people, existence to lose them, to very many women, to very many men this comes to be as a religion in them, this makes religion a real thing to them. Some love themselves so much immortality can have no meaning for them, the younger David Hersland was such a one, there will be a long history of him sometime written. Some love themselves negatively and they like thinking about immortal living. Some love themselves or other ones so forcibly in them that death can have no meaning as an ending, these are then certain of existing, these then are made to have religion, that is certain, some do not have it then in them, really they are certain that every one is continuing, they may not know it as religion, they mostly all of them sometime know it in them. Some love themselves so completely or some other one that they think they exist when they don't, will exist when they won't, are in communication with them when they certainly are not, some of these do not make it as a religion, they have it as a conviction as a certainty in them, these have a future life feeling in their present living. This is pretty common. Some have fervent loving in them for themselves or some one with very much fear in them and some of such of them have religion in them and very many of such of them have none.

There must be much alternating all through in this writing of preparing to be describing Alfred Hersland and the living in him and Julia Dehning who came later to be marrying him. These two then will be mostly all of them in this part of this writing and always I am alternating between them and always a little preparing understanding one and a little preparing understanding the other one and so sometime perhaps everything will come to be showing something and that will be then a happy ending of all this beginning.

All this describing then of virtuous being, feeling, knowing, thinking, in men and in women makes it right now to begin the complete understanding and description of the living and the being in Alfred Hersland and every one important in his living.

There have been then now, been in this description, the three generations of men and women. There was then Mr. and Mrs. Hissen and the old Mr. and Mrs. Hersland, there was then Mr. and Mrs. David Hersland and these then had three children Martha and Alfred and David and the history of Martha has been now already mostly written, not completely altogether written but a good deal written and now there will be beginning to be written the history of Alfred Hersland and every one he ever came to know in his early living, in his marrying and in his later living.

There was then Mr. Hissen and Mrs. Hissen and Alfred Hersland had it in him to have a good deal in him Mr. Hissen being but it was a very different thing in him this being in him than it was in Mr. Hissen. Alfred never had in him at any time in him religion, he was a mixture then of old Mr. Hissen and old Mr. Hersland who was a butcher when he was a young man working and who was a man who had important feeling in him from having been a little important then in religion. Alfred Hersland then, to be certain of the being in him, was of the resisting kind of them in men and women and now then I will wait again and soon then I will be full up with him, I am now then not completely full up with him. Now I am again beginning waiting to be full up completely full up with him. I am very considerably full up now with the kind of being in him, I will be waiting and then I will be full up with all the being in him, that is certain, and so then now a little again once more then I am waiting waiting to be filled up full completely with him with all the being ever in him.

There are then some living who are saying that to be a dead one is to be really a dead one and these then are not very certain that to be a dead one is to be really a dead one. They are then some who have it in them that dead is dead and these then are not very certain that to be dead is to be a dead one. There are then very many who in living have it in them that dead is dead and these then are not certain that to be a dead one is to be a really entirely completely certainly altogether dead one. There are very many then of these always living, perhaps Alfred Hersland was one of this kind of them. Perhaps he is of this kind of men. Perhaps he is not this kind of a one, not one of this kind of them of women and men. Anyway this much is certain, he was of the resisting kind of them, he is of the resisting kind of men, of the dependent independent kind of them. He is certainly of the engulfing resisting kind in men and women.

I am very nearly full up with him with Alfred Hersland and his kind in men and women. It is all filling in me now to over flowing. Alfred Hersland was a very little one and then a child and then a boy then. He learned to understand talking and answering and it was surprising when he began this thing as it is with every one. Once one sees a little one and he is not understanding anything any one says to him and he is not trying to do anything and then in a very little while a couple of months of living and he is understanding and answering and is trying to have things, that he can have a liking for then and that is a very certain thing and Alfred Hersland had this in him and later then he was a boy in his living and then he was coming to be a very young man and he had it then in him to be wanting to be helping his sister to have freedom so then he was very certain and he wanted to be helping and to be instructing and to be a good deal an example to his brother who was a younger one and he was then beginning resisting for every one to his father then, and his mother then had about him a strong feeling of worrying when he was a little late for dinner in the evening and later to be missing him when he had left them to go to Bridgepoint for his college education and he was then certain he was a man devoted to everything and every one and he always wrote to every one then to be good ones and he was a man then and then very much later he was marrying Julia Dehning and all this then was in him as much later living and in the beginning he was a little baby and then beginning understanding and talking and then a boy then and then a boy coming to be going to be a very young man and then he was full up with public feeling for every one living in the house with him, his sister, his brother, his father, his mother, every one, in the beginning then he was a very little one, this is now then the beginning of the complete history of the being and the living of him.

It is a nice thing, it is mostly pleasant for every one when the eldest son is the eldest of the children, in family living. This was not the case with Alfred Hersland, he was the eldest son, he was not the oldest of the three Hersland children, Martha was the oldest of them, it is very certain that mostly in family living it is a pleasanter thing when the oldest one of the children is the oldest son, this most generally is pleasanter for every one, for that one who is the oldest one, it is not such a pleasant thing for that one when a woman a girl a sister is the older one when he is the oldest son, this mostly then makes it a little a difficult thing when he is a son and not the oldest one of the children, in family living. Very often in family living when one is not the oldest of the three children but is the oldest son, very often then he is such a one as I am soon going to be describing as Alfred Hersland. Very often in family living when one is not the oldest of the children but is the oldest son, very often then that one is such a one as Alfred Hersland was in his living. I know now three of such of them who have it in them to be of the kind of them that Alfred Hersland is and who have it in their living that they were the oldest son and that they had a sister who was a few years older and that put them in a position that I will now soon be describing in the early living, in the beginning of being a young man in the living of Alfred Hersland.

Alfred Hersland then is now to every one a young one, this

is now a history of him. He was a good enough looking one, many said he was a very good looking one.

Sometimes in reading, sometimes in thinking, sometimes in realising, sometimes in a kind of a way in feeling, knowing repeating knowing always everything is repeating, knowing that there will be going on living is saddening. Sometime then in reading, in realising anything, a little sometimes in feeling something it is saddening to be thinking, feeling, realising that always everything, is repeating, that sometime some one is a young one and that now some one is in their middle living and that now some one is an old one and sometimes it is a queer feeling in one this and then not anything, not writing, reading, dying, being a dead one, living, being a young one, being one is a real thing inside in one then and always then it is certain that always every one is living and every one has their being in them and every one is feeling thinking knowing something and always then it is certain that every one is like some other one and everything is existing and it is saddening then and existing is not a real thing then to some one feeling then every one as existing and being themselves inside them and some one being like some one and each one being either a young one or a middle aged one or an old one and sometimes then this is a little a dreary thing and sometimes then it is a very queer thing and mostly then it is all then something and mostly then it is certain that everything is existing and mostly then it is inside in some one that not anything is a real thing, that it is dreary to be writing.

Always then Alfred Hersland had a being in him that now I am beginning describing. Always Alfred Hersland was living to his ending. This is the being then that is in every one, they are existing until there is an end of them. Each one has their own being in them, each one is of a kind in men and women. Alfred Hersland was of a kind of men and women as I was saying, he was the eldest son but not the eldest child as I was saying and that had some effect on him as I was saying it does have on those that are eldest sons but not the eldest child in family living, and Alfred Hersland was all through his early living living with poor people near him and in a way he was of them, he did things with them as I will now be telling and then he left home to go to Bridgepoint for his college training and before that he was at the stage of being very instructive and very desirous to be the head of his family and a good citizen and after he left he was a tender feeling in his mother's living and then he had some kinds of loving in him and then as I was saying he came to be married to Julia Dehning and later then his father was losing his great fortune and then too Martha was beginning having trouble in living and later then his brother David was influencing him and later then Alfred Hersland was having very much trouble in his married living and many people came then to be important to him and then there was more and more living in him and this is now to be a complete history of him. I am now almost all through with waiting. I am now beginning to be free with the being of him inside me in my feeling. I am now completely certain that not any one is to himself inside him in his or her feeling any age inside them.

Now then, mostly every one is a good deal in pieces to my feeling, Alfred Hersland then now is such a one to my feeling, a good deal in pieces to my feeling. Always all his being is always repeating in all his living. He is a good deal in pieces to my feeling.

Of the kind of one that Alfred Hersland was in his being, the kind of them men and women having in them such kind of being range from very good ones through to pretty bad ones, have all kinds of mixtures in them, have every kind of way of living are many of them pretty successful in living, some very successful and some pretty miserably failing, some pretty steady with the being in them, some pretty intermittent and some meek and some very weak in being and all this is true of every kind there is of men and women.

Alfred Hersland, Alfy as every one then called him was as a young one of the living of poor people living in small houses in a part of Gossols where the Herslands were the only rich people living. Alfy was of the living of poor people in his daily living then as was his older sister Martha then and his brother who was then quite a little one. All three of the Hersland children were of this living for a good many years in their beginning. It was different in Alfred than it was in Martha, than it was in David Hersland, that I have already been saying. In Alfred it was his daily living then, it was nearly all the living then in him. It was half country half city living. Alfy knew very many poor people then in his young living. In a way then he was then completely of them, completely of their living then. He was different in his living with them in a way than Martha and David were. He was completely then as a young one of the living of poor people, a half city half country poor people living. He was always then with these kind of men and women and children.

He was doing all his daily living with the children and the women and the men living in small houses in that part of Gossols where the Herslands were the only rich people living. The Herslands were rich people of rich american living as the natural way of living. In a way Alfred had never had any real experiencing of this kind of way of living, he really did not know very much of any one who was living this kind of living, sometimes some with their children came to see the Herslands and then the Hersland children had to play and talk with these then these children living the rich american living, and the Hersland children mostly were not interested in them, Alfred had not any liking for them, he liked to have all the fruit picked even before it was quite ripe before it was really ready for picking so that those children who were coming to visit them should not be using their trees to pick fruit and enjoy it. Alfred never liked it that these children should be at home in his orchard, picking fruit and eating it and taking it home with them, he liked very well picking fruit and climbing trees, his own trees with those children that were in his daily living, he never did like it that children coming with their parents on a Sunday visit well to do american families should come and pick fruit in his orchard and enjoy such things then when they came occasionally to visit the Herslands in a part of Gossols where not any other rich people excepting the Herslands were living. Once when some of them were coming, Alfred with David and Martha to help picked all the fruit although most of it was green then, it was mostly cherries just then, picked it all every bit of it and put it in the barn to ripen and he did this so that the children coming to visit them should not be climbing the trees and helping themselves as if it were in an orchard of their own. He made David and Martha have such a feeling too in them, it was a mixed feeling in Alfy then, he was then just beginning to feel in him responsibility for family living, he was just beginning then to feel in him that he was an american citizen, he was just beginning to feel in him then his daily living and liking that realisation that he was then beginning to have in him. He was beginning then a little dimly to have a realisation of the fact that his mother never in her feeling had been really cut off from rich right american living. He was just then completely living with the people near him, he was doing all his living with them, living was interesting to him then, he was more and more then beginning to be really living his living with their living. He had in him not any disliking for the rich american living but he did not want the children of that living to make themselves too much at home in his garden in his orchard with the flowers and the fruit that was part of his daily living then.

Section Three

By Judy Grahn

Calling Without Naming
Gertrude Stein and Metaphysics

Poets rule the world because poets rule the word. I feel ridiculous writing this even though it is true, given that someone (a poet) said to me recently, "You can always tell poets, they are the ones with bad teeth." Poverty and neglect are hardly the attributes of who we think of as "rulers," though I mean, of course, ruler in the sense of measurer, maker, mother. Poets must again remember our true functions.

Stein was not someone who suffered from bad teeth, and in her own words she was not someone who had suffered at all in her life. She wrote that though her brother Leo had begun in his adulthood to remember having had an unhappy childhood, she herself had never had an unhappy anything. And she did certainly think of herself as a ruler, and I think of her as such. As a philosopher of language she is a supreme poet and ruler, a metapoet. Poets rule words, and words rule thoughts and thoughts rule matter, or "reality".

Describing her metaphysics in a single essay is an impossible task, besides, I don't expect to know her that well until much later in my life, if then. I have found some methods of using her ideas to play with, especially when I remember what a scientist she was, how much she used observation, how much she used language as a tool for ordering observation and for expressing ideas meticulously, macroscopically.

From time to time I have found it useful, entertaining and evocative to examine parts of Stein's work in relation to the seven metaphysical principles or laws of how the universe works, credited to an ancient Egyptian, Hermes Trismegistus, Hermes "Thrice-blessed," and generally known as Hermetic teachings.[1] Hoping to tickle your fancy in this direction, I will list them with some thoughts on how I have connected them to Stein:

1. The Principle of Mentalism.

"All is Mind," everything comes from and is, a form of thought.

Stein obviously subscribed to this or otherwise she would not have devoted her long life and thousands of pages to precise linguistic descriptions of how thought operates, what language consists of, what happens when syntax is altered or attention is paid to particular parts of speech or tenses.

"How easily we ask for what we are going to come to have," she wrote, as anyone might say today who practices meditation and projection of disciplined thought in order to manifest reality.

By using "value" in selecting the vocabulary she used for her pages of hundreds of thousands of words, she gathered around herself simple profound words of ordinary relationship and the everyday aesthetic of food, company, nature, idea, love, examination, truthfulness. "Where shall I put my shoes...I don't think I am willing to put my shoes where I am not to put them and I don't think that I will wait. I will put my shoes among shoes." *(Useful Knowledge)*. These "values" of putting her shoes among shoes, filled her life as they filled her pages, a living embodiment of the principle of mentalism.

That everything matters equally is a prerequisite to comprehending the entire network of life as a living mind of interaction. The world is thought, and thought is being. The time of being, and the time of thought, occur in the continuous present: "I wish simply to say that I remember now." (Stanza XL, "Stanzas in Meditation").

In *The Geographical History of America or the Relation of Human Nature to the Human Mind*, Stein describes two aspects of human being, Human Nature and The Human Mind. "Human nature, human nature acts as it acts when it is identified when there is an identity but it is not human nature that has anything to do with that it is that anybody is there where they are, it is that that has to do with identity, with government with propaganda with history with individualism and with communism but it has nothing nothing to do with the human mind...because the human mind writes what there is and what has identity got to do with that...nothing at all."

Human Nature as she describes it could also be called the small self, the enculturated identity; the human mind could also be called the large Self, the cosmic consciousness of creativity, intuition, insight, meaningfulness, recognized connection to the all-beingness of life. Both are aspects of thought but with different functions for our earthly existence. And in Stein's terms, human nature is occupying but not interesting. Human mind is interesting.

2. The Principle of Correspondence.

"As above, so below; as below, so above."

In Stein this principle operates within each paragraph, which is a microcosm of the whole piece. As within, so without. As it is in the sentence, so it is in the mind, and as it is in the mind, so it is in the life. As she said in *Useful Knowledge*, "All parts are principal parts...By this yes."

"Yes," as she used it metaphysically, means "endless possibility." If all parts are principal parts, then from studying small interactions we can understand the larger ones by applying the law of correspondence; as it is in the small world, so it is in the larger.

"When this you see remember me," Stein wrote frequently, with many variations, and I take the "you" in that sentence to be "objectively observed reality" and the "me" to be "subjectively experienced reality." To paraphrase (clumsily): In any present observation remember one's own inner presence. The sentence expresses a balance between these two points of view, and a valid use of memory as a reminder that we affect and are present in our own observations: "you" and "me" are connected by the act "see" and are present in the same being (sentence, relationship, entity).

Correspondence in mathematics is used to define elements that maintain the same particular relationship in a geometric figure, though the size of the figures differ, as in corresponding parts of similar triangles.

Are There Arithmetics[2]   (fragment)

Are there arithmetics. In part are there
arithmetics. There are in part, there
are arithmetics in part.
Are there arithmetics.
In part
Another example.
Are there arithmetics. In part.
As a part.
Under.
As apart.
Under.
This makes.
Irresistible.
Resisted.
This makes irresistible resisted. Resisted

as it makes.
First one to be noticed.
Another one noticed.
To be noticed.
The first one to be noticed.
First one to have been noticed.
Are there arithmetics, irresistible, a part.

In the above piece Stein shows a correspondence between small numbers being a part of larger numbers, and small groups of syllables being a part of larger groups of syllables, as the "resist" part of "resisted" is part of "irresistible"—and then irresistible itself is a part of the larger language structure. The poem additionally makes a comparison between counting and noticing; and a comparison of adding as sequencing and present and then future tenses as sequencing: noticed, to be noticed, to have been noticed—thus pointing out the arithmetical logic of grammar and vice versa.

The Law of Correspondence is also about time, and the different ways we humans use it. "Continuous present" is how Stein described the use of time in such paragraphs as: "Some have not been needing to be changing. Some one is not needing to be changing. That one is what that one is, she is not one needing to be changing." ("Four Dishonest Ones")

As any poet knows, once you enter syntax you enter time, since time is in relationship. Time and its relation to relationship is the subject of the following paragraph from "Patriarchal Poetry":

Next to next next to Saturday next to next next to Saturday next to next next to Saturday.
This shows it all.
This shows it all next to next next to Saturday this shows it all.
Once or twice or once or twice once or twice or

once or twice this shows it all or next to next this
shows it all or once or twice or once or twice or once
or twice this shows it all or next to next this shows it
all or next to next or Saturday or next to next this
shows it all or next to next or next to next or Saturday
or next to next or once or twice this shows it all or next
to next or once or twice this shows it all or Saturday
or next to next...

In the above quote I find at least five different kinds of time
described:

— Progressively linear: *next to next.* One step after
another in endless future. Also, what lies down together in
moving relationship.

— Possibly linear but with "choice" involved, and the
possibility of NOT next (as in the behavior of particles): *next
OR next.*

—Event time: *once or twice.* Modern science does not
currently accept this kind of time as acceptable proof of
reality, (because the events are not repeatable on demand, in
a controlled laboratory for instance) yet we all experience
events in our lives that profoundly influence us and that
happen only "once or twice."

— Calendric time: *Saturday,* the keeping and naming of
time created by coordinating the movements of the earth with
the moon and stars. Also, the relationship *next to Saturday,*
named and unnamed (non-Calendar) time co-existing.

—Holistic time, all time, cosmological time to the extent
that we can know it: *shows it all.* The sensation of knowing
all time at once is like being "shown" something for a breathtaking "moment" in the midst of other times. The "this" of the
longer phrase "this shows it all" can also refer to the
paragraph itself as a whole, as a microcosm of a cosmos
swirling in many kinds of time at once in the same space.

3. The principle of vibration.

Everything in the cosmos moves.

The particularity of the rate (higher, lower) produces wave qualities we perceive as sound (notes, frequencies), light (colors, intensity), forms (shapes, configurations)—and other wave qualities we recognize such as emotions, and temperature.

In Stein this is identified by her as *essence*, the "bottom nature" of each person, perceivable by noticing what it is a person repeats, and "repeating is in everyone," as she lengthily described in one of her earliest works, *The Making of Americans*.

Repeating is one word repeatedly used to describe Gertrude Stein although in her later years when she had thought a great deal about this, she said that she didn't repeat, since a word is different the second time you see it, and the third different still, and so on. She differentiated between repeating and emphasizing: *(Lectures in America)*

"Is there repetition or is there insistence. I am inclined to believe there is no such thing as repetition. And really how can there be. Think about all the detective stories everybody reads. The kind of crime is the same, and the idea of the story is very often the same...always having the same theme, that is, if you like, repetition, that is if you like the repeating that is the same thing, but once started expressing this thing, expressing any thing there can be no repetition because the essence of that expression is insistence, and if you insist you must each time use emphasis and if you use emphasis it is not possible while anybody is alive that they should use exactly the same emphasis. And so let us think seriously of the difference between repetition and insistence."

Using essence to define character and emphasis to define plot, is using the principle of vibration in literature. In Stein as in the old Hermetic teachings, *everything* vibrates and since *everything* vibrates, each rate can be understood in relation to those around it at the time of perception. One's vibratory rate is one's essence.

Having successfully described the principle in her earliest works, she began isolating it not only for human characters, but also for creatures, such as the little dog who continually says "Thank you" in "Dr. Faustus Lights the Lights," and the "daily bird" in *First Reader*, "Lesson One". She expanded out to the essential vibratory phrases of our culture itself, the building blocks of thought, what might be seen as "prefab" thought, stock phrases such as "oh well" and "how do you do" and "we were equally pleased" and thousands, hundreds of thousands more, that she took out of their usual context and collected in such paragraphs as:

> "He came and he said he was hurrying hurrying and hurrying to remain he said he said finally to be and claim it he said feeling very nearly everything as it had been as if he could be precious be precious to like like it as it had been that if he was used it would always do it good and now this time that it was as if it had been just the same as longer when as before it made it be left to be sure and soft softly then can be changed to theirs and speck a speck of it makes blue be often sooner which is shared when their is in polite and reply that in their be the same with diminish always in respect to not at all and farther farther might it be known as counted with it gain to be in retain which it is not to be because of most. This is how they do not like it."
> ("Four Saints in Three Acts")

When such building block phrases are juxtaposed to build a narrative paragraph they sound like this:

> "So Edith and William did not look at Ida, they started talking. What do you think said William what do you think if and when we decide anything what do you think it will be like. This is what William said and Edith looked out of the window. They were not in the same room with Ida but they might have been. Edith liked an opportunity to stand and so she looked out of the window. She half turned, she said to William, Did you say you said Ida. William then took to standing. This was it so they were standing..."
> *(Ida, A Novel)*

Many decades will pass before such a paragraph is "trite" or fixed (named) in time/space, because she is using the *essence* of the phrases, and thus they vibrate, they move in our minds.

Finally, Stein collected some of the archetypes and deep stories of folk tradition and antiquity, especially in the female tradition, and unnamed them as well.

In "Dr. Faustus Lights the Lights" [3] this is most evident in the characters. The goddess figure in the play is named four ancient names, she is "four in one": "Marguerite Ida and Helena Annabel," all with histories. Marguerite is the workingclass version of Helen the spinner of Troy, the betrayed peasant girl in Goethe's story of Faust. St. Margaret "was a canonized form of Aphrodite Marina, Pelagia, or Margarita, called Pearl of the Sea."[4] Ida is an old female name of the mountain, Mt. Ida, setting of events in ancient Greek stories of gods and goddesses. Helena returns us to Troy and beauty warred over in 1200 B.C.E., and Annabel is the dark goddess who ruled death as well as life, with many references to the "Anna" portion of her name, such as "Hannah" as the creation/death crone of Anatolia, the mother of Christian Mary, and synonym for Sumerian Inanna and others. Edgar Allen Poe associated her with death in "Annabel Lee," and James Joyce with rebirth and the river of life in *Finnigan's Wake*, titling her "Anna Livia Plurabelle."

With her four names, Marguerite Ida and Helena Annabel is a recombining of several old traditions that have gotten split over the centuries. Stein has no trouble integrating the goddess' broken personality and scattered powers, she simply gives her back several of her names at once. This gives her a much broader vibrational band than any one of her names carries, and the deed is done in four short strokes. Marvelous.

4. The Principle of Polarity.

Everything has poles, has duality of nature; like and unlike are the same element on a continuum.

This principle expresses the idea that heat and cold, love and hate, poverty and wealth are not categorically different but rather are opposite poles of the same vibratory element. All paradoxes may be reconciled.

Everything is and isn't at the same time, an idea frequently expressed in Stein, as that something is so and then it is not so. She frequently "defines" in the negative, by saying what are NOT characteristic of her subject, placing it in a swirl of what else to think of it. "No" is stoppage, but also formation; "Yes" is expanded landscape, infinity.

Stanza XXXVIII

Which I wish to say is this
There is no beginning to an end
But there is a beginning and an end
To beginning.

Why yes of course.
Any one can learn that north of course
Is not only north but north as north
Why were they worried.
What I wish to say is this.
Yes of course
("Stanzas in Meditation")

As she makes clear in her most overtly metaphysical work, *The Geographical History of America...*, "Yes" is the ever expanding landscape, and "No" is the stopping of expansion, is ground; "Yes" is the large-minded Human Mind of creativity and infinite capacity, while "No" is the smaller self, is identity, stoppage, occupation. They are both necessary for definition, and run through her work as usefully as though they are principles of energy, ways of categorizing and reformulating the flow of information, as computer chips do with their "yes/"no" configurations.

In the principle of polarity, phenomena manifest as polarity in form, variety and rate of vibration. Rate of vibration determines such characteristics as tone, pitch, shape. One "raises" or "lowers" the vibratory rate (of anything) by reversing polarity, such as broadening pitch band to produce a bass sound, narrowing it to produce a soprano sound. Emotional polarity is reversed when two lovers, in breaking up, express hatred for each other. In crystal healing, people reverse emotional polarity by deciding to think "positively" and wearing special stones to raise their emotional vibratory rates to a more positive valence. In chemistry, the degree of combining power of an element, its "valence," is an operative of the principle of polarity.

Stein raised the overall vibratory rate of her writing early in its development by using a method of painters: value. As I said in the first essay, value is the amount of white undertone paint mixed with each color on a given palette, to provide a harmonic balance of color tones. Stein used this technique to determine the value of her vocabulary, raising the overall vibration of the work by the location of her whole vocabulary on the continuum between yes and no; between grounded-ness and flights of fancy; between peaceful words and violent words; between emotional words and thoughtful words. The carefulness and conscientiousness of her choice of vocabulary is a highly effective use of the principle of polarity.

Her surprisingly grounded nonlinear series, "Stanzas in Meditation," is filled with positively-valenced words such as "fortunately," "wish," "gather," "easily," and "please." The stanzas frequently make reference to location, such as "of course," "north," "landscape," "up and down"; and contain many meditatively restful cognitive words such as "because," "of course," "count," "add," and "think well." Stein's own method of meditation consisted of hours of daily walking, surely one of the most grounded of all methods of meditating.

A frequent feature of Stein's landscape is twinning, the duality of two natures which even when they are perceived as running parallel to each other without connection, are polarities of existence. In *Ida, A Novel*, Ida has a twin, which she herself has created. If you make her, can you kill her? the narrative asks. Critic bp nichols [5] has done a concise study of twin Ida, by closely evaluating the first five pages of the novel to examine Ida-Ida, as *idea* and *identity*—correlatives of Human Mind and Human Nature.

What else about Ida. Ida is female Idea. Ida is the name of the mountain where the Muses lived, in Greece, so she is the mother of inspiration, creativity that is in-spired, "breathed in." Ida as defined in the Hindu system of yoga is the name of a particular form of female energy; she runs through the left side of the body and is accessed through specialized breathing; she has a twin, male energy, running through the right side of the body.

Twin elements also occur in some of the plays, and in *The*

Geographical History of America..., where Stein differentiates between "human nature" and "human mind," roughly little "self" and big "Self," or as the difference between one's socialized earth personality and one's higher mind. Human nature, according to Stein, confines itself to what is *occupying*, human mind goes to (or comes from) what is *interesting*.

These twinned definitions of whole fields of endeavor are descriptions of whatever—esthetically—captures our attention. "Occupying" is a term suggestive of military troops entering the yard and capturing attention, and clearly Stein considers it the less satisfying of the two approaches to life. The high drama of war is occupying, but it is not interesting, and she said of the atomic bomb that the ways of killing us are not interesting, it is the way of living that is interesting, and so the bomb is not interesting. *(Reflections on the Atomic Bomb)*. This is a use of polarity to enhance quality of life: she refuses to live in a state of manipulated fear (the little self) and instead concentrates on what the larger Self has to say about living.

5. The Principle of Rhythm.

Everything flows, out and in, in measured motion; the pendulum of events swings one way, and then the other.

Poets express this with the cadence of lines, with rising and falling inflection, with dozens of clever devices such as alliteration and sound mime, with rhyme which is a reminder of repeating subconscious relationships, of pulse. I believe that the fundamental message of any poet is carried primarily in the rhythmic scheme of the poem, a function of both *rhythm* and *vibration*.

Stein, basically a poet in style and thought, used a great deal of rhyme, often unexpectedly and as though to pull the thought back into alignment, often to reconnect a heady passage to the reader's physical body, as that is a primary function of rhyme.

Eighty years after she wrote that everyone has repeating
as their way of living, their *essence*, science philosopher
Fritjof Capra has written on the same subject, saying that
rhythmic patterns are a universal phenomenon while at the
same time allowing distinct personalities to individual enti-
ties. The unique identity by which each human can be
recognized appears to be essentially "an identity of rhythm"
and he lists these as speech patterns, movements, breathing
and in addition what he calls 'frozen' rhythmic patterns such
as fingerprints and handwriting, all "different manifestations
of the same personal rhythm, an 'inner pulse' which is the
essence of personal identity."[6]

Stein specifies how she learned to write paragraphs,
meaning how she developed prose paragraphs corresponding to her philosophy. Given her other principles, how does
she know how to group her thoughts together, when to begin
and end any sequences. Having decided that the structure of
sentences does not apply to paragraphs, she learned to write
paragraphs by listening to a dog drink water. She does not
mean this facetiously or condescendingly, she was always
respectful of animals. She is talking about breathing, about
the dog lap-lap-lapping and then breathing; about taking in
as much as possible before needing to exhale. This is a
function of rhythm. As applied to paragraphs it was very
useful as a principle since it gave her a way to break up her
long and very interconnected thoughts without resorting to
old rules of grammar that had to do with linear plots and
conclusive conclusions, which she usually does not use in
any case.

Breathing while thinking and expressing gave her the in-
and-out flowing she needed to construct paragraphs that
move with the text. Her paragraphs do not usually climax or
conclude, but they do exhale and inhale; they do ebb and
flow; they do exchange energy; they do express the principle
of rhythm.

6. *The Principle of Cause and Effect.*

Scientists and engineers have especially liked this one in the form of the familiar law of mechanics: *For every action there is an opposite and equal reaction.* In Newtonian/Cartesian physics, mechanics, and medicine: *For every effect there is a cause, for every cause, an effect.*

Stein particularly challenged the usual and linear understanding of this principle by stepping into the middle of *being*, where time is not linear but concurrent, and where cause (past) and effect (future) are co-existing in *now*—the only place where they can possibly shift places. And in Stein, they do.

In the middle of *being*, the usual active/passive dynamic of cause/effect is shot to hell. Using Steinian syntax some cause/effect dynamics become probable, that our language ordinarily, with its fixed subject acting upon its fixed object, does not give us. Really entering the syntactical philosophy of Stein's language alters reality, because being in the continual present alters outcome. Without a known or remembered past the future is not a foregone conclusion, and meaning (hence reality) can shift.

Nowhere is linear cause and effect stressed more emphatically in storytelling than in the murder mystery. But though she read them avidly for years as she grew older, and considered them the only modern stories with originality, Stein's versions of the mystery steadfastly bypass linearity of cause and effect, as though it simply didn't apply to the more wholistic way of thinking that evolves in her writing.

In one of her plays, "Three Sisters Who are Not Sisters," a murder mystery unfolds. Of the five characters, one is murdering the others. When three are dead, the last possible victim kills the killer of the others and is then named as the killer of them all. This is as though events are littler fishes eaten by bigger fishes and finally by a biggest fish who then "causes" the deaths of all the others—because of being the last one standing in the series, as though Stein is saying there is always more to consequence than meets the eye.

In *The Geographical History of America...*, she says, "A motive is what makes you do it. But what makes you do it is not the reason why you do it."

In another of her plays, "The Mother of Us All," characters from different historic times are present simultaneously. They include the 19th century feminist Susan B. Anthony and the 17th century patriarch Daniel Webster, and a young 20th century couple preparing to marry. The young man, Jo the Loiterer, was a person (Joe Barrie) present in Stein's livingroom as she worked on the play. Much of the play revolves around the question of whether or not the young woman, Lillie, will take Jo's last name when they marry. And since this is a feminist question of course Susan B. Anthony is present for this discussion and of course so then is the oppositional voice, Daniel Webster, as they continue an argument that stretches across the centuries. The argument between Daniel Webster and Susan B. Anthony is cause and effect of itself as well as cause of the argument between Jo and Lillie, which current argument has as one effect that Susan and Daniel are also present in it.

As a woman-centered philosopher, Stein increasingly as her work developed, exchanged linear heroic plot with plot as living place/time. There are at least two meanings of plot, one is in the sense of the hero's journey to slay dragons, have adventures, prove himself and find manhood. Another meaning of plot is in place, ground, grave, land of one's "own," location. From centering in place Stein quickly identified geography with the dramatic form of play.

Place *is* play when all its elements are taken into account. Place is interaction among settings, characters, times, and observations (from an audience). This interaction of four elements is Stein's most basic use of one of the more complex aspects of the principle of cause and effect, and it is a literary parallel to quantum physics.

In quantum physics events happen in time/space, and they don't happen in a linear fixed sequence but rather in a dance of probablity that when one particle (or character) meets another, there will be an interaction in a particular direction. The *probablity* of this sentence is what gives the events individuality, continual motion, and effects of the will on form. Many of Stein's plays explore probable meaning, and interactive characterization, to such an extreme that numbers, acts and parts of speech become characters. This prevents the passivity inherent in the model of a particular cause always producing the same effect. Instead, the metaphysical dance of twenty-first century physics is on, moving us, somewhat jarringly at times, beyond the mechanistic age.

7. The Principle of Gender

Everything has its Masculine and Feminine Principles; Gender manifests on all planes.

Gender is a subject our culture takes with deadly seriousness, and as if it pertained only to sexual role behaviors. The principle of gender in its Hermetic sense refers to all creativity, to the basic laws that govern the making of anything. In that sense, even masculine and feminine lie on a continuum of interaction between forces, forces that do not have fixed qualities such as "active" and "passive," but whose powers explode into creation by the mixture their *differences*, at any given time, exert on each other.

Completely functional in a male-dominated world, while at the same time producing work that is solidly woman-centered, Stein moved beyond gender, beyond definitions or names. The playfulness that she brought to the subject of gender in our time is most evident in two long poems, "Lifting Belly" and "Patriarchal Poetry."

"Patriarchal Poetry" takes apparent and genuine aim at

the system of patriarchal thought as exemplified, say, by her father Daniel Stein, a cold, remote pedagogue, or by "too much fathering" that she believed led to the two great wars of her age. But having taken such aim the poem then steadfastly refuses to land on any such easy polemical target as "the men," for instance, instead diffusing into little electron arrows seeking whatever is rigid and prejudiced in me, the reader, of whatever gender or other names I might go by in daily life.

She is calling, and calling out, without naming, and while her work does this throughout, to do the calling with gender itself is particularly daring, since gender so often appears to be one of the apparently fixed poles of our society, a primary axis of social orientation. But "Please be the man," Stein writes in "Lifting Belly," and the axis turns, and is not fixed.

In "Lifting Belly" the playfulness of the calling mixes with female sexuality in provocative lushness, with lines such as "Little nature which is mine /fairy ham/Is a clam." Where are we in this poem, in a dialogue? Are Gertrude and Alice in bed talking, using a special lover's language we are being let in on? If so, the husband is not necessarily a male, but is agreed on, "Please be the man," and the wife never agreed to obey him. "Husband, obey your wife," the text says, in a reversal of gender role expectations of the early twentieth century.

There is much reversal of male role in the poem, such as in the word play over "Caesars," a multiple pun on "scissors" said with a Spanish accent—Alice loved all things Spanish—and Gertrude's "Caesar" haircut, which Alice gave her, and "seize her," and "the Caesars are docile," a joke on the great conqueror Julius Caesar. These are recognizably and actually typical Lesbian jokes, jokes about being seen as imitators of men, or imitators of husbands and wives, of being different from other people, jokes about roles and expectations, even those expectations that are taken seriously within the Gay community—of love and sexuality, of romance, of aggressiveness and docility.

Stein and Toklas knew the other active Lesbians of Paris but she and Alice were apart from them. The two were beyond their own families for the most part and they were beyond the Lesbian underground, they were beyond any generic expectations of naming, including gender.

In "Lifting Belly" gender is a place one engages with, a changeable character called upon at a given time like any other, an *act* as a number or a part of speech is an act, as any event in the continuous present is an act. How many acts are there in it? she asked. And the answer is legion.

To return once again to the first Hermetic principle: Everything is Thought, or the Steinian, and more currently accurate statement: *everything is thinking.* Thinking is not name. Name, in Stein's philosophy, is not yes.

She doesn't rename, she unnames. She UNNAMES! She calls, not names. It is in calling that everything becomes equal, and not only is everything equal in the paragraph, every single word and hence every possible relationship—the meaning of this is that everything is equally alive, everything is thinking, for if there are no inanimate words there are no inanimate objects either; if there are no inanimate parts of speech there are no inanimate parts of life either. Moreover thinking takes place in the present, is the present. Thinking is not the same as thought, which is a memory, or tomorrow we will get organized, or connected, or fulfilled. Thinking is the present. "Everything is thinking" establishes a theology of place.

This is such a radical view there is no way yet to fit it into our noun-driven everyday linear reality based as it is in a hierarchy of consciousness without which our society could not function as it is for a single minute of a single day. Or so we still imagine.

As I have said, I believe it will be the middle of the next

century before we "know" Gertrude Stein's mind, and this comes about because as we practice thinking we absorb, little by little, enough of her principles, and then we act them out in our technology, our social and biospheric relationships, and the philosophies and theologies of our future. She is there as we develop, every step of the way.

Essential Clues for Really Reading Her:

1. *Go ahead and use your own head.*

Often critics approach an author's work so strictly from the point of view of her life and times it seems impossible to approach the text with whatever ideas one has as a reader. Without discarding the reality of Stein's life, I feel it is important to engage directly with her text.

Since she was such a scientist of a writer, let's approach her with our most scientific selves.

Interesting parts of Stein's work reveal themselves when they are compared with ideas from such fields as quantum mechanics, modern music, Taoism, physics, feminist theology, and New Age healing.

2. *What are your favorite sciences and how can you engage them with Stein's work? And conversely, how can Stein's work help you feel more at home in any sciences?*

As always, approach expecting to be puzzled at first, and be selective. Remember to have fun, and also that she is a serious philosopher. Be patient, remember that she is ahead of us, in time.

Here are some possible relationships I can think of that might be helpful to your happy search:

Psychology: Three Lives, Fernhurst, Q.E.D., The Making

of Americans, Mrs. Reynolds.

Numbers: Her plays, Mrs. Reynolds, Advertisements.

Computer technology, and yes and no: Her grammatical texts; Patriarchal Poetry.

Physics and the meaning of being: The Geographical History of America, the plays; Patriarchal Poetry.

Graphic Portraits: Lucy Church, Amiably; Tender Buttons; her many portraits of individuals.

Linguistics and the nature of thought: Everything, and also How Writing is Written and Lectures in America

Psychism, nature and the arising Goddess: Dr. Faustus Lights the Lights, The World Is Round, The Mother of Us All, Three Saints in Four Acts, many short plays; Marguerite or a Simple Novel of High Life, Ida: A Novel

Biocentrism, land and play: Stanzas In Meditation, the geographies of America, France and England and Italy.

Notes

1. *Kybalion, The*, Hermetic Philosophy, by Three Initiates, The Yogi Publication Society, Masonic Temple, Chicago, Illinois, copyright 1912 and 1947.

2. G. Stein, "Are There Arithmetics," *Oxford* magazine, edited by Geofrey Brereton, May, 1927, p.28. In the Yale Collection of American Literature, Beinecke Rare Manuscript Library, Yale University.

3. See "Would a viper have stung her if she had only had one name": *Dr. Faustus Lights the Lights*, by Shirley Neuman for some of the matriarchal background to this play. In *Gertrude Stein and the Making of Literature*, ed. Shirley Neuman and Ira B. Nadel, Boston, Northeastern University Press, 1988.

4. B. Walker, *The Women's Encyclopedia of Myths and Secrets*, New York, Harper and Row, 1983.

5. bp nichols, "When the Time Came," in *Gertrude Stein and the Making of Literature*, Boston, Northeastern University Press, 1988.

6. F. Capra, *The Turning Point*, pp. 300-301, Simon and Schuster, New York, 1982.

By Gertrude Stein

Ida

(excerpt)

Part One

The road is awfully wide.
With the snow on either side.
    She was walking along the road made wide with snow.
The moonlight was bright. She had a white dog and the dog
looked gray in the moonlight and on the snow. Oh she said
to herself that is what they mean when they say in the night
all cats are gray.
    When there was no snow and no moonlight her dog had
always looked white at night.
    When she turned her back on the moon the light sud-
denly was so bright it looked like another kind of light, and
if she could have been easily frightened it would have frightened her but you get used to anything but really she never did
get used to this thing.
    She said to herself what am I doing, I have my genius and
I am looking for my Andrew and she went on looking.
    It was cold and when she went home the fire was out and
there was no more wood. There was a little girl servant, she
knew that the servant had made a fire for herself with all that
wood and that her fire was going. She knew it. She knocked
at her door and walked in. The servant was not there but the
fire was. She was furious. She took every bit of lighted wood

and carried it into her room. She sat down and looked at the fire and she knew she had her genius and she might just as well go and look for her Andrew. She went to bed then but she did not sleep very well. She found out next day that Andrew came to town every Sunday. She never saw him. Andrew was very good looking like his name. Ida often said to herself she never had met an Andrew and so she did not want to see him. She liked to hear about him.

She would if it had not been so early in the morning gone to be a nurse. As a nurse she might seek an Andrew but to be a nurse you have to get up early in the morning. You have to get up early in the morning to be a nun and so although if she had been a nun she could have thought every day about Andrew she never became a nun nor did she become a nurse. She just stayed at home.

It is easy to stay at home not at night-time but in the morning and even at noon and in the afternoon. At nighttime it is not so easy to stay at home.

For which reason, Andrew's name changed to Ida and eight changed to four and sixteen changed to twenty-five and they all sat down.

For which all day she sat down. As I said she had that habit the habit of sitting down and only once every day she went out walking and she always talked about that. That made Ida listen. She knew how to listen.

This is what she said.

She did not say Ida knew how to listen but she talked as if she knew that Ida knew how to listen.

Every day she talked the same way and every day she took a walk and every day Ida was there and every day she talked about his walk, and every day Ida did listen while she talked about his walk. It can be very pleasant to walk every day and to talk about the walk and every day and it can be very pleasant to listen every day to him talk about his every-day walk.

You see there was he it came to be Andrew again and it was Ida.

If there was a war or anything Andrew could still take a walk every day and talk about the walk he had taken that day.

For which it made gradually that it was not so important that Ida was Ida.

It could and did happen that it was not so important.

Would Ida fly, well not alone and certainly it was better not to fly than fly alone. Ida came to walking, she had never thought she would just walk but she did and this time she did not walk alone she walked with Susan Little.

For this they did not sing.

Such things can happen, Ida did not have to be told about it nor did she have to tell about it.

There was no Andrew.

Andrew stayed at home and waited for her, and Ida came. This can happen, Andrew could walk and come to see Ida and tell her what he did while he was walking and later Ida could walk and come back and not tell Andrew that she had been walking. Andrew could not have listened to Ida walking. Andrew walked not Ida. It is perhaps best so.

Anybody can go away, anybody can take walks and anybody can meet somebody new. Anybody can like to say how do you do to somebody they never saw before and yet it did not matter. Ida never did, she always walked with some one as if they had walked together any day. That really made Ida so pleasant that nobody ever did stay away.

And then they all disappeared, not really disappeared but nobody talked about them any more.

So it was all to do over again, Ida had Andrew that is she had that he walked every day, nobody talked about him any more but he had not disappeared, and he talked about his walk and he walked every day.

So Ida was left alone, and she began to sit again.

And sitting she thought about her life with dogs and this

was it.

The first dog I ever remember seeing, I had seen cats before and I must have seen dogs but the first dog I ever remember seeing was a large puppy in the garden. Nobody knew where he came from so we called him Prince.

It was a very nice garden but he was a dog and he grew very big. I do not remember what he ate but he must have eaten a lot because he grew so big. I do not remember playing with him very much. He was very nice but that was all, like tables and chairs are nice. That was all. Then there were a lot of dogs but none of them interesting. Then there was a little dog, a black and tan and he hung himself on a string when somebody left him. He had not been so interesting but the way he died made him very interesting. I do not know what he had as a name.

Then for a long time there were no dogs none that I ever noticed. I heard people say they had dogs but if I saw them I did not notice them and I heard people say their dog had died but I did not notice anything about it and then there was a dog, I do not know where he came from or where he went but he was a dog.

It was not yet summer but there was sun and there were wooden steps and I was sitting on them, and I was just doing nothing and a brown dog came and sat down too. I petted him, he liked petting and he put his head on my lap and we both went on sitting. This happened every afternoon for a week and then he never came. I do not know where he came from or where he went or if he had a name but I knew he was brown, he was a water dog a fairly big one and I never did forget him.

And then for some time there was no dog and then there were lots of them but other people had them.

A dog has to have a name and he has to look at you. Sometimes it is kind of bothering to have them look at you.

Any dog is new.

The dogs I knew then which were not mine were mostly very fine. There was a Pekinese named Sandy, he was a very large one, Pekineses should be tiny but he was a big one like a small lion but he was all Pekinese, I suppose anywhere there can be giants, and he was a giant Pekinese.

Sandy was his name because he was that color, the color of sand. He should have been carried around, Pekinese mostly are but he was almost too heavy to carry. I liked Sandy. When he stood up on a table all ruffled up and his tail all ruffled up he did look like a lion, a very little lion, but a fierce one.

He did not like climbing the mountains, they were not real mountains, they were made of a man on two chairs and Sandy was supposed to climb him as if he were climbing a mountain. Sandy thought this was disgusting and he was right. No use calling a thing like that climbing the mountains, and if it has been really mountains of course Sandy would not have been there. Sandy liked things flat, tables, floors and paths. He liked waddling along as he pleased. No mountains, no climbing, no automobiles, he was killed by one. Sandy knew what he liked, flat things and sugar, sugar was flat too, and Sandy never was interested in anything else and then one day an automobile went over him, poor Sandy and that was the end of Sandy.

So one changed to two and two changed to five and the next dog was also not a big one, his name was Lillieman and he was black and a French bull and not welcome. He was that kind of a dog he just was not welcome.

When he came he was not welcome and he came very often. He was good-looking, he was not old, he did finally die and was buried under a white lilac tree in a garden but he just was not welcome.

He had his little ways, he always wanted to see something that was just too high or too low for him to reach and so everything was sure to get broken. He did not break it but it did just get broken. Nobody could blame him but of course he was not welcome.

Before he died and was buried under the white lilac tree, he met another black dog called Dick. Dick was a French poodle and Lillieman was a French bull and they were both black but they did not interest each other. As much as possible they never knew the other one was there. Sometimes when they bumped each other no one heard the other one bark it was hard to not notice the other one. But they did. Days at a time sometimes they did.

Dick was the first poodle I ever knew and he was always welcome, round roly-poly and old and gray and lively and pleasant, he was always welcome.

He had only one fault. He stole eggs, he could indeed steal a whole basket of them and then break them and eat them, the cook would hit him with a broom when she caught him but nothing could stop him, when he saw a basket of eggs he had to steal them and break them and eat them. He only liked eggs raw, he never stole cooked eggs, whether he liked breaking them, or the looks of them or just, well anyway it was the only fault he had. Perhaps because he was a black dog and eggs are white and then yellow, well anyway he could steal a whole basket of them and break them and eat them, not the shells of course just the egg.

So this was Dick the poodle very playful very lively old but full of energy and he and Lillieman the French bull could be on the same lawn together and not notice each other, there was no connection between them, they just ignored each other. The bull Lillieman died first and was buried under the white lilac, Dick the poodle went on running around making love to distant dogs, sometimes a half day's run away and running after sticks and stones, he was fourteen years old and very lively and then one day he heard of a dog far away and he felt he could love her, off he went to see her and he never came back again, he was run over, on the way there, he never got there he never came back and alas poor Dick he was never buried anywhere.

Dogs are dogs, you sometimes think that they are not but they are. And they always are here there and everywhere.

There were so many dogs and I knew some of them I knew some better than others, and sometimes I did not know whether I wanted to meet another one or not.

There was one who was named Mary Rose, and she had two children, the first one was an awful one. This was the way it happened.

They say dogs are brave but really they are frightened of a great many things about as many things as frighten children.

Mary Rose had no reason to be frightened because she was always well and she never thought about being lost, most dogs do and it frightens them awfully but Mary Rose did get lost all the same not really lost but for a day and a night too. Nobody really knew what happened.

She came home and she was dirty, she who was always so clean and she had lost her collar and she always loved her collar and she dragged herself along she who always walked along so tidily. She was a fox-terrier with smooth white hair, and pretty black marks. A little boy brought back her collar and then pretty soon Chocolate came, it was her only puppy and he was a monster, they called him Chocolate because he looked like a chocolate cake or a bar of chocolate or chocolate candy, and he was awful. Nobody meant it but he was run over, it was sad and Mary Rose had been fond of him. Later she had a real daughter Blanchette who looked just like her, but Mary Rose never cared about her. Blanchette was too like her, she was not at all interesting and besides Mary Rose knew that Blanchette would live longer and never have a daughter and she was right. Mary Rose died in the country, Blanchette lived in the city and never had a daughter and was never lost and never had any worries and gradually grew very ugly but she never suspected it and nobody told her so and it was no trouble to her.

Mary Rose loved only once, lots of dogs do they love only once or twice, Mary Rose was not a loving dog, but she was a tempting dog, she loved to tempt other dogs to do what they should not. She never did what she should not but they did when she showed them where it was.

Little things happen like that, but she had to do something then when she had lost the only dog she loved who was her own son and who was called Chocolate. After that she just was like that.

I can just see her tempting Polybe in the soft moonlight to do what was not right.

Dogs should smell but not eat, if they eat dirt that means they are naughty or they have worms, Mary Rose was never naughty and she never had worms but Polybe, well Polybe was not neglected but he was not understood. He never was understood. I suppose he died but I never knew. Anyway he had his duty to do and he never did it, not because he did not want to do his duty but because he never knew what his duty was.

That was what Polybe was.

He liked moonlight because it was warmer than darkness but he never noticed the moon. His father and his sister danced on the hillside in the moonlight but Polybe had left home so young that he never knew how to dance in it but he did like the moonlight because it was warmer than the dark.

Polybe was not a small dog he was a hound and he had stripes red and black like only a zebra's stripes are white and black but Polybe's stripes were as regular as that and his front legs were long, all his family could kill a rabbit with a blow of their front paw, that is really why they danced in the moonlight, they thought they were chasing rabbits, any shadow was a rabbit to them and there are lots of shadows on a hillside in the summer under a bright moon.

Poor Polybe he never really knew anything, the shepherds said that he chased sheep, perhaps he did thinking they were rabbits, he might have made a mistake like that, he easily might. Another little little dog was so foolish once he always thought that any table leg was his mother, and would suck away at it as if it was his mother. Polybe was not as foolish as that but he almost was, anyway Mary Rose could always lead him astray, perhaps she whispered to him that sheep were rabbits. She might have.

And then Mary Rose went far away. Polybe stayed where he was and did not remember any one. He never did. That was Polybe.

And he went away tied to a string and he never did try to come back. Back meant nothing to him. A day was never a day to Polybe. He never barked, he had nothing to say.

Polybe is still some place today, nothing could ever happen to him to kill him or to change anything in any way.

The next dog was bigger than any other dog had been.

When a dog is really big he is very naturally thin, and when he is big and thin when he moves he does not seem to be moving. There were two of them one was probably dead before I saw the second one. I did not know the first one but I heard what he could do I saw him of course but when I saw him he came along but he was hardly moving.

It did not take much moving to come along as fast as we were going. There was no other dog there which was lucky because they said that when he saw another dog well he did not move much but he killed him, he always killed any dog he saw although he hardly moved at all to kill him. I saw this dog quite a few times but there was never any other dog anywhere near. I was glad.

The other one well he looked gentle enough and he hardly moved at all and he was very big and he looked thin although he really was not.

He used to walk about very gently almost not at all he was

so tall and he moved his legs as if he meant them not to leave the ground but they did, just enough, just a little sideways just enough, and that was all. He lived a long time doing nothing but that and he is still living just living enough.

The next dog and this is important because it is the next dog. His name is Never Sleeps although he sleeps enough.

He was brown not a dark brown but a light brown and he had a lot of friends who always went about together and they all had to be brown, otherwise Never Sleeps would not let them come along. But all that was later, first he had to be born.

It was not so easy to be born.

There was a dog who was an Alsatian wolf-hound a very nice one, and they knew that in the zoo there was a real wolf quite a nice one. So one night they took the dog to see the wolf and they left her there all night. She liked the wolf and the wolf was lonesome and they stayed together and then later she had a little dog and he was a very nice one, and her name was Never Sleeps. She was a gentle dog and liked to lie in the water in the winter and to be quiet in the summer. She never was a bother.

She could be a mother. She met a white poodle he was still young and he had never had a puppy life because he had not been well. His name was Basket and he looked like one. He was taken to visit Never Sleeps and they were told to be happy together. Never Sleeps was told to play with Basket and teach him how to play. Never Sleeps began, she had to teach catch if you can or tag, and she had to teach him pussy wants a corner and she taught him each one of them.

She taught him tag and even after he played it and much later on when he was dead another Basket he looked just like him went on playing tag. To play tag you have to be able to run forward and back to run around things and to start one way and to go the other way and another dog who is smaller and not so quick has to know how to wait at a corner and go around the other way to make the distance shorter. And sometimes just to see how well tag can be played the bigger quicker dog can even stop to play with a stick or a bone and still get away and not be tagged. That is what it means to play tag and Never Sleeps taught Basket how to play. Then he taught him how to play pussy wants a corner, to play this there have to be trees. Dogs cannot play this in the house they are not allowed to and so they have to have at least four trees if there are three dogs and three trees if there are two dogs to play pussy wants a corner. Never Sleeps preferred tag to pussy wants a corner but Basket rather liked best pussy wants a corner.

Ida never knew who knew what she said, she never knew what she said because she listened and as she listened well the moon scarcely the moon but still there is a moon.

Very likely hers was the moon.

Ida knew she never had been a little sister or even a little brother. Ida knew.

So scarcely was there an absence when some one died.

Believe it or not some one died.

And he was somebody's son and Ida began to cry and he was twenty-six and Ida began to cry and Ida was not alone and she began to cry.

Ida had never cried before, but now she began to cry.

Even when Andrew came back from his walk and talked about his walk, Ida began to cry.

It's funny about crying. Ida knew it was funny about crying, she listened at the radio and they played the national anthem and Ida began to cry. It is funny about crying.

But anyway Ida was sitting and she was there and one by one somebody said Thank you, have you heard of me. And she always had. That was Ida.

Even Andrew had he had heard of them, that was the way he had been led to be ready to take his walk every day because he had heard of every one who came in one after the other one.

And Ida did not cry again.

One day, she saw a star it was an uncommonly large one and when it set it made a cross, she looked and looked and she and did not hear Andrew take a walk and that was natural enough she was not there. They had lost her. Ida was gone.

So she sat up and went to bed carefully and she easily told every one that there was more wind in Texas than in San Francisco and nobody believed her. So she said wait and see and they waited.

She came back to life exactly day before yesterday. And now listen.

Ida loved three men. One was an officer who was not killed but he might have been, one was a painter who was not in hospital but he might have been one and one was a lawyer who had gone away to Montana and she had never heard from him.

Ida loved each one of them and went to say good-bye to them.

Good-bye, good-bye she said, and she did say good-bye to them.

She wondered if they were there, of course she did not go away. What she really wanted was Andrew, where oh where was Andrew.

Andrew was difficult to suit and so Ida did not suit him. But Ida did sit down beside him.

Ida fell in love with a young man who had an adventure. He came from Kansas City and he knew that he was through. He was twenty years old. His uncle had died of meningitis, so had his father and so had his cousin, his name was Mark and he had a mother but no sisters and he had a wife and sisters-in-law.

Ida looked the other way when they met, she knew Mark would die when he was twenty-six and he did but before that he had said, For them, they like me for them and Ida had answered just as you say Mark. Ida always bent her head when she saw Mark she was tall and she bent her head when she saw Mark, he was tall and broad and Ida bent her head when she saw him. She knew he would die of meningitis and he did. That was why Ida always bent her head when she saw him.

Why should everybody talk about Ida.

Why not.

Dear Ida.

By Gertrude Stein

Three Sisters Who Are Not Sisters

A Melodrama

JENNY, HELEN *and* ELLEN
SAMUEL *and* SYLVESTER

We are three sisters who are not sisters, not sisters. We are three sisters who are orphans.

We are three sisters who are not sisters because we have not had the same mother or the same father, but because we are all three orphans we are three sisters who are not sisters.

Enter two brothers.

We are two brothers who are brothers, we have the same father and the same mother and as they are alive and kicking we are not orphans not at all, we are not even tall, we are not brave we are not strong but we never do wrong, that is the kind of brothers we are.

JENNY: And now that everybody knows just what we are what each one of us is, what are we going to to.

SYLVESTER: What are we going to do about it.

JENNY *(impatiently):* No not what are we going to do about it there is nothing to do about it, we are three sisters who are not sisters, and we are three orphans and you two are not, there is nothing to do about that. No what I want to know is what are we going to to now. Now what are we going to do.

SAMUEL: I have an idea a beautiful idea, a fine idea, let us play a play and let it be a murder.

JENNY:

HELEN: Oh yes let's.

ELLEN:

SYLVESTER: I won't be murdered or be a murderer. I am not that kind of a brother.

SAMUEL: Well nobody says you are, all you have to do is to be a witness to my murdering somebody.

HELEN: And who are you going to murder.

SAMUEL: You for choice. Let's begin.

ELLEN: Oh I am so glad I am not a twin, I would not like to be murdered just because I had a sister who was a twin.

JENNY: Oh don't be silly, twins do not have to get murdered together, let's begin.

Scene 2

A room slightly darkened, a couch, and a chair and a glass of water, the three sisters sitting on the couch together, the light suddenly goes out.

JENNY: Look at the chair.

HELEN: Which chair.

JENNY: The only chair.

ELLEN: I can't see the only chair.

JENNY: *(with a shriek):* Look at the only chair.

All three together: There is no chair there.

SAMUEL: No there is no chair there because I am sitting on it.

SYLVESTER: And there is no him there because I am sitting on him.

JENNY: Which one is going to murder which one.

SAMUEL: Wait and see.

Suddenly the light goes up there is nobody in the room and Sylvester is on the floor dead.

[CURTAIN]

ACT II

Scene I

The light is on.

Sylvester is on the floor dead.
Jenny is asleep on the couch.
She wakes up and she sees Sylvester on the floor dead.
Oh he is dead Sylvester is dead somebody has murdered him, I wish I had a sister a real sister oh it is awful to be an orphan and to see him dead, Samuel killed him, perhaps Helen killed him, perhaps Ellen but it should be Helen who is dead and where is Helen.
She looks under the bed and she bursts out crying.
There there is Helen and she is dead, Sylvester killed her and she killed him. Oh the police the police.
There is a knock at the door and Samuel comes in dressed like a policeman and Jenny does not know him.
JENNY: Yes Mr. Policeman I did kill them I did kill both of them.
SAMUEL: Aha I am a policeman but I killed both of them and now I am going to do some more killing.
JENNY: *(screaming):* Ah ah.
And the lights go out and then the lights go up again and Jenny is all alone, there are no corpses there and no policeman.
JENNY: I killed them but where are they, he killed them but

where is he. There is a knock at the door I had better hide.
She hides under the bed.

Scene 2

SAMUEL *(as a policeman comes in):* Aha there is nobody
dead and I have to kill somebody kill somebody dead. Where
is somebody so that I can kill them dead.
*He begins to hunt around and he hears a sound, and he
is just about to look under the bed when Ellen comes in.*
ELLEN: I am looking for Helen who is not my twin so I do
not have to be murdered to please her but I am looking for
her.
*Samuel the policeman comes out of the corner where he
has been hiding.*
SAMUEL: Aha you killed her or aha you killed him, it does
not make any difference because now I am going to do some
killing.
ELLEN: Not me dear kind policeman not me.
SAMUEL: I am not a policeman I am a murderer, look out
here I come.
*The light goes out. When it comes on again, the policeman
is gone and Ellen murdered is on the floor.*
*Jenny looks out timidly from under the bed and gives a
shriek:*
Oh another one and now I am only one and now I will be
the murdered one.
And timidly she creeps back under the bed.

[CURTAIN]

ACT III

Jenny under the bed. Samuel this time not like a policeman but like an apache comes creeping in.

SAMUEL: Aha, I am killing some one.

JENNY *(under the bed):* He can't see me no he can't, and anyway I will kill him first, yes I will.

Suddenly the room darkens and voices are heard.

I am Sylvester and I am dead, she killed me, every one thinks it was Samuel who killed me but it was not it was she.

HELEN'S VOICE: I am Helen and I am dead everybody thinks it was Samuel who killed me but not at all not all not at all it was she.

A THIRD VOICE: I am Ellen and I am dead, oh so dead, so very very dead, and everybody thinks it was Samuel but it was not it was not Samuel it was she oh yes it was she.

The light goes up and Jenny alone looks out fearfully into the room from under the bed.

JENNY: Oh it was not Samuel who killed them it was not, it was she and who can she be, can she be me. Oh horrible horrible me if I killed all three. It cannot be but perhaps it is, *(and she stretches up very tall)* well if it is then I will finish up with him I will kill him Samuel and then they will all be dead yes all dead but I will not be dead not yet.

The light lowers and Samuel creeps in like an apache.

SAMUEL: They say I did not kill them they say it was she but I know it was me and the only way I can prove that I murdered them all is by killing her, aha I will find her I will kill her and when I am the only one the only one left alive they will know it was I that killed them all, I Samuel the apache.

He begins to look around and suddenly he sees a leg of Jenny sticking out under the bed. He pulls at it.

SAMUEL: Aha it is she and I will kill her and then they will know that I Samuel am the only murderer.

He pulls at her leg and she gives a fearful kick which hits him on the temple. He falls back and as he dies,

SAMUEL: Oh it is so, she is the one that kills every one, and that must be so because she has killed me, and that is what they meant, I killed them each one, but as she was to kill me, she has killed all of them all of them. And she has all the glory, Oh Ciel.

And he dies.

Jenny creeps out from under the bed.

JENNY: I killed him yes I did and he killed them yes he did and now they are all dead, no brothers no sisters no orphans no nothing, nothing but me, well there is no use living alone, with nobody to kill so I will kill myself.

And she sees the glass of water.

JENNY: Aha that is poison.

She drinks it and with a convulsion she falls down dead.
The lights darken and the voices of all of them are heard.

We are dead she killed us, he killed us sisters and brothers orphans and all he killed us she killed us she killed us he killed us and we are dead, dead dead.

The lights go up and there they all are as in the first scene.

JENNY: Did we act it are we dead, are we sisters, are we orphans, do we feel funny, are we dead.

SYLVESTER: Of course we are not dead, of course we never were dead.

SAMUEL: Of course we are dead, can't you see we are dead, of course we are dead.

HELEN *(indignantly):* I am not dead, I am an orphan and a sister who is not a sister but I am not dead.

ELLEN: Well if she is not dead then I am not dead. It is very nice very nice indeed not to be dead.

JENNY: Oh shut up everybody, shut up, let's all go to bed, it is time to go to bed orphans and all and brothers too.

And they do.

[FINIS]

By Gertrude Stein

Look and Long

A Play In Three Acts

FOUR COUSINS
TWO BROTHERS: OLIVER, SILLY
TWO COUSINS: MURIEL, SUSIE
AN APPARITION

Scene: In front of a house with trees

Enter Oliver, profoundly sad, he stops and looks about and folds his arms and looks up at the sky.
OLIVER: I wonder, oh I wonder.
Silence.
From the other side enters Muriel, she too is profoundly sad and her eyes are cast down on the ground as she stands. Suddenly she sees a spider.
MURIEL: Araignee de matin, fait chagrin, and it is morning.
She stops and crouches behind a chair in an agony of despair.
In rush Susie and Silly.
SUSIE: Oh I have I have seen a goat a white goat and I milked him oh a lovely goat a lovely white goat.
SILLY: Silly Susie a goat is a she if she gives milk to three,

beside it was not a goat, it was a chicken and it was an egg not milk even if it was white do you see.

Silly and Susie dance around and suddenly they see Oliver that is to say they bump against him.

SUSIE: Oh I thought he was a tree. When this you see remember me.

Oliver pays no attention he continues to gloom looking up at the sky with folded arms.

SILLY: Oh look Susie look what is there, there behind that chair.

Susie and Silly steal around quietly behind the chair and there is Muriel her eyes fixed on the ground in despair.

MURIEL (*murmurs*): The spider the spider oh the spider it is not there.

OLIVER (*gives a start*): It was a cuckoo and (*with a bitter cry*) I have no money in my purse no money anywhere. Oh why did that cuckoo try to cry when I had no money no money, none.

MURIEL: No money.

SUSIE AND SILLY: No money.

OLIVER: No money, none.

Just then there was a funny noise and in the middle of the four of them was a dancing apparition.

All together: Oh (*and they watch her dance*).

SUSIE: Is it pretty.

OLIVER: Is it ugly.

MURIEL: Who is it.

SILLY: Where does it come from.

APPARITION (*dancing*): I come from the moon, I come from the sun and I come to look at you one by one.

And then suddenly stopping she points a finger at Oliver: You you, one of these days you will split in two, you you.

OLIVER (*disdainfully*): I wonder.

APPARITION: You will wonder when it comes like thunder that you will split in two all through.

And suddenly pointing her finger at Muriel:

APPARITION: And you.

MURIEL: Well what of it I have no share nor any care of anything that happens to him.

APPARITION: No but you will get thin, get thin oh so thin, that you can slip through a ring and when you slip through a ring nobody can find you nobody can find where you have been nobody, nobody, nobody not even he and this is what the spider said and he was red the spider and this is what he said.

MURIEL: Oh (*and she began to sigh*) Oh my.

APPARITION (*pointing one finger at Susie and another at Silly*): Silly will turn into Willy and Susie will turn into an egg and Willie will sit on the egg, and so they will wed Willie and the egg, although the egg was bad. Oh dear (*the apparition began to giggle and giggle*) oh dear (*and she faded away giggling*).

OLIVER (*gloomily*): I don't care for my share.

MURIEL (*with a gentle sigh*): I like to be thin, it is so interesting.

Susie and Silly holding hands just laugh and laugh and the curtain falls.

ACT II

Oliver comes in very gloomily and all tied up with string.

OLIVER: I'll fool her, when I split in two if I do this string will hold me together whatever I do, so nobody can know not even she, and she is ugly, that I am not one but two, she'll see.

Muriel coming in and in each hand a huge bottle of milk.

MURIEL: No I won't, yes I will, it would be a thrill to be thin and go through a ring, but I'll fool her yes I will, hullo Oliver are you in two, then I will be as thin as either one of you.

OLIVER (*gloomily*): Go to bed.

MURIEL: Go to bed yourself, what do I care what happens to you.

OLIVER: You do too.

Muriel begins to cry: Boohoo

Just then Susie and Silly come in giggling.

SUSIE: I am an egg and I am cracked and Silly is Willy and he is so silly, see me crack, hear me crack.

SILLY: And the egg you are is addled at that.

And they giggle and giggle and the other two continue to be gloomy.

SILLY: Hush I hear a noise, let us each get behind a tree so she cannot see and then we will know what she can do. Hush. (*And they each get behind a tree*).

The apparition comes in disguised as an old woman picking up sticks. As she picks them up she dances.

APPARITION: One stick is one two sticks are two three sticks are three four sticks are four, four sticks are four, three sticks are three, two sticks are two, one stick is one. Which one, which won (*and she begins to giggle*). This one.

OLIVER: She is ugly but not the same, I don't know her name she is ugly all the same, but she is not she, so I must not be scared when she says this you see.

MURIEL: If I say one two three and she is she she will look at me. (*She puts her head out and she calls out very loud*) One two three if you are she then look at me.

The old woman pays no attention but goes on picking up and throwing away sticks, always repeating.

APPARITION: One stick is one, this one, two sticks are two for which one, three sticks are three, suits me, four sticks are four, no more. Four sticks are four, three sticks are three, two sticks are two, one stick is one.

SUSIE: Oh Silly she scares me.

SILLY: Don't be silly but she scares me too.

SUSIE: Ouch.

SILLY: Ouch.

Both together: We wish we were brave but we are not, not, not, not.

Just then the old woman says:

APPARITION: One stick is one (*and she suddenly hits Oliver on the back*).

APPARITION: One stick is one whack on the back.

OLIVER: Oh oh, I am in two oh in two in two. It is only the string holds me together. Oh.

The old woman then hits Muriel on the back shouting:

APPARITION: Two sticks are two take that.

MURIEL (*dropping both bottles of milk which smash*): Oh I am getting thin it is most distressing, my milk, my milk, my ring oh I am getting so thin.

APPARITION (*behind Silly*): Three sticks are three (*and gives him a whack*).

SILLY: Oh I am not Silly I am only Willy and I do not want to be Willy I want to be Silly, oh.

Apparition goes behind Susie.

Four sticks are four and there are no more whack on your back.

SUSIE: Oh I am an egg, a white egg, not even a brown egg, a dirty white egg and it is addled and never now can I wed with dear Silly who is only Willy.

And they all throw themselves on the ground lamenting and the old woman dances away singing:

APPARITION: One stick is one two sticks are two three sticks are three four sticks are four, four sticks are four, three sticks are three two sticks are two one stick is one and now I am done.

OLIVER: I'll see to it that she never comes back.

MURIEL: Oh oh.

OLIVER (*grimly*): I'll see to it that she never comes back, the ugly, I am in two but she will never get through to us again.

MURIEL: I am so thin, my ring my ring, I am so thin.

SUSIE AND SILLY: Oh oh.

The curtain falls.

ACT III

Enter Oliver this time beside the string he has sticking plaster all down the front and the back of him holding him together and in his hand a large cardboard and wire and pincers.

Muriel coming in with a doll's carriage filled with butter sugar milk and bread. Susie is a large white egg and Silly is Willy. They come in slowly looking all around and sadly shaking their heads.

OLIVER: I may be a twin but she will never get in.

MURIEL: Oh dear I am getting so thin, I eat milk and bread and sugar and butter and they say of butter, one pound of butter makes two pounds of girl and oh dear butter, butter, I get thinner and thinner and my ring oh dear I am so thin.

SUSIE: Oh I wish I was a fish and not an egg and then I could swim and not do anything.

SILLY: I wish I wish I was not Willy, I wish I wish I wish I was Silly so I could marry Susie oh dear.

OLIVER (*darkly*): Well wait she cannot get in, see what I am doing.

He commences to stop up the entrance between the trees with wire and in the middle of it he puts a large sign NO TRESPASSING

OLIVER: There what do I care if I am a twin, she never will get in never never.

MURIEL: Oh dear I am so thin, it is not interesting, oh dear I am so thin, oh dear where is my ring. I slip through my ring oh dear I am so thin.

SUSIE AND SILLY: Oh dear oh dear.

Just then the apparition appears disguised as a french poodle. She comes along barking and jumping.

OLIVER: Oh what a pretty dog. Dogs lick wounds and they heal perhaps he could lick me where I am in two and then I would be one, oh happy me not to be two but one. Which one. Oh happy day. Which one. One. One. One.

MURIEL: And perhaps he has a bone, bones make you fat oh it is that, I want to be fat, being thin is not interesting, being fat oh I want to be that.

SUSIE: Oh Willie sit on me quick it would be awful if he bit.

WILLY: If he bit he might make me Silly instead of Billy.

The poodle comes in barking and rushing around and they all say:

and what a pretty dog. I would like a pretty dog like that.

The dog comes up to Oliver barking and jumping.

APPARITION: Am I pretty am I witty and would you like to have a dog like that.

OLIVER: You bet I would, I'd give my hat, I'd give my bat to have a pretty dog like that.

APPARITION (*to Muriel*): Am I pretty am I witty and would you like to have a pretty dog like that.

MURIEL: Thin or fat I would oh I would like to have a pretty dog like that and I would make him a pretty hat of roses and daisies if I had a pretty dog like that.

APPARITION *to Susie and Silly* (*Willie is sitting on Susie*): Am I pretty am I witty and would you like a pretty dog like that.

SUSIE AND SILLY: We would that.

Apparition barking and dancing licks Oliver up and down saying:

I lick you front and back do you feel that.

OLIVER: You bet I do and it tickles too but it is funny now I know I am one and not two, thank you, thanks pretty doggie thanks for that.

Apparition kisses Muriel.

MURIEL: Oh happy day oh little by little I am getting fat, a pound to-day, not like yesterday, a pound every day oh I am getting fat. Oh thank you witty pretty doggie thank you for that.

Apparition jumps over Willie and Susie and they scream.

Oh we are Susie and we are Silly and thanks pretty dog for that.

Oliver goes over to the wire and takes down the cardboard NO TRESPASSING *and gives it to the dog who begs and takes it and dances with it tearing it up while the four cousins dance around the dog singing:*

The doggie is pretty the doggie is witty we all always want to have a dog like that.

[CURTAIN]

By Gertrude Stein

Doctor Faustus Lights the Lights

1938

ACT I

Faust standing at the door of his room, with his arms up at the door lintel looking out, behind him a blaze of electric light.

Just then Mephisto approaches and appears at the door.

Faustus growls out.	The devil what the devil what do I care if the devil is there.
Mephisto says.	But Doctor Faustus dear yes I am here.
Doctor Faustus.	What do I care there is no here nor there. What am I. I am Doctor Faustus who knows everything can do everything and you say it was through you but not at all, if I had not been in a hurry and if I had taken my time I would have known how to make white electric light and day-light and night light and what did I do I saw you miserable devil I saw you and and I was deceived and I believed miserable devil I thought I needed you, and I thought I was tempted by the devil and

I know no temptation is tempting unless the devil tells you so. And you wanted my soul what the hell did you want my soul for, how do you know I have a soul, who says so nobody says so but you the devil and everybody knows the devil is all lies, so how do you know how do I know that I have a soul to sell how do you know Mr. Devil oh Mr. Devil how can you tell you can not tell anything and I I who know everything I keep on having so much light that light is not bright and what after all is the use of light, you can see just as well without it, you can go around just as well without it you can get up and go to bed just as well without it, and I I wanted to make it and the devil take it yes you devil you do not even want it and I sold my soul to make it. I have made it but have I a soul to pay for it.

Mephisto coming nearer and trying to pat his arm.

Yes dear Doctor Faustus yes of course you have a soul of course you have, do not believe them when they say the devil lies, you know the devil never lies, he deceives oh yes he deceives but that is not lying no dear please dear Doctor Faustus do not say the devil lies.

Doctor Faustus.

Who cares if you lie if you steal, there is no snake to grind under one's heel, there is no hope there is no death there is no life there is no breath, there

just is every day all day and when
there is no day there is no day, and
anyway of what use is a devil unless he
goes away, go away old devil go away,
there is no use in a devil unless he
goes away, how can you remember a
devil unless he goes away, oh devil
there is no use in your coming to stay
and now you are red at night which is
not a delight and you are red in the
morning which is not a warning go
away devil go away or stay after all
what can a devil say.

Mephisto.

A devil can smile a devil can while
away whatever there is to give away,
and now are you not proud Doctor
Faustus yes you are you know you are
you are the only one who knows what
you know and it is I the devil who tells
you so.

Faustus.

You fool you devil how can you know,
how can you tell me so, if I am the only
one who can know what I know then
no devil can know what I know and no
devil can tell me so and I could know
without any soul to sell, without there
being anything in hell. What I know I
know, I know how I do what I do when
I see the way through and always any
day I will see another day and you old
devil you know very well you never see
any other way than just the way to
hell, you only know one way. You only
know one thing, you are never ready
for anything, and I everything is al-

ways now and now and now perhaps
through you I begin to know that it is
all just so, that light however bright
will never be other than light, and any
light is just a light and now there is
nothing more either by day or by night
but just a light. Oh you devil go to hell,
that is all you know to tell, and who is
interested in hell just a devil is interested in hell because that is all he can
tell, whether I stamp or whether I cry
whether I live or whether I die, I can
know that all a devil can say is just
about going to hell the same way, get
out of here devil, it does not interest
me whether you buy or I can sell, get
out of here devil just you go to hell.

Faustus gives him an awful kick, and Mephisto moves
away and the electric lights just then begin to get very gay.

Alright then

The Ballet

Doctor Faustus sitting alone surrounded by electric
lights.

His dog comes in and says
Thank you.

One of the electric lights goes out and again the dog says
Thank you.

The electric light that went out is replaced by a glow.

The dog murmurs.

My my what a sky.

And then he says
Thank you.
I shall not.

No I shall not.

    Faustus addresses little boy and dog

Night is better than day so please go away

    The boy says

But say

When the hay has to be cut every day then there is the devil
to pay

    The dog starts and then he shrinks and says

Thank you

    Faustus half turns and starts

I hear her

    he says

I hear her say

Call to her to sing

To sing all about

to sing a song

All about

day-light and night light.

Moonlight and star-light

electric light and twilight

every light as well.

    The electric lights glow and a chorus in the distance sings

    Her name is her name is her name is Marguerite Ida and
Helena Annabel.

    Faustus sings

I knew it I knew it the electric lights they told me so no dog
can know no boy can know I cannot know they cannot know
the electric lights they told me so I would not know I could not
know who can know who can tell me so I know you know they
can know her name is Marguerite Ida and Helena Annabel
and when I tell oh when I tell oh when I when I when I tell, oh
go away and go away and tell and tell and tell and tell and tell,
oh hell.

    The electric lights commence to dance and one by one
    they go out and come in and the boy and the dog begin to

sing.

Oh very well oh Doctor Faustus very very well oh very well, thank you says the dog oh very well says the boy her name her name is Marguerite Ida and Helena Annabel, I know says the dog I know says the boy I know says Doctor Faustus no no no no no nobody can know what I know I know her name is not Marguerite Ida and Helena Annabel, very well says the boy it is says the boy her name is Marguerite Ida and Helena Annabel, no no no says Doctor Faustus, yes yes yes says the dog, no says the boy yes says the dog, her name is not Marguerite Ida and Helena Annabel and she is not ready yet to sing about day-light and night light, moonlight and star-light electric light and twilight she is not she is not but she will be. She will not be says Doctor Faustus never never never, never will her name be Marguerite Ida and Helena Annabel never never never never well as well never Marguerite Ida and Helena Annabel never Marguerite Ida and Helena Annabel.

There is a sudden hush and the distant chorus says
It might be it might be her name her name might be Marguerite Ida and Helena Annabel it might be.

And Doctor Faustus says in a loud whisper
It might be but it is not, and the little boy says how do you know and Faustus says it might be it might not be not be not be, and as he says the last not be the dog says
Thank you.

Scene II

I am I and my name is Marguerite Ida and Helena Annabel, and then oh then I could yes I could I could begin to cry but why why could I begin to cry.

And I am I and I am here and how do I know how wild the wild world is how wild the wild woods are the wood they call the woods the poor man's overcoat but do they cover me and if they do how wild they are wild and wild and wild they are, how do I know how wild woods are when I have never ever seen a wood before.

I wish (*she whispered*) I knew why woods are wild why animals are wild why I am I, why I can cry, I wish I wish I knew, I wish oh how I wish I knew. Once I am in I will never be through the woods are there and I am here and am I here or am I there, oh where oh where is here oh where oh where is there and animals wild animals are everywhere.

　　　　　She sits down.

I wish (*she says conversationally*) I wish if I had a wish that when I sat down it would not be here but there there where I could have a chair there where I would not have to look around
Will he tell
And then she stops again
And the bite might he make it a bite.
Doctor Faustus a queer name
Might he make it a bite
　　　And so she disappears.

　　　　　　　　Scene III

Doctor Faustus the dog and the boy all sleeping, the dog dreaming says thickly
Thank you, thank you thank you thank you thank you, thank you thank you.
Doctor Faustus turns and murmurs
Man and dog dog and man each one can tell it all like a ball with a caress no tenderness, man and dog just the same each one can take the blame each one can well as well tell it all as they can, man and dog, well well man and dog what is the difference between a man and a dog when I say none do

I go away does he go away go away to stay no nobody goes away the dog the boy they can stay I can go away go away where where there there where, dog and boy can annoy I can go say I go where do I go I go where I go, where is there there is where and all the day and all the night too it grew and grew and there is no way to say I and a dog and a boy, if a boy is to grow to be a man am I a boy am I a dog is a dog a boy is a boy a dog and what am I I cannot cry what am I oh what am I

And then he waits a moment and he says
Oh what am I.

Just then in the distance there is a call
Doctor Faustus Doctor Faustus are you there Doctor Faustus I am here Doctor Faustus I am coming there Doctor Faustus, there is where Doctor Faustus oh where is there Doctor Faustus say it Doctor Faustus are you there Doctor Faustus are you there.

The dog murmurs
Thank you thank you
and the boy says
There is somebody of course there is somebody just there there is somebody somebody is there oh yes somebody is there.

and all together they say
Where is there nobody says nobody is there. Somebody is there and nobody says that somebody is not there. Somebody somebody is there somebody somebody somebody somebody says there is where where is it where is it where is it where, here is here here is there somebody somebody says where is where.

Outside the voice says
Doctor Faustus are you there Doctor Faustus anywhere, Doctor Faustus are you there.

And then there is a knock at the door.
The electric lights glow softly and Marguerite Ida and

Helena Annabel comes in.

Well and yes well, and this is yes this is Doctor Faustus Doctor Doctor Faustus and he can and he can change a bite hold it tight make it not kill not kill Marguerite Ida not kill Helena Annabel and hell oh hell not a hell not well yes well Doctor Faustus can he can make it all well.

And then she says in a quiet voice
Doctor Faustus have you ever been to hell.
Of course not she says of course you have not how could you sell your soul if you had ever been to hell of course not, no of course not.
Doctor Faustus tell me what did they give you when you sold your soul, not hell no of course not not hell.

And then she goes on.
I I am Marguerite Ida and Helena Annabel and a viper bit or stung it is very well begun and if it is so then oh oh I will die and as my soul has not been sold I Marguerite Ida and Helena Annabel perhaps I will go to hell.

The dog sighs and says
Thank you
  and the little boy coming nearer says
what is a viper, tell me Marguerite Ida and Helena Annabel I like you being Marguerite Ida and Helena Annabel what is a viper do I know it very well or do I not know it very well please tell you are Marguerite Ida and Helena Annabel what is a viper.

  Doctor Faustus says
Little boy and dog can be killed by a viper by Marguerite Ida and Helena Annabel not very well no not very well
    (*He bursts out*)
Leave me alone
Let me be alone
Little boy and dog let me be alone, Marguerite Ida and Helena Annabel let me be alone, I have no soul I had no soul I sold it sold it here there and everywhere.

What did I do I knew
I knew that there could be light not moon-light star light day-
light and candle light, I knew I knew I saw the lightening light,
I saw it light, I said I I I must have that light, and what did I
do oh what did I too I said I would sell my soul all through but
I knew I knew that electric light was all true, and true oh yes
it is true they took it that it was true that I sold my soul to
them as well and so never never could I go to hell never never
as well. Go away dog and boy go away Marguerite Ida and
Helena Annabel go away all who can die and go to heaven or
hell go away oh go away leave me alone oh leave me alone. I
said it I said it was the light I said I gave the light I said the
lights are right and the day is bright little boy and dog leave
me alone let me be alone.

The country woman with the sickle looks in at the window
and sings Well well this is the Doctor Faustus and he has not
gone to hell he has pretty lights and they light so very well and
there is a dog and he says thank you and there is a little boy
oh yes little boy there you are you just are there yes little boy
you are and there is Marguerite Ida and Helena Annabel and
a viper did bite her, oh cure her Doctor Faustus cure her what
is the use of your having been to hell if Marguerite Ida and
Helena Annabel is not to be all well.

And the chorus sings
What is the use Doctor Faustus what is the use what is the
use of having been to hell if you cannot cure this only only this
Marguerite Ida and Helena Annabel.

Dr. Faustus says
I think I have thought thought is not bought oh no thought
is not bought I think I have thought and what have I bought
I have bought thought, to think is not bought but I I have
bought thought and so you come here you come you come
here and here and here where can I say that not to-day not
any day can I look and see, no no I cannot look no no I cannot
see and you you say you are Marguerite Ida and Helena

Annabel and I I cannot see I cannot see Marguerite Ida and
I cannot see Helena Annabel and you you are the two and I
cannot cannot see you.

Marguerite Ida and Helena Annabel
Do not see me Doctor Faustus do not see me it would terrify
me if you did see do not see me no no do not see me I am
Marguerite Ida and Helena Annabel but do not see me cure
me Doctor Faustus do the viper bit the viper stung his sting
was a bite and you you have the light cure me Doctor Faustus
cure me do but do not see me, I see you but do not see me cure
me do but do not see me I implore you.

Doctor Faustus
A dog says thank you but you you say do not see me cure me
do but do not see me what shall I do.

He turns to the dog
The dog says
Thank you
and the boy says
What difference does it make to you if you do what difference
oh what difference does it make to you if you do, whatever you
do do whatever you do do what difference does it make to you
if you do.

Marguerite Ida and Helena Annabel
What difference does it make to you if you do what difference
does it make to you but I a viper has had his bite and I I will
die but you you cannot die you have sold your soul but I I have
mine and a viper has come and he has bitten me and see see
how the poison works see see how I must die, see how little
by little it is coming to be high, higher and higher I must die
oh Doctor Faustus what difference does it make to you what
difference oh what difference but to me to me to me to me a
viper has bitten me a bitter viper a viper has bitten me.

The dog
Oh Thank you thank you all all of you thank you thank
you oh thank you everybody thank you he and we thank you,

a viper has bitten you thank you thank you.
    The boy
A viper has bitten her she knows it too a viper has bitten her
believe it or not it is true, a viper has bitten her and if Doctor
Faustus does not cure her it will be all through her a viper has
bitten her a viper a viper.
    Dog
Thank you
    Woman at the window
A viper has bitten her and if Doctor Faustus does not cure her
it will be all through her.
    Chorus in the distance
Who is she
She has not gone to hell
Very well
Very well
She has not gone to hell
Who is she
Marguerite Ida and Helena Annabel
And what has happened to her
A viper has bitten her
And if Doctor Faustus does not cure her
It will go all through her
And he what does he say
He says he cannot see her
Why cannot he see her
Because he cannot look at her
He cannot look at Marguerite Ida and Helena Annabel
But he cannot cure her without seeing her
They say yes yes
And he says there is no witness
And he says
He can but he will not
And she says he must and he will
And the dog says thank you

And the boy says very well
And the woman says well cure her and she says she is
Marguerite Ida and Helena Annabel.

There is silence the lights flicker and flicker, and Marguerite Ida and Helena Annabel gets weaker and weaker and the poison stronger and stronger and suddenly the dog says startlingly
Thank you
Doctor Faustus says
I cannot see you
The viper has forgotten you.
The dog has said thank you
The boy has said will you
The woman has said
Can you
And you, you have said you are you
Enough said.
You are not dead.
Enough said
Enough said.
You are not dead.
No you are not dead.
Enough said
Enough said
You are not dead.

All join in enough said you are not dead you are not dead enough said yes enough said no you are not dead yes enough said, thank you yes enough said no you are not dead.

And at the last
In a low whisper
She says
I am Marguerite Ida and Helena Annabel and enough said I am not dead.

Curtain

ACT II

Someone comes and sings
Very
Very
Butter better very well
Butcher whether it will tell
Well is well and silver sell
Sell a salted almond to Nell
Which she will accept
And then
What does a fatty do
She does not pay for it.
No she does not
Does not pay for it.
By this time they know how to spell very
Very likely the whole thing is really extraordinary
Which is a great relief
All the time her name is Marguerite Ida Marguerite Ida
    They drift in and they sing
Very likely the whole thing is extraordinary
Which is a great relief
All the time her name is Marguerite Ida
Marguerite Ida
    Then they converse about it.
Marguerite Ida is her name Marguerite Ida and Helena
Annabel
who can tell if her name is Marguerite Ida or Helena Annabel
Sillies all that is what makes you tall.
To be tall means to say that everything else is layed away.
Of course her names is Marguerite Ida too and Helena
Annabel as well.
    A full chorus
Of course her names is Marguerite Ida too and Helena
Annabel as well.

A deep voice asks
Would a viper have stung her if she had only had one name
would he would he.
How do you know how do you know that a viper did sting her.
How could Doctor Faustus have cured her if there had not
been something the matter with her.
Marguerite Ida and Helena Annabel it is true her name is
Marguerite Ida and Helena Annabel as well and a viper has
stung her and Doctor Faustus has cured her, cured her
cured her, he has sold his soul to hell cured her cured her
cured he he has sold his soul to hell and her name is
Marguerite Ida and Helena Annabel and a viper had to bite
her and Doctor Faustus had to cure her cure her cure her
cure her.

The curtain at the corner raises and there she is Marguerite Ida and Helena Annabel and she has an artificial viper
there beside her and a halo is around her not of electric light
but of candle light, and she sits there and waits.

The chorus sings
There she is
Is she there
Look and see
Is she there
Is she there
Anywhere
Look and see
Is she there
Yes she is there
There is there
She is there
Look and see
She is there.
There she is
There there
Where

Why there
Look and see there
There she is
And what is there
A viper is there
The viper that bit her
No silly no
How could he be there
This is not a viper
This is what is like a viper
She is there
And a viper did bite her
And Doctor Faustus did cure her
And now
And now
And now she is there
Where
Why there
Oh yes there.
Yes oh yes yes there.
There she is
Look and see
And the viper is there
And the light is there
Who gave her the light
Nobody did
Doctor Faustus sold his soul
And so the light came there
And did she sell her soul.
No silly he sold his soul
She had a viper bite her
She is there
Oh yes she is there
Look there
Yes there

She is there.

Marguerite Ida begins to sing
I sit and sit with my back to the sun I sat and sat with my back
to the sun. Marguerite Ida sat and sat with her back to the
sun. The sun oh the sun the lights are bright like the sun set
and she sat with her back to the sun sat and sat

She sits

A very grand ballet of lights.
Nobody can know that it so
They come from everywhere
By land by sea by air
They come from everywhere
To look at her there.
See how she sits
See how she eats
See how she lights,
The candle lights.
See how the viper there,
Cannot hurt her.
No indeed he cannot.
Nothing can touch her,
She has everything
And her soul,
Nothing can lose her,
See how they come
See how they come
To see her.
See how they come.
Watch
They come by sea
They come by land
They come by air
And she sits
With her back to the sun
One sun

And she is one
Marguerite Ida and Helena Annabel as well.
　　They commence to come and more and more come and
　　they come from the sea from the land and from the air.
　　And she sits.
　　A man comes from over the seas and a great many are
　　around him
　　He sees her as she sits.
　　And he says
Pretty pretty dear
She is all my love and always here
And I am hers and she is mine
And I love her all the time
Pretty pretty pretty dear.
No says the chorus no.
She is she and the viper bit her
And Doctor Faustus cured her.
The man from over seas repeats
Pretty pretty pretty dear
She is all my love and always here
And I am hers and she is mine
And I love her all the time.
　　Marguerite Ida and Helena Annabel suddenly hears
something and says
What is it.
　　He comes forward and says again
Pretty pretty pretty dear she is all my love and she is always
here.
　　She sings slowly
You do or you do not.
　　He
Pretty pretty dear she is all my love and she is always here.
Well well he says well well and her name is Marguerite Ida and
Helena Annabel and they all say it was a viper, what is a viper,
a viper is a serpent and anybody has been bitten and not

everybody dies and cries, and so why why say it all the time,
I have been bitten I I I have been bitten by her bitten by her
there she sits with her back to the sun and I have won I have
won her I have won her.

  She sings a song
You do or you do not
You are or you are not
I am there is no not
But you you you
You are as you are not
    He says
Do you do what you do because you knew all the way through
that I I was coming to you answer me that.
    She turns her back on him.
    And he says
I am your sun oh very very well begun, you turn your back
on your sun, I am your sun, I have won I have won I am your
sun.
    Marguerite Ida and Helena Annabel rises. She holds the
viper she says
Is it you Doctor Faustus is it you, tell me man from over the
sea are you he.
    He laughs.
Are you afraid now afraid of me.
    She says
Are you he.
    He says
I am the only he and you are the only she and we are the only
we. Come come do you hear me come come, you must come
to me, throw away the viper throw away the sun throw away
the lights until there are none. I am not any one I am the only
one, you have to have me because I am that one.
    She looks very troubled and drops the viper but she
instantly stoops and picks it up and some of the lights go out
and she fusses about it.

And then suddenly she starts,
No one is one when there are two, look behind you look
behind you you are not one you are two.
She faints.
And indeed behind the man of the seas is Mephistopheles
and with him is a boy and a
girl.
Together they sing the song the boy and the girl.
Mr. Viper think of me. He says you do she says you do and
if you do dear Mr. Viper if you do then it is all true he is a boy
I am a girl it is all true dear dear Mr. Viper think of me.
The chorus says in the back,
Dear dear Mr. Viper think of them one is a boy one is a girl
dear dear viper dear dear viper think of them.
Marguerite Ida and Helena Annabel still staring at the
man from over the seas and Mephisto behind them.
She whispers,
They two I two they two that makes six it should be seven they
two I two I two they two five is heaven.
Mephisto says
And what if I ask what answer me what, I have a will of iron
yes a will to do what I do. I do what I do what I do, I do I do.
And he strides forward,
Where where where are you, what a to do, when a light is
bright there is moon-light, when a light is not so bright then
it is day-light, and when a light is no light than it is electric
light, but you you have candle light, who are you.
The ballet rushes in and out.
Marguerite Ida and Helena Annabel lifts the viper and
says
Lights are all right but the viper is my might.
Pooh says Mephisto, I despise a viper, the viper tries but the
viper lies. Me they cannot touch no not any such, a viper, ha
ha a viper, a viper, ha ha, no the lights the lights the candle
lights, I know a light when I see a light, I work I work all day

and all night, I am the devil and day and night, I never sleep by any light by any dark by any might, I never sleep not by day not by night, you cannot fool me by candle light, where is the real electric light woman answer me.

The little boy and girl creep closer, they sing.

Mr Viper dear Mr. Viper, he is a boy I am a girl she is a girl I am a boy we do not want to annoy but we do oh we do oh Mr. Viper yes we do we want you to know that she is a girl that I am boy, oh yes Mr. Viper please Mr. Viper here we are Mr. Viper listen to us Mr. Viper, oh please Mr. Viper it is not true Mr. Viper what the devil says Mr. Viper that there is no Mr. Viper, please Mr. Viper please Mr. Viper, she is a girl he is a boy please Mr. Viper you are Mr. Viper please Mr. Viper please tell us so.

The man from over the seas smiles at them all, and says It is lovely to be at ease.

Mephisto says

What you know I am the devil and you do not listen to me I work and I work by day and by night and you do not listen to me he and she she and he do not listen to me you will see you will see, if I work day and night and I do I do I work day and night, then you will see what you will see, look out look out look out for me.

He rushes away

And Helena Annabel and Marguerite Ida shrinks back, and says to them all

What does he say

And the man from over seas says

Pretty pretty dear she is all my love and she is always here. and then more slowly

I am the only he you are the only she and we are the only we, and the chorus sings softly

And the viper did bite her and Doctor Faustus did cure her. And the boy and girl sing softly.

Yes Mr. Viper he is a boy she is a girl yes Mr. Viper.

And the ballet of lights fades away.

Curtain.

ACT III Scene I

Doctor Faustus' house
Faustus in his chair, the dog and the boy, the electric
lights are right but the room is dark.
Faustus
Yes they shine
They shine all the time.
I know they shine
I see them shine
And I am here
I have no fear
But what shall I do
I am all through
I cannot bear
To have no care
I like it bright
I do like it bright
Alright I like it bright,
But is it white
Or is it bright.
Dear dear
I do care
That nobody can share.
What if they do
It is all to me
Ah I do not like that word me,
Why not even if it does rhyme with she. I know all the words
that rhyme with bright with light with might with alright, I

know them so that I cannot tell I can spell but I cannot tell
how much I need to not have that, not light not sight, not light
not night not alright, not night not sight not bright, no no not
night not sight not bright no no not bright.

There is a moment's silence and then the dog says
Thank you.

He turns around and then he says
Yes thank you.

And then he says
Not bright not night dear Doctor Faustus you are right, I am
a dog yes I am just that I am I am a dog and I bay at the moon,
I did yes I did I used to do it I used to bay at the moon I always
used to do it and now now not any more, I cannot, of course
I cannot, the electric lights they make it be that there is no
night and if there is no night then there is no moon and if
there is no moon I do not see it and if I do not see it I cannot
bay at it.

The dog sighs and settles down to rest
and as he settles down he says
Thank you.

The little boy cuddles up close to him and says
Yes there is no moon and if there is a moon then we do not
bay at the moon and if there is no moon then no one is crazy
any more because it is the moon of course it is the moon that
always made them be like that, say thank you doggie and I
too I too with you will say thank you.

They softly murmur
Thank you thank you thank you too.

They all sleep in the dark with the electric light all bright,
and then at the window comes something.
Is it the moon says the dog is it the moon says the boy is it
the moon do not wake me is it the moon says Faustus.
No says a woman no it is not it is not the moon, I am not the
moon I am at the window Doctor Faustus do not you know
what it is that is happening.

No answer.

Doctor Faustus do not you know what is happening.

Back of her a chorus

Doctor Faustus do not you know what is happening.

Still no answer

All together louder

Doctor Faustus do not you know do not you know what it is that is happening.

Doctor Faustus.

Go away woman and men, children and dogs moon and stars go away let me alone let me be alone no light is bright, I have no sight, go away woman and let me boy and dog let me be alone I need no light to tell me it is bright, go away go away, go away go away.

No says the woman no I am at the window and here I remain till you hear it all. Here we know because Doctor Faustus tells us so, that he only he can turn night into day but now they say, they say, (her voice rises to a screech) they say a woman can turn night into day, they say a woman and a viper bit her and did not hurt her and he showed her how and now she can turn night into day, Doctor Faustus oh Doctor Faustus say you are the only one who can turn night into day, oh Doctor Faustus yes do say that you are the only one who can turn night into day.

The chorus behind says

Oh Doctor Faustus oh Doctor Faustus do say that you are the only one who can turn night into day.

Faustus starts up confused he faces the woman, he says, What is it you say.

And she says imploringly,

Oh, Doctor Faustus do say you are the only one who can turn night into day.

Faustus slowly draws himself erect and says

Yes I do say I am the only one who can turn night into day.

And the woman and the chorus say,

He is the only one who can turn night into day.
And the dog says
He is the only one who can turn night into day, there is no
moon any night or any day he is the only one to turn night into
day,
and the little boy says
Yes he is the only one to turn night into day.
And the woman then says
But come Doctor Faustus come away
come and see whether they say that
they can turn night into day
Who says
says Doctor Faustus
She says
says the woman
Who is she
says Doctor Faustus
The answer
Marguerite Ida or Helena Annabel
She
says Doctor Faustus
Who said I could not go to hell.
She she
says the woman
She she
says the chorus
Thank you
said the dog
Well
said Doctor Faustus
Well then I can go to hell, if she can turn night into day then
I can go to hell, come on then come on we will go and see her
and I will show her that I can go to hell, if she can turn night
into day as they say then I am not the only one very well I am

not the only one so Marguerite Ida or Helena Annabel listen
well you cannot but I I can go to hell. Come on every one never
again will I be alone come on come on every one.
They all leave.

Scene II

The scene as before, Marguerite Ida or Helena Annabel
sitting with the man from over the seas their backs to the sun,
the music to express a noon-day hush.
Everybody dreamily saying
Mr. Viper please Mr. Viper,
    some saying
Is he is he Doctor Faustus no he isn't no he isn't, is he is he
is he all he loves her is he is he all she loves him, no one can
remember anything but him, which is she and which is he
sweetly after all there is no bee there is a viper such a nice
sweet quiet one, nobody any body knows how to run, come
any one come, see any one, some, come viper sun, we know
no other any one, any one can forget a light, even an electric
one but no one no no one can forget a viper even a stuffed one
no no one and no one can forget the sun and no one can forget
Doctor Faustus no no one and and no one can forget Thank
you and the dog and no one can forget a little boy and no one
can forget any one no no one.
    (*These words to be distributed among the chorus*)
    and the man from over seas murmurs dreamily
Pretty pretty pretty dear here I am and you are here and yet
and yet it would be better yet if you had more names and not
only four in one let it be begun, forget it oh forget it pretty one,
and if not I will forget that you are one yes I will yes I will pretty
pretty one yes I will.
    Marguerite Ida or Helena Annabel stiffens a little
Well will you yes I will, no one can know when I do not tell then
so that they cannot know anything they know, yes I know, I

do know just what I can know, it is not there well anywhere,
I cannot come not for any one I cannot say what is night and
day but I am the only one who can know anything about any
one, am I one dear dear am I one, who hears me knows me
I am here and here I am, yes here I am.

    The chorus gets more lively and says
Yes there she is
Dear me
    says the man from over seas.
    Just them out of the gloom appears at the other end of the
    stage Faust and the boy and the dog, nobody sees them,
    just then in front of every one appears Mephisto, very
    excited and sings
Which of you can dare to deceive me which of you he or she
can dare to deceive me, I who have a will of iron I who make
what will be happen I who can win men or women I who can
be wherever I am which of you has been deceiving which of
you she or he which of you have been deceiving me.

    He shouts louder
If there is a light who has the right, I say I gave it to him, she
says he gave it to her or she does not say anything, I say I am
Mephisto and what I have I do not give no not to any one, who
has been in her who has been in him, I will win.

    The boy and girl shrilly sing
She is she and he is he and we are we Mr. Viper do not forget
to be. Please Mr. Viper do not forget to be, do not forget that
she is she and that he is he please Mr. Viper do not forget me.

    Faustus murmurs in a low voice
I sold my soul to make it bright with electric light and now no
one not I not she not they not he are interested in that thing
and I and I I cannot go to hell I have sold my soul to make
a light and the light is bright but not interesting in my sight
and I would oh yes I would I would rather go to hell be I with
all my might and then go to hell oh yes alright.

    Mephisto strides up to him and says

You deceived me.
I did not
    says Faustus
    Mephisto.
You deceived me and I am never deceived
Faust, you deceived me and I am always deceived,
Mephisto, you deceived me and I am never deceived.
    Faustus
Well well let us forget it is not ready yet let us forget and now
oh how how I want to be me myself all now, I do not care for
light let it be however light, I do not care anything but to be
well and to go to hell. Tell me oh devil tell me will she will
Marguerite Ida and Helena Annabel will she will she really
will she go to hell.
    Mephisto
I suppose so.
    Faustus
Well then how dear devil how how can I who have no soul I
sold it for a light how can I be I again alright and go to hell.
    Mephisto
Commit a sin
    Faustus
What sin, how can I without a soul commit a sin.
    Mephisto
Kill anything
    Faustus
Kill
    Mephisto
Yes kill something oh yes kill anything.
Yes it is I who have been deceived I the devil who no one can
deceive yes it is I I who have been deceived.
    Faustus
But if I kill what then will.
    Mephisto
It is I who have an iron will.

Faustus
But if I kill what will happen then.
Mephisto
Oh go to hell.
Faustus
I will
He turns he sees the boy and dog he says
I will kill I will I will
He whispers
I will kill I will I will.
He turns to the boy and dog and he says
Boy and dog I will kill you two I will kill I will I will boy and dog
I will kill you kill you, the viper will kill you but it will be I who
did it, you will die.
The dog says
Thank you, the light is so bright there is no moon tonight I
cannot bay at the moon the viper will kill me. Thank you,
and the boy says
And I too, there is no day and night there is no dog to-night
to say thank you the viper will kill me too, good-bye to you.
In the distance the voices of the boy and girl are heard
saying
Mr. Viper please listen to me he is a boy she is a girl.
There is a rustle the viper appears and the dog and the
boy die.
Faustus
They are dead yes they are dead, dear dog dear boy yes you
are dead you are forever ever ever dead and I I can because
you die nobody can deny later I will go to hell very well very
well I will go to hell Marguerite Ida and Helena Annabel I come
to tell to tell you that I can go to hell.
Mephisto
And I, while you cry I who do not deny that now you can go
to hell have I nothing to do with you.
Faustus

No I am through with you I do not need the devil I can go to hell all alone. Leave me alone let me be alone I can go to hell all alone.

Mephisto

No listen to me now take her with you do I will make you young take her with you do Marguerite Ida and Helena Annabel take her with you do.

Faustus

Is it true that I can be young.

Mephisto

Yes.

Faustus

Alright.

> He is young he approaches Marguerite Ida and Helena
> Annabel who wakes up and looks at him. He says

Look well I am Doctor Faustus and I can go to hell.

Marguerite Ida and Helena Annabel

You Doctor Faustus never never Doctor Faustus is old I was told and I saw it with my eyes he was old and could not go to hell and you are young and can go to hell, very well you are not Doctor Faustus never never.

Faustus

I am I am I killed the boy and dog when I was an old man and now I am a young a man and you Marguerite Ida and Helena Annabel and you know it well and you know I can go to hell and I can take some one too and that some one will be you.

Marguerite Ida and Helena Annabel

Never never, never never, you think you are so clever you think you can deceive, you think you can be old and you are young and old like any one but never never, I am Marguerite Ida and Helena Annabel and I know no man or devil no viper and no light I can be anything and everything and it is always always alright. No one can deceive me not a young man not an old man not a devil not a viper I am Marguerite Ida and Helena Annabel and never never will a young man be an old

man and an old man be a young man, you are not Doctor
Faustus no not ever never never
and she falls back fainting into the arms of the man from
over the seas who sings
Pretty pretty pretty dear I am he and she is she and we are
we, pretty pretty dear I am here yes I am here pretty pretty
pretty dear.
Mephisto strides up
Always deceived always deceived I have a will of iron and I am
always deceived always deceived come Doctor Faustus I have
a will of iron and you will go to hell.
Faustus sings
Leave me alone let me be alone, dog and boy boy and dog leave
me alone let me be alone
and he sinks into the darkness and it is all dark and the
little boy and the little girl sing
Please Mr. Viper listen to me he is he and she is she and we
are we please Mr. Viper listen to me.

Curtain

By Gertrude Stein

Patriarchal Poetry

(excerpt)

Patriarchal poetry makes no mistake makes no mistake in estimating the value to be placed upon the best and most arranged of considerations of this in as apt to be not only to be partially and as cautiously considered as in allowance which is one at a time. At a chance at a chance encounter it can be very well as appointed as appointed not only considerately but as it as use.

Patriarchal poetry to be sure to be sure to be sure candidly candidly and aroused patriarchal to be sure and candidly and aroused once in a while and as a circumstance within that arranged within that arranged to be not only not only not only not not secretive but as one at a time not in not to include cautiously cautiously cautiously at one in not to be finally prepared. Patriarchal poetry may be mistaken may be undivided may be usefully to be sure settled and they would be after a while as establish in relatively understanding a promise of not in time but at a time wholly reconciled to feel that as well by an instance of escaped and interrelated choice. That makes it even.

Patriarchal poetry may seem misplaced at one time.

Patriarchal poetry might be what they wanted.

Patriarchal poetry shall be as much as if it was counted from one to one hundred.

From one to one hundred.

From one to one hundred.
From one to one hundred.
Counted from one to one hundred.
Nobody says soften as often.
From one to one hundred.
Has to say happen as often.
Laying while it was while it was while it was. While it was.
Patriarchal poetry while it was just as close as when they were then being used not only in here but also out there which is what was the thing that was not only requested but also desired which when there is not as much as if they could be while it can shall have and this was what was all when it was not used just for that but simply can be not what is it like when they use it.
As much as that patriarchal poetry as much as that.
Patriarchal poetry as much as that.
To like patriarchal poetry as much as that.
To like patriarchal poetry as much as that is what she did.
Patriarchal poetry usually.
In finally finding this out out and out out and about to find it out when it is neither there nor by that time by the time it is not why they had it.
Why they had it.
What is the difference between a glass pen and a pen what is the difference between a glass pen and a pen what is the difference between a glass pen and a pen to smile at the difference between a glass pen and a pen.
To smile at the difference between a glass pen and a pen is what he did.
Patriarchal poetry makes it as usual.
Patriarchal poetry one two three.
Patriarchal poetry accountably.
Patriarchal poetry as much.
Patriarchal poetry reasonably.
Patriarchal poetry which is what they did.

One Patriarchal Poetry.

Two Patriarchal Poetry.

Three Patriarchal Poetry.

One two three.

One two three.

One Patriarchal Poetry.

Two Patriarchal Poetry.

Three Patriarchal Poetry.

When she might be what it was to be left to be what they had as they could.

Patriarchal Poetry as if as if it made it be a choice beside.

The Patriarchal Poetry.

At the time that they were sure surely certain certainly aroused arousing laid lessening let letting be it as if it as if it were to be to be as if it were to be letting let it nearly all it could be not be nearly should be which is there which is it there.

Once more a sign.

Signed by them.

Signed by him.

Signed it.

Signed it as it was.

Patriarchal Poetry and rushing Patriarchal Poetry and rushing.

Having had having had having had who having had who had having having had and not five not four not three not one not three not two not four not one not one done.

Patriarchal poetry recollected.

Putting three together all the time two together all the time two together all the time two together two together two together all the time putting five together three together all the time. Never to think of Patriarchal Poetry at one time.

Patriarchal poetry at one time.

Allowed allowed allowed makes it be theirs once once as they had had it have having have have having having is the same.

Patriarchal Poetry is the same.

Patriarchal Poetry.

It is very well and nicely done in Patriarchal Poetry which is begun to be begun and this was why if when if when when did they please themselves indeed. When he did not say leave it to that but rather indeed as it might be that it was not expressed simultaneously was expressed to be no more as it is very well to trouble him. He will attend to it in time. Be very well accustomed to this in that and plan. There is not only no accounting for tastes but very well identified extra coming out very well identified as repeated verdure and so established as more than for it.

She asked as she came down should she and at that moment there was no answer but if leaving it alone meant all by it out of it all by it very truly and could be used to plainly plainly expressed. She will be determined determined not by but on account of implication implication re-entered which means entered again and upon.

This could be illustrated and is and is and is. There makes more than contain contained mine too. Very well to please please.

Once in a while.

Patriarchal poetry once in a while.

Patriarchal Poetry out of pink once in a while.

Patriarchal Poetry out of pink to be bird once in a while.

Patriarchal Poetry out of pink to be bird left and three once in a while.

Patriarchal Poetry handles once in a while.

Patriarchal Poetry once in a while.

Patriarchal Poetry once in a while.

Patriarchal Poetry to be added.

Patriarchal Poetry reconciled.

Patriarchal Poetry left alone.

Patriarchal Poetry and left of it left of it Patriarchal Poetry left of it Patriarchal Poetry left of it as many twice as many patriarchal poetry left to it twice as many once as it was once it was once every once in a while patriarchal poetry every once in a while.

Patriarchal Poetry might have been in two. Patriarchal Poetry added to added to to once to be once in two Patriarchal poetry to be added to once to add to to add to patriarchal poetry to add to to be to be to add to to add to patriarchal poetry to add to.

One little two little one little two little one little at one time one little one little two little two little two little at one at a time.

One little one little two little two little one little two little as to two little as to two little as to one little as to one two little as to two two little two. One little one little one little two little two little one little two one little two.

Need which need which as it is need which need which as it is very need which need which it is very warm here is it.

Need which need which need need in need need which need which is it need in need which need which need which is it.

Need in need need which is it.

What is the difference between a fig and an apple. One comes before the other. What is the difference between a fig and an apple one comes before the other what is the difference between a fig and an apple one comes before the other.

When they are here they are here too here too they are here too. When they are here they are here too when they are here they are here too.

As out in it there.

As not out not out in it there as out in it out in it there as out in it there as not out in it there as out in as out in it as out in it there.

Next to next next to Saturday next to next next to Saturday next to next next to Saturday.

This shows it all.

This shows it all next to next next to Saturday this shows it all.

Once or twice or once or twice once or twice or once or twice this shows it all or next to next this shows it all or once or twice or once or twice or once or twice this shows it all or next to next this shows it all or next to next or Saturday or next to next this shows it all or next to next or next to next or Saturday or next to next or once or twice this shows it all or next to next or once or twice this shows it all or Saturday or next to next this shows it all or once or twice this shows it all or Saturday or next to next or once or twice this shows it all or once or twice this shows it all or next to next this shows it all or once or twice this shows it all or next to next or once or twice or once or twice this shows it all or next to next this shows it all or once or twice this shows it all or next to next or once or twice this shows it all or next to next or next to next or next to next or once or twice or once or twice or next to next or next to next or once or twice this shows it all this shows it all or once or twice or next to next this shows it all or next to next this shows it all or next to next this shows it all or next to next this shows it all or once or twice or once or twice this shows it all or once or twice or next to next this shows it all this shows it all or next to next or shows it all or once or twice this shows it all or shows it all or next to next or once or twice or shows it all or once or twice or next to next or next to next or once or twice or next to next or next to next or shows it all or shows it all or next to next or one or twice or shows it all or next to next or shows it all or next to next or shows it all or once or twice or next to next or next to next or next to next or next or next or next or next or shows it all or next or next or next to next or shows it all or next to next to next to next to next.

Not needed near nearest.
Settle it pink with pink.
Pinkily.

Find it a time at most.

Time it at most at most.

Every differs from Avery Avery differs from every within.

As it is as it is as it is as it is in line as it is in line with it.

Next to be with it next to be with it with it with with with it next to it with it with it. Return with it.

Even if it did not touch it would you like to give it would you like to give it give me my even if it did not touch it would you like to give me my. Even if you like to give it if you did not touch it would you like to give me my.

One divided into into what what is it.

As left to left left to it here left to it here which is not queer which is not queer where when when most when most and best what is the difference between breakfast lunch supper and dinner what is the difference between breakfast and lunch and supper and dinner.

She had it here who to who to she had it here who to she had it here who to she had it here who to she had it here who to who to she had it here who to. Who to she had it here who to.

Not and is added added is and not added added is not and added added is and not added added added is not and added added not and is added added is and is added added and is not and added added and is not and added added is and is not added added is and not and added added is and not and added.

Let leave it out be out let leave it out be out be out let leave it out be out let leave it out be out. Let leave it out be out let leave it out be out. Let leave it out be out. Let leave it out. Let leave it out. Let. Let leave it out. Let leave it out. Let leave it out.

Eighty eighty one which is why to be after one one two Seattle blue and feathers they change which is why to blame it once or twice singly to be sure.

A day as to say a day two to say to say a day a day to say

to say to say to say a day as to-day to say as to say to-day. To dates dates different from here and there from here and there.

Let it be arranged for them.

What is the difference between Elizabeth and Edith. She knows. There is no difference between Elizabeth and Edith that she knows. What is the difference. She knows. There is no difference as she knows. What is the difference between Elizabeth and Edith that she knows. There is the difference between Elizabeth and Edith which she knows. There is she knows a difference between Elizabeth and Edith which she knows. Elizabeth and Edith as she knows.

Contained in time forty makes forty-nine. Contained in time as forty makes forty-nine contained in time contained in time as forty makes forty-nine contained in time as forty makes forty-nine.

Forty-nine more or at the door.

Forty-nine or more or as before. Forty-nine or forty-nine or forty-nine.

I wish to sit with Elizabeth who is sitting. I wish to sit with Elizabeth who is sitting I wish to sit with Elizabeth who is sitting. I wish to sit with Elizabeth who is sitting.

Forty-nine or four attached to them more more than they were as well as they were as often as they are once or twice before.

As peculiarly mine in time.

Reform the past and not the future this is what the past can teach her reform the past and not the future which can be left to be here now here now as it is made to be made to be here now here now.

Reform the future not the past as fast as last as first as third as had as hand it as it happened to be why they did. Did two too two were sent one at once and one afterwards.

Afterwards.

How can patriarchal poetry be often praised often praised.

To get away from me.
She came in.
Wishes.
She went in.
Fishes.
She sat in the room
Yes she did.
Patriarchal poetry.
She was where they had it be nearly as nicely in arrangement.
In arrangement.
To be sure.
What is the difference between ardent and ardently.
Leave it alone.
If one does not care to eat if one does not care to eat oysters one has no interest in lambs.
That is as usual.
Everything described as in a way in a way in a way gradually.
Likes to be having it come.
Likes to be.
Having it come.
Have not had that.
Around.
One two three one two three one two three one two three four.
Find it again.
When you said when.
When you said
When you said
When you said when.
Find it again.
Find it again
When you said when.
They said they said.

They said they said they said when they said men.

Men many men many how many many many many men men men said many here.

Many here said many many said many which frequently allowed later in recollection many many said when as naturally to be sure.

Very many as to that which which which one which which which which one.

Patriarchal poetry relined.

It is at least last let letting letting letting letting it be theirs.

Theirs at least letting at least letting it be theirs

Letting it be at least be letting it be theirs.

Letting it be theirs at least letting it be theirs.

When she was as was she was as was she was not yet neither pronounced so and tempted.

Not this this is the way that they make it theirs not they.

Not they.

Patriarachal Poetry makes mistakes.

One two one two my baby is who one two one two one two my baby or two one two. One two one one or two one one one one one one one one one or two. Are to.

It is very nearly a pleasure to be warm.

It is very nearly a pleasure to be warm.

It is very nearly a pleasure to be warm.

A line a day book.

One which is mine.

Two in time

Let it alone

Theirs as well

Having it now

Letting it be their share.

Settled it at once.

Liking it or not

How do you do.

It.

Very well very well seriously.

Patriarchal Poetry defined.

Patriarchal Poetry should be this without which and organisation. It should be defined as once leaving once leaving it here having been placed in that way at once letting this be with them after all. Patriarchal Poetry makes it a master piece like this makes it which which alone makes like it like it previously to know that it that that might that might be all very well patriarchal poetry might be resumed.

How do you do it.

Patriarchal Poetry might be withstood.

Patriarchal Poetry at peace.

Patriarchal Poetry a piece.

Patriarchal Poetry in peace.

Patriarchal Poetry in pieces.

Patriarchal Poetry as peace to return to Patriarchal Poetry at peace.

Patriarchal Poetry or peace to return to Patriarchal Poetry or pieces of Patriarchal Poetry.

Very pretty very prettily very prettily very pretty very prettily.

By Gertrude Stein

Stanzas in Meditation

Stanza II

It is very often that they like to care
That they have it there that the window is open
If the fire which is lit and burning well
Is not open to the air.
Think well of that is open to the air
Not only which but also nearly patiently there
It is very often why they are nearly
Not only with but also with the natural wine
Of the country which does not impoverish
Not only that but healthily with which they mean
That they may be often with them long.
Think of anything that is said
How many times have they been in it
How will they like what they have
And will they invite you to partake of it
And if they offer you something and you accept
Will they give it to you and will it give you pleasure
And if after a while they give you more
Will you be pleased to have more
Which in a way is not even a question
Because after all they like it very much.
It is very often very strange
How hands smell of woods
And hair smells of tobacco

And leaves smell of tea and flowers
Also very strange that we are satisfied
Which may not be really more than generous
Or more than careful or more than most.
This always reminds me of will they win
Or must they go or must they be there
They may be often led to change.
He came and when he went he said he was coming
And they can not be more in agreement
Than cakes are virtuous and theirs is a pleasure
And so they either or a splendid as a chance
Not to be seen to be not impervious
Or which they were not often as a chance
To be plainly met not only as anxious.
Will they come here I wonder why
If not will they try if they wonder why
Or not at all favorably
Just as can as in a way
A cow is and little cows are
He said it so and they meant more
Which it is for this an occasion or not
Just as they please
Can they be just as careful as if they have a chance
To be not only without any trouble
Or can be they came

Stanza III

They can lightly send it away to say
That they will not change it if they can
Nor indeed by the time that it is made
They can indeed not be careful that they were thankful

That they should distinguish which and whenever
They were not unlikely to mean it more
Than enough not to decide that they would not
Or well indeed if it is not better
That they are not cautious if she is sleepy
And well prepared to be close to the fire
Where it is as if outside it did resemble
Or can be they will relinquish.
I think I know that they will send an answer.
It can be sensibly more than they could
That one sheep has one lamb and one sheep has two lambs
Or they can be caught as if when they had been
Not only as they like but she can say
He can say too two can be more that is to say
Three can be more than one more
And only after they have five nobody
Has quarreled not only for them but after a while
She knows that they know that they
Are not remarkable.
It is often more which they use that they
Knowing that there is a month to-day
In which often they use or can they use
Which they knew it could be in no venture
That they will use he will carefully await
And leave it like that to be carefully watching
Will we come and will we come then
They can to which can they be to which they use
Or not at all as in a fashion
More than kind.
It is often so that they will call them
Or can be there for which they will not see them
Nor can they us what they will like
In for instance will they change this for them.
Coming by themselves for them in no matter
Could one ask it is not usual

That if they are polite they are politer
Or either of them not to be one for them
Which they can call on their account for them.
It is all all of which they could be generous
If no one gave more to them
They could be with them all who are with them
For them can they be more than many
Not only but righteous and she would be
Not angry now not often for them
With not as told not by them
It is very well to have no thorough wishes
Wish well and they will call
That they were remarkable
And it is well to state that rain makes hills green
And the sky blue and the clouds dark
And the water water by them
As they will not like what they do not have
As nobody has been indifferent
Not only will she regret
But they will say one two three
Much as they use.
It is very well to know.
More than to know
What they make us of
Although it is cold in the evening
Even if a fire is burning and
Summer is of use to them

Stanza IV

All who have hoped to think of them or wonder
Or can be they will like what they have had
More than they should if they went away freshly

And were very modest about not knowing why it was
That they were not denied their pleasure then
For which they can be more than not inclined
Which makes it plainly that in one way it made no difference
That they were always said to be just when they came
There where they liked and they were not allowed
Not only ordinarily but just now
They were agreeable which is why they are they
They hesitate they more they come where they are standing
They will take courage which they will not want
Nor will they worry very much as why they wait
They will not be often there
Think well of how very agreeable it is to meet them
To say yes we will go we know where we have been
We will say yes it is not without trouble that we came
Nor do we manage definitely to share.
But we must with one and all go there.
It will be often fortunately that strawberries need straw
Or can they yes indeed have marsh grass ready
It will support all who will have support
And she will kindly share hers with them
His with them
More than that they will stop this for them
Not only certainly but very surely
No one needs kindly any disappointment
Will they step in and out and can easily
One heel be well and one heel one be well
Or as an ever ready change for once in a while
There can be reasons too why there are reasons why
If they can be said as much
That they will stay behind not only here but there
For them in a way they stay

Stanza V

Be careful that it is not their way not to like that
Not only not to be careful but to be very much obliged
Also moreover not to be the cause of their going
But which they will endeavor not to change
Not only for this but by the time
That which they knew there they must remain
If for them not at all it is not only why they like
But which they may wish from foolishness
Once at a glance.
It is not only why they are careful to replace
Not only which they can as they disturb
Or any weakness of wishing they would come there
More often than they do or carefully not at all
As it is their care to bestow it at one time
Should they because or in or influence
Not only called but very likely called a sneeze
From first to last by them in this way introduces
Them one at one time.
It is at once after that they will be better than theirs
All alike or all alike as well or rather better not
It can only not do not do all of which
They prefer elaborate to why they while away
Their time as they can accidentally manage
As a chance in which provocation is what they can call
Or while they went they gathered more
To make room for placing there
The more it needs if not only it needs more so
Than which they came

Stanza XIII

But it was only which was all the same

Stanza XIV

It is not only early that they make no mistake
A nightingale and a robin.
Or rather that which can which
Can which he which they can choose which
They know or not like that
They make this be once or not alike
Not by this time only when they like
To have been very much absorbed.
And so they find it so
And so they are
There
There which is not only here but here as well as there
They like whatever I like.

Stanza XVII

Come which they are alike
For which they do consider her
Make it that they will not belie
For which they will call it all
Make them be after not at least ready
Should they be settled strangely
Coming when they like an allowance
Naming it that they change more for them

With which which is certainly why they waited
They can be more regularly advised
In their case they will be able
Not only which they know but why they know
It is often that do their best
Not only as it is but which in change
They can be as readily which it is alike
Theirs as they better leave
All which they like at once
Which nearly often leave
This is the time in which to have it fasten
That they like all they like
More than which they can redeem.
It is often very well to if they prey
Should they could should they
They will not be imagined fairer
If they next from then on
Have it as not diminished
They can place aisle to exile
And not nearly there
Once in a while they stammer but stand still
In as well as exchange.
Once in a while very likely.
It is often their choice to feel it
As they could if they left it all
A ball fall.
Not two will give
Not one will give one two
Which they can add to change.
They will change what they like
Just what they do.
One two three or two

Stanza XVIII

She can be kind to all
If she wishes chickens to share
Her love and care
But they will think well of this
Which can not be amiss
If they like.
Two dogs for one or some one.
It is a happy wish
For some one.

Stanza II

I think very well of Susan but I do not know her name
I think very well of Ellen but which is not the same
I think very well of Paul I tell him not to do so
I think very well of Francis Charles but do I do so
I think very well of Thomas but I do not not do so
I think very well of not very well of William
I think very well of any very well of him
I think very well of him.
It is remarkable how quickly they learn
But if they learn and it is very remarkable how quickly they
    learn
It makes not only but by and by
And they can not only be not here
But not there
Which after all makes no difference
After all this does not make any does not make any difference
I add added it to it.
I could rather be rather be here.

By Gertrude Stein

The Geographical History of America or the Relation of Human Nature to the Human Mind

(excerpt)

And human nature well human nature is not interesting not at all interesting.

Chapter II

It is a remarkable thing not remarkable but remarked. Is there any difference between remarked and remarkable.

There are a great many people always living who are mixed up with anything and that is known as events.

But.

Only one sometimes two mostly only one sometimes none but certainly mostly only one in a generation can write what goes on existing as writing.

It is absurd when you think about it as absurd as any superstition but there it is there is only one in a generation not likely more than one in many a generation not even one that can write what goes on existing.

Now what have you to say to that.

That when you come to think about it it is astonishing but when you hear that there is no relation between human nature and the human mind it is no longer as astonishing.

How often as I have been walking and looking at so many who are studying and walking and I can say to myself why should not one of them write something that will be that that which it is and they will not no they will not and what is that that which it is.

It is writing of course it is the human mind and there is no relation between human nature and the human mind no no of course not.

And what has that to do with flat land or any land the flatter the land oh yes the flatter land but of course the flatter the land and the sea is as flat as the land oh yes the flatter the land the more yes the more it has may have to do with the human mind.

After number I

Number one I cannot be often enough surprised at what they do and that they do it so well, so much is written and they do do it so well.

And then I wonder as they do it so well as so many do it so many do it so very very well, I mean writing how is it that after all only one and that one only one in a generation and very often very many generations no one does it at all that is writing.

It has all to do with the fact that there is no relation between human nature and the human mind.

Those all those that do it so well and they do they do do it so well all those that do do it so well do it with human nature as human nature that is with remembering and forgetting.

Think anything you say has to do with human nature and if you write what you say if you write what you do what is done then it has to do with human nature and human nature is occupying but it is not interesting.

No you all know you all know that human nature is not

interesting, you watch any dog with affection no human nature is not interesting it is occupying but it is not interesting and therefore so much writing is done. But is it done oh yes of course it is done. Done and done. That is the way they used to bet.

Now you take anything that is written and you read it as a whole it is not interesting it begins as if it is interesting but it is not interesting because if it is going to have a beginning and middle and ending it has to do with remembering and forgetting and remembering and forgetting is not interesting it is occupying but it is not interesting.

And so that is not writing.

Writing is neither remembering nor forgetting neither beginning or ending.

Being dead is not ending it is being dead and being dead is something. Think of any crime of course being dead is something.

Now and that is a great American contribution only any flat country has and can be there that being dead is actually something.

Americans are like that.

No Europeans and so no European can ever invent a religion, they have too much remembering and forgetting too much to know that human nature is anything.

But it is not because it is not interesting no not any more interesting than being drunk. Well who has to listen to anything. Any European but not any American.

Number two.

That would be sad.

What.

That any American would hear what any one is saying.

Number three.

I found that any kind of a book if you read with glasses

and somebody is cutting your hair and so you cannot keep the glasses on and you use your glasses as a magnifying glass and so read word by word reading word by word makes the writing that is not anything be something.

Very regrettable but very true.

So that shows to you that a whole thing is not interesting because as a whole well as a whole there has to be remembering and forgetting, but one at a time, oh one at a time is something oh yes definitely something.

Number four.

Why if only one person in a generation and often not one in a generation can really write writing why are there a number of them that can read it quite a number of them in any generation.

There is a question.

Why do they as well as can they.

Number Five.

Do they as well as can they.

Number six.

One two three four five six seven all good children go to heaven some are good and some are bad one two three four five six seven.

So you see that this is the question.

How is it that a number a certain number in any generation can read what is written but only one in any number of generations can write what is written.

She dropped something.

Number six and seven.

Another thing.

What is the relation of anything to anything.

Not human nature and not the human mind.

Human nature is not that thing and the human mind. Nor the human mind.

First Example.
The relation of the human mind to the universe.
What is the universe.
Human nature is not in any relation to the universe anybody can understand that thing.
That is not understanding that is unanswerable that human nature has no relation to the universe.
What is the universe.

Second Example.
There are so many things which are not the same identity, human nature, superstition, audience, and the human mind. And the only one that is the one that makes writing that goes on is the human mind.
Identity and audience.
No one is identical but any one can have identity.
And why.
Because what is the use of being a little boy if you are going to grow up to be a man.

Example Four.
Another thing that there is is the Universe.
Identity has nothing to do with the universe identical might have if it could have but identity certainly not certainly not identity.

Example Five.
Nothing should follow something because in this way there will come to be a middle and a beginning and an end and of course that does make identity but not the human mind or not the human mind.
If you write one thing that is any word and another word

is used to come after instead of come or of come again then that may have something not to do with identity but with human nature.

And human nature has nothing to do with the human mind.

Now about anything nothing can grow but after all as nothing can grow there is no identity.

Not of course not even naturally not but just not, not at all.

But anything can grow.

But what is the use of being a little boy if he is going to grow up to be a man.

Do you see what a mistake it is to say that.

Example six.

The universe.

What is extra is not a universe.

No indeed.

Play I
Characters.

Identity, human nature, human mind, universe, history, audience and growing.

Play II

I do not think I would care about that as a play.

Play I

The human mind.

The human mind at play.

Play II

Human nature.

The dog if he is lost knows very well he will be found.

Human Nature.
But perhaps he will not be found.

Play III
Very often he is not found he is run over.

Play IV
Sometimes he is not run over but he is not found.

Play I
Identity.
If I know that I say that I will go away and I do not I do not.
That makes identity.
Thank you for identity even if it is not a pleasure.

Play I
Identity is not as a pleasure.

Play I
Identity has nothing to do with one and one.

Play I
The Universe.
The Universe well if there is a way to have it be that they can lay a universe away.

Play II
But they cannot.

Play III
Of course they can.

Play IV
Of course they can. They do not. But they can.

Play V
A universe if it is layed away, they cannot. Of course they cannot.

Play V
A universe cannot.

Play I
An audience.
An audience cannot be layed away. Of course it can. It can but is it. Of course it can.
Any audience can be layed away of course it can.

Play II
Growing.
There is no of course it can to growing.
Growing has no connection with audience.
Audience has no connection with identity.
Identity has no connection with a universe.
A universe has no connection with human nature.

Play I
Human nature.
Human nature is not interesting. Human nature is not a play.

Play II
Human nature is not interesting.
Examples seven and eight
The more likely a universe is to be connected with identity the less likely is a universe to be a universe.
No one likes the word universal to be connected with a universe.
Part II
All the parts are part II.

I once knew a man who never had part one he always had part 2.

I always knew.

Part III
Now what has any one to do with Part III

Part I
If every day it is necessary to have an uncle killed that is if he kills himself instead of a father that too has nothing to do either with identity or with human nature.

Part IV
It is very strange that although only one in ever so often can write a great many can read what the one has written. But is that only because they can read writing or has it to do with the one who is writing.

That is what I want to know.

The human mind writes only once in a very little or big so often but every time every time size has nothing to do with anything because the universe every once in a while the universe is that size and so does it make any difference since the human mind has what it has does what it does and writes what it writes and that has nothing to do with identity or audience or history or events, and yet only once oh only once in every few generations the human mind writes. That is all because of human nature and human nature is not interesting everybody says it is but it is not.

Part I
He needs what he can please

Part I
Every time they change, I mean the earth I mean why mean the earth and which makes more than what is on it

in it.

Part II
Once they like an earth

Part II
Once they like a heaven

Part II
Once they like a heaven and earth

Part III
No heaven

Part III
No earth

Part I
They come later not to know there ever had been a heaven.

Part III
Certainly it lasted heaven a very little time all things considered that is considered as long as anything is.

No earth yes no earth.

No heaven yes certainly no heaven.

Part III
Now this which I want you to think about is this.

Every once in so often is every once in so often and anybody can decide what nothing is.

Please excuse me.

If nothing is anything any one every once in so often can decide what anything is.

That is the way it is.

Part I

Every time there is a human mind it is or it is not all the universe which is or is not.

That is what the human mind is.

Think what the human mind is.

Part II

It has nothing to do with anything but is one yes well yes that is what the human mind is.

Part III

Is one yes that is what the human mind is.

Part IV

Human nature no.

Human nature never is one that is not what the human mind is human nature is not what the human mind is.

Part IV

Romance.

There is some relation between romance and the human mind but no relation between human nature and romantic anything because human nature is not interesting but romance is.

Part I

Lolo.

Part II

I cannot begin too often begin to wonder what money is. Has it to do with human nature or the human mind. Human nature can use it but cannot refuse it. Can human nature know it know what money is or only the human mind and remember now there is no heaven and of course no earth, not in America perhaps not anywhere but there is the human mind and any one which is more than not enough may perhaps know what money and romance is.

Part I
I am not confused in mind because I have a human mind.

Part II
Yes which is.

Part I
Romance and money one by one.

Part II
Lolo.

Part II
Care fully for me.
As often as carefully.
Each one of these words has to do with nothing that is not romance and money.

Part III
Romance has nothing to do with human nature.

Part III
Neither has money.

Part I
Lolo.

Part II
Where he lived and when he died.
Some see some sun.

Part III
He died naturally

Part I
She says he says he says she says what is done is not done.

Number one.
It is not to discourage to say that each time although each time is such a very few times that there is a different way to say that the sun is far away each time that there is a different way to say that anything is far away although at any time that there is a universe now at any time that there is a universe anything is very near.

Number two.
That is just that and that has nothing to do with the human mind or human nature that is just that.

Number one.
It happens it changes a little any day it happens though that any day some one can say something that makes any one know that the larger is smaller but not that the smaller is larger.

Now suppose everybody says pioneering is over that means that the larger is smaller but not that the smaller is larger and that well that no that that has nothing to do with the human mind.

But has the human mind anything to do with romance not human nature perhaps human nature. Who likes human nature. Not I. And the human mind. And romance oh yes I do like romance that is what makes landscapes but not flat land.

Flat land is not romantic because you can wander over it and if you can wander over it then there is money and if there is money then there is the human mind and if there is the human mind there is neither romance nor human nature nor governments nor propaganda.

There should be none of these if the land is flat.

Flat land as seen from above.

Above what.

Above the flat land.

Is there any human nature in red indians or chinamen there should not be.

But there is.

Alright there is.

But there should not be.

Is there any romance.

All right there should not be.

But there is.

Alright there should not be.

And government, no there is no government where the land is flat.

There should not be.

And there is not.

And why not.

Because anybody can wander and if anybody can wander then there should not be any human nature.

And romance

No there should not be.

And yet romance has nothing to do with human nature.

No nothing.

Nothing at all

Nothing at all.

Nothing at all at all

Nothing at all.

Number II

Lolo.

There is no romance if anybody is to die by and by.

But to die
Yes to die.
Not only not to die.
Not by and by.
And so romance is delicious.
But not to die by and by.
Lolo.

Number three.

Lolo was one no matter that he had a father.
No matter that he had a father.
Nobody cries out loud no matter that he had a father.
It was not mentioned often or again.
Lolo was himself romantic and he is dead not by and by but dead.
And as I pass where he had not had a father there where he is not dead by and by but as he is then there there where he is he was not where he is. Lolo is dead and any father had a mother he had a mother but none of this is dead.
He is dead.
Lolo is dead.
There where there is no other.

Number III

Do you see what romance is.

Number III

Do you see that it has nothing to do with human nature or the human mind.

Number III

So many things have nothing to do with human nature.
Romance did.
It had nothing to do with human nature.
And the human mind.

Nothing did.
Nothing did have nothing to do with the human mind.
Romance did.
Oh romance did.
Romance had nothing to do with the human mind nor
with human nature.
Romance did.

Number III
It has to do with neither with flat land or money or the
human mind or human nature.
Now anybody might think that romance and adventure
was the same but it is not.
Adventure has to do with small things being bigger and
big things being smaller but not romance no not romance.
Romance has nothing to do with anything being bigger or
being smaller and therefore although romance has nothing
to do with the human mind they come together.
They have nothing either one of them has nothing to do
with human nature. Oh no nothing to do with human nature.
Lolo.
Nothing to do with human nature.

Number I
Every time any one can come to be one then there is no
human nature no not in that one.
Human nature has to do with identity but identity has
nothing to do with any one being one.
Not not anything in any one.
No no no.

Number II
Be a credit to beware.
Does it make any difference how you felt to-day.
No not any

Does it make any difference how you felt yesterday
No not any.

Does it make any difference if a dog does not know the difference between a rubber ball and a piece of paper.

No not any why he does.

Bibliography
Gertrude Stein's Work Used In This Book

Autobiography of Alice B. Toklas, The (New York: Harcourt Brace, 1933; reprinted New York: Vintage Press).

Blood on the Dining-Room Floor (Berkeley: Creative Arts Book Company, 1982; edited and with an afterword by John Herbert Gill).

Everybody's Autobiography (New York: Vintage Press, 1973).

Fernhurst, Q.E.D., and Other Early Writings (New York: Liveright Publishing Corporation, 1973 and 1983).

Geography and Plays (New York: Something Else Press, Inc., 1922, reissued in 1968; introduction by Sherwood Anderson).

Gertrude Stein's America (New York: Liveright, 1965).

How Writing Is Written, Volume II of the Previously Uncollected Writings of Gertrude Stein (Los Angeles: Black Sparrow Press, 1974; edited by Robert Bartlett Haas).

Ida A Novel (New York: Random House, 1941; New York: Cooper Square, 1971; New York: Vintage Books, 1972).

Last Operas and Plays (New York: Vintage Books, 1975; edited and with an introduction by Carl Van Vechten).

Lectures in America (Boston: Beacon Press, 1957).

Lucy Church Amiably (Hastings-on Hudson, New York: Ultramarine Publishing Co., Inc.).

Making of Americans, The (New York: Harcourt, Brace and World, 1962).

Mrs. Reynolds (Los Angeles: Sun & Moon Classics, 1988).

Paris France (New York: Liveright, 1970).

Picasso, The Complete Writings (Boston: Beacon Press, 1985; edited by Edward Burns, foreword by Leon Katz and Edward Burns).

Primer for the Gradual Understanding of Gertrude Stein, A (Los Angeles: Black Sparrow Press, 1971; edited by Robert Bartlett Haas).

Reflections of the Atomic Bomb, Volume I of the Previously Uncollected Writings of Gertrude Stein (Los Angeles: Black Sparrow Press, 1974; edited by Robert Bartlett Haas).

Selected Writings of Gertrude Stein (New York: Vintage Press, 1972, edited by Carl Van Vechten with an essay by F.W. Dupee).

Three Lives (New York: Vintage Press, copyright 1909 and 1936 by Gertrude Stein).

What Are Masterpieces (New York: Pitman Publishing Corporation, 1970; afterword by Robert Haas).

World Is Round, The (San Francisco: North Point Press, 1988; with pictures by Clement Hurd).

Yale Gertrude Stein, The (New Haven, Ct.: Yale University Press, 1980; edited with an introduction by Richard Kostelanetz).